New Performance/New Writing

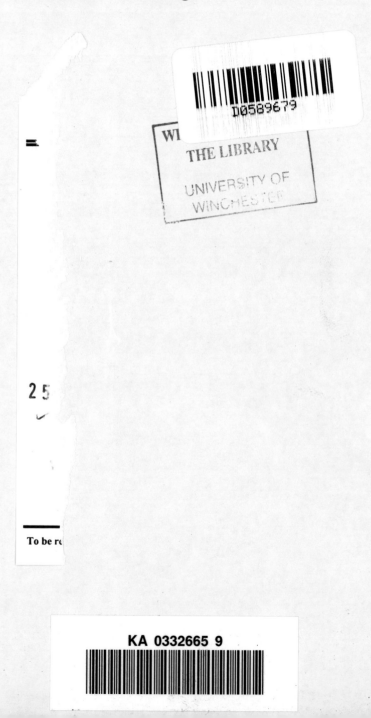

New Performance/
New Writing

John Freeman

palgrave
macmillan

First published 2007 by
PALGRAVE MACMILLAN
Houndmills, Basingstoke, Hampshire RG21 6XS and
175 Fifth Avenue, New York, N.Y. 10010
Companies and representatives throughout the world

PALGRAVE MACMILLAN is the global academic imprint of the Palgrave
Macmillan division of St. Martin's Press, LLC and of Palgrave Macmillan Ltd.
Macmillan® is a registered trademark in the United States, United Kingdom
and other countries. Palgrave is a registered trademark in the European
Union and other countries.

ISBN-13: 978–1–4039–9813–2   hardback
ISBN-10: 1–4039–9813–2   hardback
ISBN-13: 978–1–4039–9814–9   paperback
ISBN-10: 1–4039–9814–0   paperback

This book is printed on paper suitable for recycling and made from fully
managed and sustained forest sources. Logging, pulping and manufacturing
processes are expected to conform to the environmental regulations of
the country of origin.

A catalogue record for this book is available from the British Library.

Library of Congress Cataloging-in-Publication Data
Freeman, John, 1959–
  New performance/new writing : texts and contexts in postmodern
    performance / John Freeman.
       p. cm.
  Includes bibliographical references and index.
  ISBN-13: 978–1–4039–9813–2 (hardback : alk. paper)
  ISBN-10: 1–4039–9813–2 (hardback : alk. paper)
  ISBN-13: 978–1–4039–9814–9 (pbk.)
  ISBN-10: 1–4039–9814–0 (pbk.)
  1. Experimental theater. 2. Performing arts. 3. Performance art.
    4. Playwriting. I. Title.
PN2193.E86F74 2007
792.02′2—dc22
                                                      2007021729

10   9   8   7   6   5   4   3   2   1
16   15   14   13   12   11   10   09   08   07

Printed and bound in China

For H.

Contents

List of Case Studies

Acknowledgements

I have been fortunate enough to work with some outstanding colleagues and students. To those whose varied contributions to this book were always useful and rarely acknowledged, I offer thanks here. Thanks go particularly to my colleagues on performance-writing modules at De Montfort and Brunel, Colin Chambers and David Lane.

Acknowledgement needs to be made to the Head of the School of Arts at Brunel University, for providing space, time and support for this book to be brought to a close.

Thanks, above all, to Kate Wallis, Kitty van Boxel and Sonya Barker at Palgrave.

TIMELINE: 1900 TO THE NEARLY NOW

1900: Population of the world is at 1.6 billion. Luis Buñuel is born. Nietzsche dies. Oscar Wilde dies.

1901: Anton Chekhov's *Three Sisters*. The term 'Expressionism' is used for the first time. Sigmund Freud's *Interpretation of Dreams* is published. Lee Strasberg is born. Jacques Lacan is born. Walt Disney is born.

1902: August Strindberg writes *A Dream Play*. First performance of Büchner's *Danton's Death*. Gorky writes *The Lower Depths*. Émile Zola dies. Los Angeles Theater shifts from vaudeville to cinema.

1903: Wright brothers' first flight.

1904: Salvador Dalí is born. Chekhov writes *The Cherry Orchard*. Chekhov dies. The Academy of Dramatic Art (ADA) founded in London.

1905: Edward Gordon Craig writes *On the Art of the Theatre*. Jean-Paul Sartre is born. First neon signs appear. In Berlin, Isadora Duncan establishes the first school of modern dance.

1906: First sound-on-film motion picture. Frank Wedekind's *Spring's Awakening*. Cézanne dies. Samuel Beckett is born. Ibsen dies. San Francisco earthquake.

1907: Strindberg opens his Initimate Theatre and writes *The Ghost Sonata*.

1908: Arthur Adamov is born. Simone de Beauvoir is born.

1909: *The Founding and Manifesto of Futurism* published by F. T. Marinetti. The New York Times publishes the world's first movie review.

1910: Jean Anouilh is born. Jean Genet is born. Jean-Louis Barrault is born. First staging of Futurist performance in Trieste. Tolstoy dies. By now there are 9,000 movie theatres in the U.S.

1911: Tennessee Williams is born.

$\rightarrow$

→

1912: Jacques Copeau opens the Théâtre du Vieux-Colombier. The Titanic sinks. John Cage is born. The term 'Surrealism' is first used. Eugène Ionesco is born. August Strindgerg dies. In Britain, the Lord Chamberlain legalises the word 'bloody' (in Shaw's *Pygmalion*).

1913: First performance of Büchner's *Woyzeck*. Piscator begins his theatre apprenticeship in Munich. Ferdinand de Saussure dies.

1914: Joan Littlewood is born. World War I starts. Dylan Thomas is born. Brecht's first poems are published.

1915: Arthur Miller is born. Tadeusz Kantor is born. Roland Barthes is born.

1916: Cabaret Voltaire established in Zürich. Beginnings of Dada. The last stagecoach robbery in the U.S. is solved.

1917: Jung's *Psychology of the Unconscious* is translated into English. Bolshevik Revolution in Russia. Marcel Duchamp exhibits a porcelain urinal called *Fountain*. Herbert Beerbohm Tree dies.

1918: Frank Wedekind dies. Guillame Apollinaire dies. World War I ends. Brecht writes his first play, *Baal*.

1919: German film expressionism is established with the first screening of *The Cabinet of Dr Caligari*.

1920: State Theatre, Moscow founded by Meyerhold. Academy of Dramatic Art is awarded Royal Charter and becomes RADA. Irish Civil War begins.

1921: Luigi Pirandello writes *Six Characters in Search of an Author*. Jacques Lecoq is born. Joseph Beuys is born.

1922: T. S. Eliot writes *The Wasteland*. Eugene O'Neill writes *The Hairy Ape*. Erving Goffman is born.

1923: Meyerhold Theatre founded. Moscow Arts Theatre visits New York. Sarah Bernhardt dies. Brecht writes *In the Jungle of the Cities*. Harlem's Cotton Club opens, presenting all-black performances to white-only audiences.

→

→

1924: Konstantin Stanislavski writes *My Life in Art*. Sean O'Casey writes *Juno and the Paycock*. André Breton writes the *First Surrealist Manifesto*. Marinetti publishes *Futurism and Fascism*. Marlon Brando is born. Walt Disney's first cartoon film, *Alice in Wonderland*. Franz Kafka dies.

1925: Coward's *Hay Fever* first performed in London. Hitler publishes *Mein Kampf*. Peter Brook is born. Lenny Bruce is born. First television transmission, leading to the first broadcast soap opera, *The Smith Family*.

1926: Opening of Fritz Lang's *Metropolis*. Antonin Artaud creates the Théâtre Alfred Jarry. Michel Foucault is born. Dario Fo is born. Peter and Anthony Shaffer are born. Stanisalvski's *An Actor Prepares* first published in English. Martha Graham gives her first New York performance.

1927: Erwin Piscator takes over the Berlin Volksbuhne. Artaud writes *The Spurt of Blood* in the same year that he is expelled from the Surrealist Movement. Kenneth Tynan is born. Allan Kaprow is born. Isadora Duncan dies.

1928: Bertolt Brecht writes *Threepenny Opera*. Edward Albee is born. Thomas Hardy dies. Adolphe Appia dies.

1929: Wall Street Crash. First talking movie released. Piscator writes *The Political Theatre*. John Osborne is born. Heiner Müller is born.

1930: Harold Pinter is born. John Arden is born. Andy Warhol is born. Brecht writes the *Rise and Fall of the City of Mahogonny*.

1931: Lorca's 'La Baracca' founded in Madrid. Fernando Arrabal is born. Eugene O'Neill writes *Mourning Becomes Electra*. Piscator's Drama Workshop founded in New York. Augusto Boal is born.

1932: Artaud's first manifesto of the *Theatre of Cruelty*. Athol Fugard is born. Arnold Wesker is born.

→

→

1933: Adolf Hitler comes to power in Germany. Brecht leaves Germany. Artaud writes his second manifesto. Lorca writes *Blood Wedding*. Jerzy Grotowski is born. Joe Orton is born. Yoko Ono is born. Piero Manzoni is born. Black Mountain College is formed. The first drive-in cinema opens in the U.S.

1934: Edward Bond is born. Charles Marowitz is born.

1935: Joseph Chaikin is born. John McGrath is born. Brecht is stripped of his German citizenship.

1936: Spanish Civil War starts. Pirandello dies. Václav Havel is born. Lorca dies. Brecht's first recorded use of the term *verfremdungseffekt*.

1937: Tom Stoppard is born. Richard Foreman is born. Peter Stein is born. Steven Berkoff is born.

1938: In an essay called *The Popular and the Realistic*. Brecht writes that the theatre of today cannot operate on yesterday's techniques. Artaud writes *The Theatre and its Double*. Caryl Churchill is born. Sartre writes *Nausea*. Ariane Mnouchkine is born. Stanislavski dies.

1939: World War II began. Brecht writes *Galileo* and *Mother Courage*. Shelagh Delaney is born.

1940: Brecht writes *Good Woman of Setzuan*. American Negro Theater founded in Harlem. Pina Bausch is born. Vito Acconci is born. Vsevolod Meyerhold dies.

1941: Attack on Pearl Harbour. Brecht exiled to America. Virginia Woolf dies.

1942: Spalding Gray is born. Peter Handke is born. Howard Brenton is born.

1943: Sam Shepard is born. Mike Leigh is born. Wallace Shawn is born. Oskar Schlemmer dies.

1944: German and Austrian theatres closed. Tennessee Williams writes *The Glass Menagerie*. Elizabeth LeCompte is born. Marinetti dies.

→

→

1945: First atomic bomb is dropped on Japan. Joan Little-wood establishes her Theatre Workshop. Rainer Werner Fassbinder is born. Brecht writes *Caucasian Chalk Circle*. World War II ends with 55 million dead. Tennessee Williams' *The Glass Menagerie.*

1946: Marina Abramović is born. Ulay is born. Chris Burden is born. Gertrude Stein dies. Arts Council of Great Britain is formed.

1947: Actors' Studio founded in New York. Avignon Festival founded in France. Edinburgh Festival founded in Scotland. La Jolla Playhouse founded in California. Julian Beck and Judith Molina create the Living Theatre. Tennessee Williams writes *Streetcar Named Desire*. Jean Genet writes *The Maids*. Jackson Pollock paints *Reflection of the Big Dipper*. Miller writes *All My Sons* and *Death of a Salesman*. David Mamet is born. David Hare is born. Liz Lochhead is born. Laurie Anderson is born. Orlan is born.

1948: Brecht writes his *Short Organum for the Theatre*. David Edgar is born. Apartheid is established in South Africa. Ntozake Shange is born. Artaud dies.

1949: Brecht and Helena Weigel set up the Berliner Ensemble. Eliot writes *The Cocktail Party*. Andy Kaufman is born.

1950: Eugène Ionesco writes *The Bald Soprano*. Samuel Beckett writes *Waiting for Godot*. George Bernard Shaw dies.

1951: Timberlake Wertenbaker is born.

1952: Williams writes *The Rose Tattoo*. John Cage's *4'33"* performed by David Tudor at Black Mountain College. First production of *Waiting for Godot*. Agatha Christie's *The Mousetrap* opens in the West End (still running). Roger Vitrac dies.

1953: Arthur Miller writes *The Crucible*. Sophie Calle is born. Eugene O'Neill dies. Dylan Thomas dies. Joseph Stalin dies.

→

→

1954: Berliner Ensemble performs at the first Paris Festival. Joe Papp founds New York Shakespeare Festival. Jackson Pollock dies.

1955: Miller writes *View from the Bridge*. Guillermo Gómez-Peña is born. Albert Einstein dies. Williams writes *Cat on a Hot Tin Roof*.

1956: Berliner Ensemble visits London. John L. Austin first uses the term 'performative'. Karen Finley is born. John Osborne writes *Look Back in Anger*. Brecht dies.

1957: Beckett writes *Endgame*. Osborne writes *The Entertainer*. Harold Pinter writes *The Birthday Party*. Hermann Nitsch begins developing ideas for the Orgien Mysterien Theater. *West Side Story* is on Broadway. Robert Lepage is born. Sarah Daniels is born. Peter Sellars is born. Barthes writes *Mythologies*.

1958: Jim Cartwright is born. Edward Albee writes *The Zoo Story*.

1959: Grotowski forms his Polish Laboratory Theatre. Arnold Wesker writes *Roots*. John Arden writes *Serjeant Musgrave's Dance*. Allan Kaprow presents his *18 Happenings* at Black Mountain College. Erving Goffman publishes *The Presentation of Self in Everyday Life*. Off-Off Broadway Movement begins when Joe Cino stages plays at Caffe Cino. Deborah Warner is born.

1960: Yves Klein stages his *Leap Into the Void*. Franko B is born. Anne Teresa de Keersmaeker is born.

1961: Berlin Wall erected. La Mama Experimental Theatre Club, New York. Beckett writes *Happy Days*. Piero Manzoni cans and labels his faeces. Yoko Ono creates *A Grapefruit in the World of Park*. Emergence of the Fluxus Movement in New York City. Edward Albee writes *Who's Afraid of Virginia Woolf?* Shakespeare Memorial Theatre becomes the Royal Shakespeare Company.

→

→

1962: Martin Esslin writes *The Theatre of the Absurd*. Peter Brook directs *King Lear* at the RSC. Bread and Puppet Theater founded in New York. Yves Klein watches a film of his own work and dies later that evening.

1963: John F. Kennedy assassinated. The Living Theatre stage *The Brig*. Joan Littlewood stages *Oh! What a Lovely War*. Manzoni dies. Tristan Tzara dies.

1964: Civil Rights Act adopted in the U.S. The Living Theatre tour-work in Europe. Sean O'Casey dies. Peter Weiss writes *Marat/Sade*. Grotowski stages *Akropolis*. Brook & Marowitz stage their Theatre of Cruelty season. Pinter writes *The Homecoming*. Carolee Schneemann presents *Meat Joy*. Odin Teatret (Nordic Theatre Arts Laboratory) founded in Oslo by Eugenio Barba. Ono performs *Cut Piece*. Peter Shaffer writes *The Royal Hunt of the Sun*.

1965: The Vietnam War begins. American Conservatory Theatre (ACT) founded in Pittsburgh. Brook directs *Marat/Sade*. Living Theatre stage *Frankenstein*. Edward Bond writes *Saved*. Shigeko Kubota performs *Vagina Painting*. T. S. Eliot dies.

1966: Peter Handke writes *Offending the Audience*. Joseph Beuys performs *How to Explain Paintings to a Dead Hare*. Walt Disney dies. The People Show is formed. Edward Gordon Craig dies. André Breton dies. Piscator dies. Lenny Bruce dies.

1967: Barthes proclaims the 'death of the author'. Tom Stoppard writes *Rosencrantz & Guildenstern Are Dead*. Joe Orton dies.

1968: Outbreak of Paris Riots. Stage censorship lifted in Britain. Handke writes *Kaspar*. *Hair* is on Broadway, and the Living Theatre tours *Paradise Now*. Brook writes *The Empty Space*. Grotowski writes *Towards a Poor Theatre*. Dario Fo and Franca Rama found the theatre company Nuova Scene. Welfare State International is founded in Leeds. Barthes writes *The Death of the Author*.

→

→

1969: Americans land on the moon. Grotowski directs *The Constant Prince*. Robert Wilson directs *The Life & Times of Sigmund Freud*. Gilbert & George perform *The Singing Sculpture*. Yoko Ono and John Lennon present *Bed-in for Peace*. Richard Schechner directs *Dionysus in 69*. Dario Fo writes *Mistero Buffo*. Beckett wins the Nobel Prize for Literature.

1970: The International Centre for Theatre Research established in Paris. Brook directs *A Midsummer Night's Dream*. Fo writes *Accidental Death of an Anarchist*. Grotowski states his disinterest in theatre and his wish to leave the word, and all it stands for, behind.

1971: Pinter writes *Old Times*. Brook directs for the Festival at Persepolis. Robert Wilson directs *Deafman Glance*. Sarah Kane is born. Chris Burden presents *Shoot*.

1972: Stoppard writes *Jumpers*. Vito Acconci performs *Seedbed*. Wilson makes *Ka Mountain*. Laurie Anderson: *Institutional Dream Series*.

1973: McGrath founds 7:84 (Scotland). Peter Hall joins the National Theatre. Bond writes *Bingo*. Chris Burden makes *Through the Night Softly*. Linda Montano performs *Home Endurance*, in which she stayed home for one week, documenting all thoughts and actions. Noël Coward dies. Pablo Picasso dies. Beckett writes *Not I*.

1974: Stoppard writes *Travesties*. Pinter writes *No Man's Land*. Heiner Müller writes *Medeaplay*. Chris Burden is crucified to the bonnet of a Volkswagon in *Trans-Fixed*. Cardiff Laboratory Theatre founded. The Wooster Group emerge from Richard Schechner's Performance Group. Fo writes *Can't Pay? Won't Pay!*

1975: David Mamet writes *American Buffalo*. The Wooster Group stages *Sakonett Point*. Thornton Wilder dies. Gilbert & George perform *The Red Sculpture*. Carolee Schneemann performs *Interior Scroll*. Monstrous Regiment is founded in London. Abramović meets Ulay.

→

→

1976: The Vietnam War ends. Wilson directs *Einstein on the Beach*. Caryl Churchill writes *Light Shining in Buckinghamshire*. Steppenwolf Theater Company is founded in Chicago. Tara Arts is founded in London. Beckett writes *Footfalls*.

1977: Wooster Group present *Rumstick Road*.

1978: Robert Wilson directs *Death, Destruction and Detroit*.

1979: Black Theatre Co-operative (BCT) founded in London. Peter Brook's *Conference of the Birds*.

1980: The RSC stages *Nicholas Nickleby*. Chris Burden presents *Show the Hole*. Howard Brenton writes *The Romans in Britain*. Sam Shepard's *True West* opens in San Francisco. Kenneth Tynan dies. Jean-Paul Sartre dies. Roland Barthes dies.

1981: Abramovivć & Ulay perform *Nightsea Crossing*. The Wooster Group presents *Route 1 & 9*. London International Festival of Theatre (LIFT) is founded. Split Britches is founded in New York. Jacques Lacan dies.

1982: Churchill's *Top Girls* at the Royal Court. Laurie Anderson performs *O Superman*. *Cats*, *Nicholas Nickleby* and *Amadeus* on Broadway. Fassbinder dies. Impact Theatre Co-Operative tour *Songs of the Clay People*. Strasberg dies. Erving Goffman dies.

1983: Sarah Daniels writes *Masterpieces*. Theatre de Complicite is formed. Tennessee Williams dies.

1984: Daniels' *Neaptide*. Holly Hughes performs *The Well of Horniness*. The Wooster Group perform *L.S.D. (… Just the High Points …)*. Forced Entertainment is formed and makes *Jessica in the Room of Lights*. Linda Montano and Tehching Hsieh perform *Roped*. Andy Kaufman dies. Michel Foucault dies.

1985: Karen Finley performs *Don't Hang the Angel*. Holly Hughes performs *The Lady Dick*. Peter Brook directs Jean-Claude Carrière's version of *The Mahabharata*.

→

→

Laurie Anderson performs *Home of the Brave*. Julian Beck dies.

1986: Nuclear disaster at Chernobyl. Robert Wilson directs Heiner Müller's *Hamlet-machine*. Jean Genet dies. Joseph Beuys dies. Simone de Beauvoir dies.

1987: Spalding Gray performs *Swimming to Cambodia*. Eric Bogosian performs *Talk Radio*. Holly Hughes performs *Dress Suits to Hire*. John Leguizamo performs *The Bible According to Latinus Spictus*. Impact Theatre Co-Operative tour *The Carrier Frequency*. Andy Warhol dies.

1988: Abramović & Ulay walk the Wall of China for *Lovers' Walk*. Pinter writes *Mountain Language*.

1989: Salvador Dalí dies. Samuel Beckett dies.

1990: Annie Sprinkle performs *Post Porn Modernist*. Guillermo Gómez-Peña creates *Sons of Border Crisis*. Kantor dies.

1991: Collapse of the European Communist Bloc. Leguizamo writes and performs *Motor Mouth*. Gulf War I starts.

1992: John Cage dies. Forced Entertainment tour *Emanuelle Enchanted (or a Description of this World as if it Were a Beautiful Place)*. Spalding Gray performs *Monster in a Box*. Tony Kushner's *Angels in America* opens. Laurie Anderson performs *Stories from the Nerve Bible*. Peter Handke writes *The Hour When We Knew Nothing of Each Other*.

1993: Ron Athey performs *Martyrs and Saints*. La Pocha Nostra is founded by Guillermo Gómez-Peña, Nola Mariano and Roberto Sifuentes.

1994: Bill T. Jones choreographs *Still/Here*. Jean-Louis Barrault dies. John Osborne dies. The Gulf War ends. Gómez-Peña and Sifuentes stage their *Cruci-Fiction Project*. Eric Bogosian performs *Pounding Nails in the Floor with My Forehead*. Holly Hughes performs *Clit Notes*.

→

$\rightarrow$

1995: Marina Abramović performs *Cleaning the Mirror*. Eric Bogosian performs *31 Ejaculations*. Sarah Kane's *Blasted* and Jez Butterworth's *Mojo* at the Royal Court. Laurie Anderson performs *The Nerve Bible*. Heiner Müller dies.

1996: Mark Ravenhill's *Shopping & Fucking* opens. Forced Entertainment tour *Showtime* and *Quizoola*. Sarah Kane writes *Phaedra's Love*. Robert Lepage directs *Seven Streams of the River Ota*.

1997: Dario Fo awarded Nobel Prize for Literature. Shakespeare's Globe opened in London. Leguizamo performs *Freak*.

1998: Sarah Kane writes *Cleansed* and *Crave*. *The Lion King* is on Broadway.

1999: Lecoq dies. Grotowski dies. Sarah Kane writes *4.48 Psychosis*. Sarah Kane dies. Living Theatre stage *La Resistenza*. Laurie Anderson's *Songs and Stories for Moby Dick*. Holly Hughes performs *Preaching to the Perverted*.

2000: The population of the world is 6.5 billion.

2001: Franko B: *Oh Lover Boy* and *Still Life*. Anthony Shaffer dies. September 11th attack on New York City and Washington. Spalding Gray writes and performs *Life Interrupted*.

2003: Gulf War II starts. Forced Entertainment tour *Bloody Mess*. Robert Wilson directs *Temptation of St Anthony*.

2004: Jacques Derrida dies. Marlon Brando dies. Spalding Gray dies.

2005: Abramović performs *Seven Easy Pieces*. Arthur Miller dies.

2006: Forced Entertainment tour *The World in Pictures*. Allan Kaprow dies.

2007: The Wooster Group perform *Hamlet* and *La Didone*. Andy Warhol's *Green Car Crash* sells for £36 million.

Introduction: Preparing the Ground

Like Robert Wilson's text for *A Letter for Queen Victoria*, this book starts with words of introduction and intent, words stating what it is and what it is not, words that preface our restless, relentless circling around the concepts of postmodernism and the relationship between practice and theory, words that attempt a preparing of troubled ground for the application of academic discourse to creative practice.

We are beginning a four-chapter exploration of what writing for performance might mean when one is not trying to write a well-made play, of what constitutes performance writing after the historical avant-garde. This involves an eclectic array of practitioners, periods and practices, considered in non-linear ways. In moving through the early 20th century, in the first chapter, a simple, basic chronological order is established at the same time, through the inclusion of material on Peter Handke and Robert Wilson, as this chronology is compromised. Sacrificing the provision of the type of clear and logical overview that adds false order to the chaos of practice demands a certain effort from readers; it also leads to liberation, and the fact that readers have to at times make their own connections between sections is a deliberate decision. What else is deliberate is a degree of scepticism about the ability of critical discourse to adequately capture artists' ways of thinking about their process. What is accidental (and also inevitable) is my own complicity here.

The book is not a dictionary and it makes no claims to come even close to exhausting the subject of new performance and performance writing. Just the opposite: the overview is flawed and subjective. Consequently, it is also suspect. Every decision is something of a loss and in focusing on the practitioners that it does, many more of equal and sometimes greater worth are excluded.

Performance exists in all human cultures, and society has always sought to impose organisational thought – or theory – on what it is that takes place, and how, and why. As readers will quickly note, the usefulness of theory to this book is matched by an unwillingness to work within any overarching methodological approach. As the work tends towards the provisional and the resistant to closure, so does its description. The approach to theory adopted in the chapters to follow draws upon Manuel Castells' description of theoretical analysis as a tool that enables us to understand, rather than a phenomenon that seeks its end in intellectual self-enjoyment (Castells 2004: 3). This is also a means of avoiding the reliance on a language, which is 'specialized to such a degree that no one understands our theories anymore' (Gómez-Peña 2000: 268).

Gómez-Peña is correct in his observation that 'Theory has become unintelligible to most people outside our hyper-specialized fields' (Ibid.), as is Charles Marowitz when he ponders the extent to which we have 'reached a stage where scholars are simply talking to scholars in the way that computers talk to other computers, with all the rest of us wondering what all that buzzing, droning and bleeping is really all about' (Marowitz 1991: 73). This is distinct, however, from Freud's declaration that before the problem of the creative artist, analysis must lay down its arms. To side with Freud here be antithetical to the study of performance, as well as would rendering this book redundant from the very start; it would in fact amount to the denial of performance study. Study *is* theory, as theory is at once a schema that explains practice and something embedded in the practice itself. In this way theory is practice at the same time as it stands outside it.

Writing about his own directorial work, Barry Edwards informs us that 'there is no convenient theory to use as a hook (an excuse) for the words' (Edwards 1999), and that 'to theorise … is to write (about) *something else*, something – thoughts, ideas, reflections etc. – that happens *in addition to* the practice' (Ibid.). Edwards' words function as a touchstone for this book, as well as serving as a reminder that whilst the application of certain selected theoretical models of study can provide focus, there is a danger that thinking about becomes dependent upon recognisably theoretical foci. Theories are useful, inevitable even, but their value lies in the ways that they open the ground for new practice. In and of themselves, they have no value within the pages of this book.

Stating this point of view compromises one of the main thrusts of the work, as resisting a central theoretical core in this book is hindered by the imposition of an overt authorial subjectivity. Certainly, the method of organising parameters of enquiry makes my rationale explicit from the outset. Some of the structural cornerstones of the book, the case studies and the writing exercises, are included in an attempt to ground observations in a more material set of practices: practices that are explicitly pedagogical. Ultimately the overarching frame of this book is not performance writing *per se*, but rather its relationship to postmodernity, alongside an increasing indivisibility between performance writing and performance. Where the book differs from a number of other analyses of postmodern performance is through its concern with the ways in which writing has changed in its form over the last century. It is this survey of particular manifestations of writing that reappear across performance works from Marinetti to Forced Entertainment that is at the heart of the work.

The book is no teach-yourself guide to performance writing; neither is it concerned with textual analysis. Examples of performance texts are excluded from chapters and, whilst re-framed words from Robert Wilson, Christoper Knowles, Vito Acconci, Bruno Corra, Emilio Settimelli, Yoko Ono, Tim Echells, Richard Foreman, Deborah Levy, Heiner Müller, Samuel Beckett et al would provide evidence of diversity, the ephemeral nature of performance augurs against leisurely critique and what works in the now is different in the then of close critical attention. Useful as explorations such as these are, it is not the function of this book to isolate onto the page words and actions that were written to be heard and seen upon the stage. Case studies include suggestions for further reading and many of these contain examples of performed texts, as do works in the bibliography. The rise of the Internet means that written material is available now at the click of a mouse, and numerous Web sites for all of the practitioners mentioned in these pages are only a search engine away. Performance texts that were once obscure are now so freely available that to include them here seems wasteful at best and counter-productive at worst.

At times, and to assist the making of comparative points, the book depicts modernism as being primarily about unity, clarity, and immanent meaning. This is set against the more fragmented elements of postmodernism. As an early guard against claims of reductionism, it should be noted that modernist practitioners such as Joyce, Picasso, Strindberg and Stein stand in clear resistance to any claims of modernist univocality, and that modernism is not being depicted here as some binary 'bad' set against the 'good' of postmodernism. As forms bleed into one another, so do genres and movements. That said, the book has been constructed, *and is being reconstructed in the act of reading*, within the period of postmodernity, where meaning is locatable at the surface; where there appears at times to be a continuous interplay of the already said. This book embraces rather than resists that state. Chapter 1's historical focus, for example, draws at times on recent observations of phenomena that took place up to 90 years ago. This is not due to a paucity of 'original' material so much as an interest in the ways in which movements such as Futurism, Dadaism and Surrealism are impacting on the now ... about acknowledging that we can only ever view work through modern eyes.

Chapters, which appear on the page of contents to be discrete, fold in one upon the others, forming one small part of the challenge to a unilinear history and interrogating along the way the boundaries of discipline, field and scholarship. W. B. Worthen sees theatre history as 'characterised by an effervescent eclecticism' (Worthen and Holland 2004: 1). The same is true of the brief history of performance covered in this book, and the same, albeit in more modest part, is true of this writer's approach. As with theory and history so it is with research: 'research, by definition, is a course which sets about establishing "facts" in an attempt to "reach conclusions" whereas something in process does not stop' (Hughes 2000: 3).

Performance is a word of choice: the term used most often in this book. It stands for contemporary work that is sometimes more and often knowingly less than theatre, as it is usually described. The names of forms and approaches overlap, so that one spectator's 'theatre' is another's 'performance', which in turn might be 'performance art' for another and 'live art' for another still. Davis and Postlewait highlight the problems of attempting clean distinctions when they ask 'if performance art is defined in opposition to theatre, do they both share the trait of theatricality (Davis and Postlewait 2003: 27)? One of the definitions suggested by Davis and Postlewait is that 'in opposition to conventional theatre [performance art] subverted, as much as possible, the recognizable iconic, deictic, and symbolic codes' (Ibid.). The one thing we know is that forms bleed. Distinctions between fine art and performance as well as poetry and performance, like those between dance and theatre, are no longer safe, if they ever were. The edges blur. The word performance is offered as shorthand for work that subverts the conventional codes of theatre. It follows that the types of performance writing this book seeks to explore are those where the written is only one element among many. These are performance writings which 'open out and question the continuing assumptions of a reified conception of the artwork as a static object whose meanings are inherent in its form or structure and [are] easily disclosed to the knowing interpreter' (Jones and Stephenson 1999: 7). The approaches to performance articulated in this book are about strategies for interruption, about indications of uncertainty and about doubt.

Written principally at a university desk and intended primarily to have an educational application, this book

1. Aims not to restrict writing solely to the textual.

2. Acknowledges that writing is somehow related to inscription, to the attempt to present thought and bodily activity in forms that challenge conventional or assumed modes of representation.

3. Investigates the continuous reinvention of the word in performance.

4. Invites readers to think about what we do when we are faced with the new, with the experience of something that tests many of our assumed ways of understanding.

5. Offers suggestions for further reading, alongside suggestions as to practice.

6. Seeks to embody through its writing something of the fragmented nature of the work it describes.

7. Aims for provocation in lieu of prescription.

The timeline at the start of this book is almost a chapter in itself. In the first instance, it is longer and more detailed than is usual in a book such as this. In the second, it is unashamedly limited, indicative as it is of *this writer's interests*, rather than suggesting that it speaks objectively for major shifts in a century or so of theatre-based performance. The timeline thus reflects the current critical unease with accepting the givens of theatre history, even as it reinforces many of them. This contradiction means that for every event I *believe* to be demanding of inclusion, there are thirty more that are included because it is impossible for me, shackled as I am to the canons of Western theatre, to write any history that excludes them. Thirdly, it is an attempt at emphasising the conflicting as well as continuous nature of the last hundred years of performance. A useful early exercise is to copy out the timeline and to delete those events that you regard as insignificant whilst writing in your own, making inclusions and erasures that strengthen the list. The exercise is useful not least in its exposing of the bias at work in authorial preconceptions.

Peter Harrop's identification of three areas of development in contemporary performance forms an astute contribution to our introductory comments. Harrop cites 'the mainstream – new voices for old forms; the avant-garde – new forms for new voices; and the interventionist – new contexts for new forms for new voices' (Harrop 1996: 126). For Harrop, interventionism is aligned to active spectatorship, exemplified by Augusto Boal's 'spectactor', 'the participant who alternates between watching, listening and doing' (Owens and Holtham 2006), and he makes this case persuasively. For our purposes, however, intervention is being used in a different (and differently discriminating) way, as a model for the type of postmodern practice that seeks, in Peggy Phelan's terms, 'representation without reproduction' (Phelan 1993: 3).

CASE STUDY 1.1: AUGUSTO BOAL

Augusto Boal, (1931–) a Brazilian theatre director, writer and politician, has been confronting oppression in various forms for over 40 years. Raised in Rio de Janeiro, Boal was trained in chemical engineering and attended Columbia University in the late 1940s and early 1950s. His belief that theatre can be used as a means to create a better future has inspired numerous groups all over the world to use his techniques, and to do so in a multitude of settings. Boal is permanently connected to the term 'Theatre of the Oppressed', a form of rehearsal theatre designed, in principle, for people who want to learn ways of fighting back against oppression in their daily lives.

Boal sees oppression as a power dynamic which is based on monologue rather than dialogue; as a situation of domination that prohibits the oppressed from exercising their basic human rights. Accordingly, the Theatre of the Oppressed is intended to function as a participatory theatre that fosters democratic and cooperative forms of interaction among participants. In this way, theatre becomes less about spectacle than a site for interventionist process.

The origins of this work began in the 1960s when Boal employed a device whereby audience members could stop a performance and suggest different actions for the actors, who would then carry out the audience suggestions. On one occasion (or so legend has it) a female spectator was so frustrated with what she saw that she entered the playing space and showed the performers what to do. Boal's approach to theatre was transformed. From this point on, he began inviting spectators with suggestions for change onto the stage to demonstrate their ideas, discovering through this participatory act ways in which the spectators became empowered ... not only to imagine change but to actually practice that change, reflect collectively on the suggestion and become empowered to generate social action. As ever, one needs to approach claims like these with a degree of caution and seek evidence of this framed empowerment having currency beyond the workshop walls.

$\rightarrow$

→
Boal served as Artistic Director of the Sao Paulo Arena Theatre from 1956 to 1971. At the end of this period he came under attack by the Brazilian government and was imprisoned and subsequently exiled.

Recommended Reading:
Boal, Augusto. 1992. *Games for Actors and Non-Actors*. London & New York: Routledge.
Schutzman, Mady and Jan Cohen-Cruz. 1993. *Playing Boal: Theatre, Therapy, Activism*. London: Taylor & Francis.
Boal, Augusto.1994. *The Rainbow of Desire*. London & New York: Routledge.
——. 1998. *Legislative Theatre*. London & New York: Routledge.
——. 2000. *Theatre of the Oppressed*. London: Pluto.

Brief case studies such as these will appear irregularly throughout the book. They comprise many of the usual suspects of British and American contemporary performance practice and analysis, as well as one or two names less expected in a work such as this. The case studies function almost as performed asides: as with the timeline, they are part of the text and also elements slightly and always apart. Aimed as prompts for further study, they punctuate lengthy chapters and an equally long introduction, providing readers with necessary rest stops along the way.

Like performance making, writing is always an exercise in complication, and where this book's chapters seek to categorise practitioners and practices, the aim is to create associative links rather than limitations. Despite their best intentions, chapters in books can create and subsequently impose an awkward split between mutually supporting foci. Notwithstanding this, this book, just like any other, needs to be broken down into manageable sections. The chapters that follow provide for this at the same time as they offer no clean breaks: writing about the space is also writing about the body in space; writing about the body is also writing about the self; writing the group segues into acts of rewriting, of deconstruction. Chapters bleed and fray, challenging indexical divisions. In this, the writing in this book is at its closest perhaps to the phenomena it describes. Performance is always about more than one thing, and performance writing, the blueprint for something other than itself, for something that will never quite be what it intends, is this difference writ large.

For Phelan, performance emerges from discrete historical traditions. As a 'counterpoint to realism … from the history of painting' (Phelan 2004: 21) and as 'a return to investigations of the body most fully explored by shamans, yogis and practitioners of alternative healing arts' (Ibid.). Herbert Blau notes performance's historical address to 'shattering language, abandoning texts and going for broke with the body, or extolling *body* language' (Blau 1996: 1). Performance is, as Carlson reminds us, an 'essentially contested concept' (Carlson 1996: 1) and that which was once seemingly secure has become unfixed and at times unfathomable, a network of ideas spilling out of a knowingly punctured frame.

There is a connection here with interdisciplinarity, where differing and sometimes deliberately contrasting forms of performative mediation are used collaboratively. No clear distinctions between performance and theatre, or performance writing and performance composition exist and there is no intention to create them here. That aside, we are able to take performance as an umbrella term that encompasses work wherein words 'may be spoken live, re corded, or presented visually … [where] text is merely one element of the work, not privileged above other elements or disciplines, and [which] *interrogates* the interpretative conventions and formulae of traditional forms of theatre' (Lennard & Luckhurst 2002: 269).

Whatever the banner under which staged work functions it does so in ways that are mediated. A visual artist can leave marks on a canvas that remain as those marks, broadly at least, regardless of the passing of time and the shifting perspectives of viewers; likewise, a novelist's words, once published, stay as they are, despite the vagaries of font. Yet even when a performer such as Laurie Anderson writes words for her own voice, the voice that speaks is radically different to the voice on the page.

CASE STUDY 1.2:   LAURIE ANDERSON

Laurie Anderson (1947–) studied for an MFA in Sculpture at Columbia University. Anderson has often created performance on a massive scale, both in terms of physical size and length. She often incorporates her own 'home made' and invented instruments to produce digitised sounds, alongside slide and film projection. An example of this can be found in her 1992 work *Stories from the Nerve Bible* in which Anderson used computerised imagery and holograms to create a

→

→

spectacular visual context for her songs. The performance art world of the early 1970s fostered an experimental attitude among many young artists in downtown New York and Anderson quickly became part of this. In one of her most noted early works, *As:If,* Anderson stood on a block of ice, playing her violin whilst wearing a pair of ice skates. When the ice melted the performance ended. The violin has a sound range closer than any other to the female voice and Anderson's work exploits this similarity, with the violin often being used as a surrogate for the artist's voice.

An accomplished musician, Anderson achieved international recognition in 1982 with the eight-minute single *O Superman.* Since then she has collaborated with, amongst others, William Burroughs, Peter Gabriel, David Sylvian, Spalding Gray, Andy Kaufman, Robert Lepage, Wim Wenders, Bill T. Jones and Lou Reed. In 2003, Anderson became artist-in-residence for NASA, an occasion which inspired her performance piece, *The End of the Moon.*

With worldwide status as a leader in the groundbreaking use of technology in the arts, Laurie Anderson recently collaborated with Interval Research Corporation, in the exploration of new creative tools, including her own invention, the 'Talking Stick'. Anderson wrote the entry on New York for the Encyclopaedia Britannica, hosted the PBS special Art 21, received the 2001 Tenco Prize for Songwriting, in San Remo, Italy, and the 2001 Deutsche Schallplatten prize for *Life on a String.*

Chronology (Selected):
As:If (1974)
At the Shrink's (1975)
Handphone Table (1978)
Americans on the Move, Part 1 (1979)
Big Science (1982)
United States Parts I–IV (1983)
Language is a Virus from Outer Space (1984)
Home of the Brave (1985)

→

→

Empty Places (1990)
Blood Fountain (1994)
The Nerve Bible (1995)
The Speed of Darkness (1997)
Songs and Stories for Moby Dick (1999)

Recommended Reading:

Sayre, Henry M. 1989. *The Object of Performance: The American Avant-Garde since 1970*. Chicago: Chicago University Press.

Anderson, Laurie and Germano Celant. 1998. *Laurie Anderson: Dal Vivo*. Milan: Fondazione Prada.

Bonney, Jo (ed.) 2000. *Extreme Exposures: An Anthology of Solo Performance Texts from the Twentieth Century*. New York: Theater Communications Group.

Goldberg, RoseLee and Laurie Anderson. 2000. *Laurie Anderson*. New York: Harry N. Abrams.

Grosenick, Uta (ed.) 2005. *Women Artists in the 20th and 21st Century*. Koln: Taschen.

The term performance suggests the body, even at times clichés of the body: naked, self-referential, bloodied or abused. The term is less suggestive of text, of text-as-word. This book can be regarded as that which explores and exposes the margins of the already-marginalised, through an associative consideration of a diverse array of textual approaches that utilise performance, and vice versa. The focus throughout is on those writers, directors and performers whose work is linked by an interest in the ephemeral and the conceptual, whose approach to performance writing is (to use a currently unfashionable and almost taboo term) *experimental*. We can say that what it is that identifies performance writing as new is not automatically connected to the time at which it was written; rather, it is about approaches to writing that challenge mainstream sensibilities in ways that are both provocative and original. In this way texts for performance from 100 years ago might be addressed in the following chapters, whilst certain works from the more recent past might well be ignored. What remains constant is that the emphasis of the book is on work that advances our thinking about what performance writing and making might mean.

The structure of this book, with its various chapter-length concentrations on self, body, group etc, only sets up these distinctions in order to reveal their absence of fixity. Like the approaches to work they describe, the focus of particular chapters provide ways in to performance rather than limits to the ways in which they are read. It is after all precisely this instability that defines the field. In the writing that follows this introduction, Chapter 1 provides a survey of the first half of the 20th century, locating movements such as Surrealism, Dada and Futurism as clear precursors of contemporary performance work. Chapter 2 explores space in performance and makes a case for installation art as the bridge between modern and postmodern performance, almost perversely omitting specific references to performance writing until its final pages. Chapter 3 examines the ways in which practitioners employ autobiographical performance modes to challenge and subvert spectatorial assumptions about 'self' and 'other', whilst Chapter 4 concentrates on links between originality and appropriation, group devising and authorial identity. Other than on very limited occasions, I have decided to spare readers from the distractions of footnote numbers in the text. Those spared readers are urged to view this book as one among many and to regard the opinions herein in the light of other works.

In seeking similarities we create ubiquities. Where this book slips into prescription, it does so without intention. We *are* able, as Adrian Heathfield suggests, to 'identify an uneven presence of certain shared urges ... a commitment to undermine the dominant orders of the text; an interest in intense physicality and sensory impression; an avant-gardist suspicion of the values of consensus inherent within the popular' (Heathfield 1997: 1), but this falls short (let it always be hoped) of performance writing by rote, of the dread recipe offered by Jacqueline Martin of post-holocaustic angst played out in a fractured, non-linear and solution-free landscape (Martin 1991: 119). What is the dread here is not that Martin's reading of contemporary performance is inaccurate; on the contrary, it is the accuracy of her appraisal that reminds us how quickly once-subversive performance becomes the very thing it so recently sought to displace.

The writing undertaken here has been both hampered and helped by a growing unease with the idea of authority. This position is referred to explicitly on a number of occasions, and the tension it creates is a constant feature: a book of words, often about words, that does not fully trust the thing that it is. Pages impose linearity. Pages are numbered and progressive. Connected ideas create chapters. One page, one line, one word is read at a time. These, with some notable exceptions, are the rules of the book, for reader and writer alike, giving permanent form to the temporal and order to the random. Where performance is always in the moment, critique is always in the past, so that documentation is only ever a surrogate. Like evidence submitted in a trial, it adds to the establishment of the facts of a given event, testifying to phenomena beyond its self. Documentation does not exist in isolation from intention, and each example points at and persuades our attention to external actions. In recording time-based work within space-based media, problems inevitably emerge, and writing *about* performance is an innately flawed endeavour in ways that writing *for* performance manages to avoid. Where the former corrals the subversive, the latter is able to release it. Beckett's writing of text for the character named Vladimir creates performance; John Peter's critical appraisal, published as *Vladimir's Carrot* (Peter 1988), good as it is, is like swimming on dry land.

CASE STUDY 1.3:   SAMUEL BECKETT

Samuel Beckett (1906–89) studied French and Italian at Trinity College Dublin. Amongst the many honours subsequently awarded to him was the Nobel Prize for Literature in 1969.

Beckett created work which has extended the possibilities of performance and literature in unprecedented ways, bringing to the theatre an acute awareness of the absurdity of human existence, exemplified through our desperate search for meaning, our individual isolation and the gulf between our desires and the language in which these can find and be given expression.

Beckett's work can be placed in two main categories, effectively, amounting to before and after *Waiting for Godot*, which was written around 1950. The latter period brought Beckett international eminence in theatre, radio and television, and he concentrated more and more on the search for dramatic minimalism. His writing became ever shorter and more distilled, resulting in plays which he termed 'dramaticules'. These plays would often amount to no more than a few pages, or less, of text. The pre-Godot period, when Beckett was finding his way as a writer and was virtually unknown reveals much more variety. Beckett was catapulted into celebrity in 1952 by the first production of *En attendant Godot*, which was translated as *Waiting for Godot* in 1954. The play, famously, concerns two tramps in conversation about the awaited Godot, who never arrives and whose mystery is ever sustained.

→

$\rightarrow$

There have been a number of recent attempts to regard Beckett as a postmodernist. Despite this, Beckett's work is resolutely modernist, with his plays revealing a consistent concern with human suffering and survival and where his characters are struggling with meaninglessness and an existential world. Beckett's entire output, the narrative prose as well as the dramatic works, reduces basic existential problems to their most essential features. In this way his concerns are fundamental, but never simplistic: the ephemerality of life; time and eternity; the individual's sense of loneliness and alienation and above all the mystery of self. What *can* be read as postmodern is the knowingly constructed manner of acting suggested in Beckett's work, with characters, particularly in *Endgame*, *Krapp's Last Tape* and *Waiting for Godot*, seemingly conscious of their own acted and performing selves.

Beckett's legacy of innovative theatrical exploration has been tempered somewhat by the guardians of his estate who resist directorial alterations to his work with an iron rule.

Chronology (Selected):
Waiting for Godot (1952)
Endgame (1957)
Krapp's Last Tape (1959)
Happy Days (1961)
Play (1964)
Not I (1973)
Footfalls (1976)
Quad (1981)

Recommended Reading:
Cohn, Ruby. 1969. *Currents in Contemporary Drama.* Bloomington: Indiana University Press.
Esslin, Martin. 1973. *The Theatre of the Absurd.* Overlook Press.
Styan, J. L. 1981. *Modern Drama in Theory and Practice 2: Symbolism, Surrealism and the Absurd.* Cambridge: Cambridge University Press.

$\rightarrow$

$\rightarrow$

Brater, Enoch and Ruby Cohn (eds). 1992. *Around the Absurd: Essays on Modern and Postmodern Drama*. Ann Arbor: University of Michigan Press.

Knowlson, James. 1996. *Damned to Fame: The Life of Samuel Beckett*. London: Bloomsbury.

Cronin, Anthony. 1997. *Samuel Beckett: The Last Modernist*. London: Harper Collins.

Beckett, Samuel. 2006. *The Complete Dramatic Works of Samuel Beckett*. London: Faber & Faber.

Where the textual practices encountered here often resist narrative, an overall narrative can still be said to exist. Notwithstanding its doubled status as a research report, this book tells a story (not *the* story) of performance making and writing across a certain period of time (the relatively recent past) and in certain (almost exclusively Western) places. Academic theorists, as Rebecca Schneider suggests, are generally granted status as people who are removed or 'disembodied' from that which they describe (Schneider 1997; 9). Such is emphatically not the case here. Whatever this book examines and describes, its authorial voice has no choice but to remain male, European, white and subjective, for how could any authorial voice deny its own persistence? Inasmuch as I am attempting to use language in a way that is as liberating as it is descriptive of liberal processes, the narrative engaged in is likely at times and in Zygmunt Bauman's terms, 'to go around in circles, rather than developing in a straight line. Some topics return later, to be looked upon once again in the light of what we have discussed in the meantime. This is how all effort of understanding works. Each step in understanding makes a return to previous stages necessary' (Bauman 1990: 19). This is explanation, not apology.

A number of questions are raised in this book. For the most part these are implicit, yet some can be articulated. They are given here to create some indication of constructive and inevitable unease:

1. Can performance writing exist when no words have been written … when none have been spoken?

2. Can the event of performance create its own text, or does text need to be prior?

3. Do these words now, written as words on a screen and read on the page, constitute text for performance? Would they, if each paragraph were allocated to a character's name and if each chapter began with a fictional location and time?

4. What about a barrister's speech? What about a news report? What about text that has been appropriated from elsewhere, recontextualised, made subject to textual harassment?

5. Have we reached the point where we no longer ask 'What can we write?' so much as 'What can we do with writing?' Not 'What can we perform?' but 'What can we do with performance?'

If the implication of 'Anything Goes' feels like too much of a catch-all, offered too early on, as a valid philosophical notion that threatens to invalidate this book before it starts, then we can say that writing for performance is that which explores tensions. These are not necessarily the tensions that occur when a character's intentions are brought face to face with an obstacle. The tension explored here is between self and other, fine art and theatre, the body and the word, truth claims and overt constructedness, between the live and the not quite, between what we want and what we sometimes get.

Contemporary performance writing questions performance writing, just as contemporary performance questions performance, and we would be narrowing things down if we considered writing as something distinct from making: the problems and challenges of one are there for the other. Attempts to define performance have never ended because its boundaries have to always remain capable of expanding to accommodate new and previously unimagined forms. All forms of performance are therefore possible, and the defining features can never be authoritatively listed: such a list would signal the end of change and *ergo* the end of the line for the new. There are already too many examples of work that take us back to the drawing board of performance for us to bask even momentarily in the false light of knowing.

Original is easy, Brecht told us, but good is hard. But what constitutes 'good' and, indeed, what, in the context of performance, constitutes 'writing'? What works well on the page may promise more than it delivers in performance. No rules exist for categorising the quality of art, and subjectivity, of thought if not language, lurks between each and every line. As a means of controlling this, of keeping things in check, this book will concentrate on the work of established practitioners whose work is accessible through further reading. Whilst this is no guarantee of objectivity, even if such were desired, it does at least guard against the inclusion of the obscure, the idiosyncratic and the inaccessible.

Writing for new performance does not always result in the creation of words to be spoken. The Austrian writer Peter Handke's 1992 play *The Hour When We Knew Nothing of Each Other* is a noted example of a text without words that is neither dance nor mime. Samuel Beckett's 1956, *Act Without Words I and II*, alongside his 1969 play *Breath*, and *Quad*, a 1982 text written for television, are others. In its broadest sense, the approach to writing taken in this book is sympathetic to Roland Barthes' distinction between readerly and writerly texts. Barthes' belief was that the ideal text was writerly, inasmuch as the textual 'networks are many and interact, without any one of them being able to surpass the rest; this text is a galaxy of signifiers, not a structure of signifieds; it has no beginning; it is reversible; we gain access to it by several entrances, none of which can be authoritatively declared to be the main one; the codes it mobilizes extend as far as the eye can reach, they are interminable' (Barthes 1974: 17).

CASE STUDY 1.4:   RONALD BARTHES

Roland Barthes (1915–80) was born in Normandy. Between 1935 and 1939 he studied at the Sorbonne, where he earned a licence in Classical Letters. In 1952, Barthes was at the Centre National de la Recherché Scientifique, where he studied Lexicology and Sociology. During his seven-year period there, he began writing a series of installments to *Les Lettres Nouvelles*, a collection of essays that attempted to dismantle key myths of popular culture. These essays were gathered together into *Mythologies*, which was published in 1957. Barthes spent the next ten years exploring the fields of Semiology and Structuralism. During this period he was made chair at a number of faculty positions around France, a career progression which allowed the continuance of his increasingly provocative and influential writings.

Barthes' most well-known work remains a 1968 essay called *The Death of the Author*. For Barthes, the notion of the author, or authorial authority, amounted to the forced projection of meaning. By imagining an intended meaning, one was able to infer an *a priori* explanation for it. Barthes saw

→

→
this as an untenable position, arguing that the unknowable state of the author's mind, alongside the array of individual and spectatorial readings made any such predictive realisation impossible. In this way Barthes sought to expose the whole notion of the 'knowable text' as little more than another delusion of bourgeois literary and intellectual culture.

The Death of the Author was part of a body of work, much of which comprised an interrogation of items of cultural material to expose how bourgeois society used them to assert its values upon others. Barthes found semiology, the study of signs, useful to him in these interrogations and it is in this way that his connection with critical thinking about performance has been solidified. Barthes' notions of 'Readerly' and 'Writerly' texts have been equally valuable to our contemporary understanding of performance, providing us with an avenue and vocabulary of critique. Barthes argued that Readerly texts are those where readers are dissuaded (often by subtle means) from writing or producing their own meanings. 'Writerly' texts, by contrast, seek to make of readers/spectators active producer of texts and therefore of meanings. Where readerly texts offer the comfort of stabilisation, writerly texts demand an engagement that is always in some ways abrasive.

Barthes was struck by a laundry truck whilst walking home in Paris and died one month later from his injuries.

Recommended Reading:

Barthes, Roland. 1973. *Mythologies*. London: Granada.
Barthes, Roland. 1974. *S/Z*. New York: Hill and Wang.
Barthes, Roland. 1977. *Roland Barthes by Roland Barthes*. London: Macmillan.
Barthes, Roland. 1977. *Image – Music – Text*. London: Fontana Press.
Wasserman, George. W. 1989. *The Ecstasies of Roland Barthes*. London: Routledge.
Rylance, Rick. 1994. *Roland Barthes*. Hemel Hempstead: Harvester Wheatsheaf.
Allen, Graham. 2003. *Roland Barthes*. London & New York: Routledge.

In creating performance where the invitation exists for the spectator to actively construct her or his own understanding of the work, writing functions as a metaphor for construction. Writing for new performance is intrinsically concerned with activity and creation; the term is also loosely bracketed with the word 'performative', a key word that is increasingly used to refer to almost every aspect of performance study. In its purest sense performativity refers to J.L. Austin's argument that words are possessed of the power to make things happen (Austin 1975), to create rather than merely describe, to utilise 'performative utterance' so that the words are also the deeds. When spoken by a police officer, the words 'you are under arrest' are indubitably performative: speaking the words makes something happen, as it does when a bride or groom says 'I do'. Conversely, the words 'I love you' are not necessarily performative, whilst the context in which they are spoken might well make them so. From the perspective of a dramatic text, words are generally rooted in either the present or the past. To be prosaic, we are more likely to hear a character say 'I am going for a walk' or 'I went for a walk' than 'I am walking'. With echoes of Gertrude Stein, Richard Foreman's practice exemplifies his desire to subvert this trend through writing primarily in the present and in response to immediate stimuli.

New Performance/New Writing provides a snapshot of new writing for new performance at the start of the century. It is also a stimulus. Theory is a neighbour to practice, not a replacement for it, and the exercises towards the creation of new work are in this book as a reminder that performance is a thing to be done, rather than something to be relentlessly and exclusively written about. Despite the inclusion of practical ideas, any and all suggestions that appear need to be approached with the knowledge that what works in one situation and at one time is no guarantee of repeated or repeatable success. On the contrary, performance writing, marked as it is by an immediacy that more often than not resists transcription, is the least permanent and most idiosyncratic of forms. No claims for some transferable and self-defined 'best practice' are made here, just as no Ben Jonsonesque rhetoric will be made in these pages that Forced Entertainment's *Speak Bitterness* or Fiona Templeton's *YOU–The City* are not texts for their age, but texts for all time. The writing discussed in this book makes an attempt to speak to its own time and to articulate the concerns of the moment. Resistance to a drive towards posterity is one of the aspects that link the artists and work under discussion.

Another linking aspect is a close and at times inseparable connection between the writer and the written, between performer and performance. In this way, the bespoke nature of the material augurs against recycling and repetition. There are exceptions to this, but the relatively recent history of performance texts tells us that few of these are notable. Spalding Gray's celebrated monologues, whilst published, were clearly written for Gray's own voice. Another performer, sitting at another table in another space or even at the same table and in the same space, could certainly perform *Swimming to Cambodia* or *Monster in a Box*, but why would s/he want to? The texts, written as they were as a kind of first-person autobiography, are not a blueprint for impersonation in the manner of *Uncle Vanya*. The narrative reconstruction is of Gray's own life story. The gap between the invented (remembered) self of Gray's written text and the remembering (inventing) self of Gray's performance may be wider than it first appears, but it is/was nevertheless bridged by Gray's status as both subject and object.

At this point in our history notions of self are no longer assumed to be secure, and are perhaps the most elusive security to seek. It may be the case, as Goffman argued, that our daily selves are constructed and created in the same ways that a Stanislavskian actor assumes the characteristics of a fictional other (Goffman 1959). Patterns of behaviour are tried out, tested and refined, and costume is chosen to suit the scene. The blurring of self and other feels at times like the oxygen of new performance. We cannot easily define 'self' and we cannot successfully reach out for something 'real' beyond performance. All that we can ever know is the reality of the performance itself. This is the only realism we can catch, and it comes without a chase. It is from this perspective that performance writing assumes a degree of importance within postmodern culture.

Postmodernism is ubiquitous in that there are many ways of understanding and of using the term. My own usage as it relates to performance is determined by the specific set of circumstances in which the work I see, read about, discuss and occasionally make takes place. In this, I am writing from a particular early 21st-century academic perspective, which is at all times and for better or worse, identifiably British. The absence of a single emanating theory means that the word, as style, as epoch and as intent can be used to cover a multitude of approaches. For the purposes of this book, the prime aspects of the postmodern condition are taken to be

1. A challenge to the liberal humanist paradigm, which sees people as rational individuals able to identify and reflect upon universal regimes of truth, art and knowledge.

2. The desire to reveal the ideological basis contained in the production of knowledge, alongside a focusing of attention on the perspectives from which work is created.

3. A concern with radical eclecticism built on juxtapositions of conflicting discourse.

4. A foregrounding of intertextuality and the revelation, rather than concealment of process.

5. An interest in shifting performative identities, through autobiography and autoethnography.

6. The absence of closure and the exposure of artifice.

In its unwillingness to create coherent scenes, characters, conventional time-scales and passive viewing, postmodernism has a complex relationship with the idea of easy entertainment. Martin reminds us that 'in this theatre, language is not used to communicate in the normal way, rather words are freed from the tyranny of the text and give place to sounds, chants and broken pieces of dialogue in an attempt to arouse connotative responses in the individual member of the audience' (Martin 1991: 119). Martin's 'tyranny of text' is a loaded term, but her recognition of the fact that spectators of postmodern performance have to work not *harder*, but *differently*, is useful to us. Because events are often thematically disconnected, spectatorship becomes an intrinsically active operation. In many ways then we can say that postmodern performance brings spectators closer to reality (as opposed to realism) through its denial of that all-seeing perspective provided by the false coherence of representational mimesis.

Postmodernism has been around long enough now for most of us, like Martin, to know it when we see it and to say what we see in recognisably postmodern terms. Heiner Müller's wry response to being called a postmodernist was to say that his understanding of the term was that he once knew a postman who was also a modernist (Müller 1984: 137). Whether Müller liked it or not, his work – performance about performance, aligned to a self-reflexive restructuring of contents and codes – checked most of the postmodern boxes.

The grand narratives of mainstream dramatic invention are built on the classical modernist idea that there are certain truths that can unify humankind. Postmodern performance writing self-reflectively challenges the rationalising assumptions of a modernist mindset by emphasising smaller narratives, 'which are concerned with localised events and individual perspectives and are often open-ended' (Page 2006: 20). By ensuring that the language forms it utilises are never hermetically sealed, postmodernism creates an oscillating displacement wherein identities are constituted from the interface between multiple spheres of presentation and representation. Marco de Marinis suggests that 'In representational theater, the *mise en scene* functions *on the whole* as a transparent semiotic system of *renvoi*, and as a fictional event, by virtue of the conventional canons that ground it. ... The exact opposite occurs with theatrical events that can be placed mostly or entirely outside the canons of representation. In these cases, the underlying production conventions cause the performance to present itself *generally* as a self-reflexive and nonfictional entity' (de Marinis 2004: 234).

Performance writing can be regarded as differing from ideas of 'dramatic text' inasmuch as the subject of articulation is likely to be regarded as being in process, as something provisional, contextual and unfinished, as a performative rather than a constative narratology. Rather than being regarded as an autonomous being, a *character*, who reflects on the world from a position of privilege, the performing self is no more than one caught up in the flow of many. As Auslander writes about the ways in which members of the Wooster Group performed in *L.S.D. (...Just the High Points...)*, the 'blurring of identity nullified the possibility of characteristic projection. It also suggested the construction of the subject under mediatization; the mediatized self-in-alterity, rather than some conception of an 'authentic' self, became the grounding' (Auslander 1997: 66). This position poses a challenge to those principles of dramatic writing that aim to reveal the presentational truth of a representational subject: the characteristically modernist approach that would have it that the 'real', the essentialist truth about the world and its people can be successfully conveyed through narrative. That is to say, that fictionalised narrative drama is able to faithfully represent a 'real' that lies beyond the phenomenology of the spectator and performer together in space. Theodor Adorno suggests that 'Works of art do not lie; what they say is literally true. Their reality however lies in the fact that they are answers to questions brought before them from outside. The tension in art therefore has meaning only in relation to the tension outside. ... The unresolved antagonisms of reality appear in art in the guise of immanent problems of artistic form' (Adorno 1984: 8). The assertion, after Picasso, that art is a lie that tells the truth is persuasive, but the performance/not performance strategies of practitioners such as Abramović and Ulay, Carolee Schneemann and Sophie Calle allow for no easy distinctions between the points where truth might end and lies begin, and this is felt as acutely by the artists as spectators. Contemporary performance writing is in many ways a search for a truth that can exist without the postmodern need for endless quotation marks and qualification, at the same time as the security blanket of certainty is continuously stripped away. What remains occupies the liminal space between essentialist faith and postmodern doubt.

The idea that there is never one single truth is one that has become increasingly, almost pervasively popular. Truth is seen as always relative: to time, to place, to culture and to individuals. And yet we are able to make distinctions between facts, which may well be true, and opinions, which are based primarily on our individual readings of these facts. As Julian Baggini puts it 'Not all points of view are equally "valid" except in the sense that we all have the right to believe what we will. Simply to claim the truth is in the eye of the beholder is the end of all attempts at intelligent discourse. Similarly, though we may not be able to prove all our beliefs, some are better supported by argument and experience than others' (Baggini and Fosl 2002: 46). Baggini's concluding comments serve as a useful reminder that some truths are more truthful than others and that remaining sceptical about claims for truth is not the same thing as opting for a denial of truth *per se*. In our insistence that nothing can stand for the 'true', we run the risk of merely swapping one form of (modernist) dogma for another (postmodern) belief system; to stagger into a kind of intellectual despair where there is no point to the search because there is nothing out there to find, and no qualitative distinction between one aim and another.

Charles Peirce used the term abduction to refer to his principle of best explanation; to make decisions as to truthfulness based on one's best reading of the evidence to hand. Peirce provides us with a philosophical term for a common sense approach, one that favours pragmatism over cynicism. Jean Baudrillard's three 1991 articles, *The Gulf War Won't Happen*, *Is The Gulf War Actually Happening?* and, most provocatively, *The Gulf War Never Happened*, create an intellectual position on the nature of truth and illusion that we can engage with without disavowing pragmatism. J. L. Styan recognises the relationship between performance and truth when he points out that 'As it is with acting, so it is with playwriting: the old gives way to the new, which in turn grows old. It is axiomatic that each generation feels that its theatre is in some way more 'real' than the last. ... It is, of course, the conception of dramatic reality which changes, and realism must finally be evaluated, not by the style of a play or performance, but by the image of truth its audience perceives' (Styan 1981: 1). There is always a space between reality and performance because some form of simulation is used as a bridge between experience and its retelling: however closely work draws on the 'real', its own inevitable acts of selection and staging bring imagination to bear on experience, and the nature of the real starts to shift.

When Yoko Ono wanted her work to be true ... to achieve truth through art by any possible means, she culled events from her own private experiences, drawing spectators into a self-reflective world where sensory acts of everyday life were isolated and made public. To Ono, performance is not a process of fabrication through rehearsal so much as a process of living, as something intuitive, spiritual, sensual and experiential, as something that is not merely a duplication of life.

CASE STUDY 1.5: YOKO ONO

Yoko Ono (1933–) is a Japanese-American musician, artist and performer who has lived most of her life in the United States. She attended the upmarket Gakushuin Academy in Tokyo from primary school to college, where she was the first female student to enroll on the Philosophy programme. At the close of the World War II, Ono moved with her family to Scarsdale, New York where she enrolled in Sarah Lawrence College to study Music.

Ono was first married in 1956 to the composer Toshi Ichiyanagi. They divorced after six years. In the year of her divorce Ono married the jazz musician, art dealer and film producer Anthony Cox. This marriage was annulled in 1963, but the couple remarried later that year, finally divorcing in 1969. In the same year Ono married John Lennon. Some critics, such as Brian Sewell regard Ono's marriage to Lennon as her sole public achievement, whilst others feel that her husband's fame did much to overshadow Ono's significance as an artist.

Ono was one of the original members of the Fluxus Movement, a collection of disaffected artists that came together at the beginnings of the 1960s in a sort of neo-Dada homage. Fluxus (the term, translated from Latin, means 'instant change') fed into and out of conceptual and performance art, and Ono, collaborating closely with John Cage, was instrumental in these areas of work.

A noted example of Ono's performance work is *Cut Piece*. In this work Ono remained passive as spectators cut her clothes off, leaving her naked on stage. Perhaps the most influential example of her conceptual practice was her book *Grapefruit*, which included a series of instructions that are to be completed in the mind of the reader.

In 2001, *YES YOKO ONO*, a 40-year retrospective of Ono's work received the International Association of Art Critics USA Award for Best Museum Show Originating in New York City. In the same year Ono received an honorary Doctorate of Laws degree from Liverpool University. In 2002 Ono received the Skowhegan Medal for work in assorted media and was presented with the honorary degree of Doctor of Fine Arts

→

$\rightarrow$

from Bard College. In 2005 the Japan Society of New York presented her with a Lifetime Achievement Award.

Chronology (Selected):
Cough Piece (1961)
Touch Poem No. 5 (1962)
Hide and Go Seek (1964)
Chair Piece (1964)
Cut Piece (1964)
No. 4 (Bottoms) (1966)
Strip Tease Show (1966)
9 Concert Pieces for John Cage (1966)
Box of Smile (1966)
Two Virgins (1968)
Life with the Lions (1969)
Bed-In for Peace (1969)
Walking on Thin Ice (1981)
Yoko Ono: En Trance (1990)
My Mummy was Beautiful (2004)

Recommended Reading:
Ono, Yoko. 1970. *Grapefruit*. New York: Simon and Schuster.
Henri, Adrian. 1974. *Total Art: Environments, Happenings, and Performance*. New York: Oxford University Press.
Goldberg, RoseLee. 1979. *Performance: Live Art 1909 to the Present*. New York: Harry N. Abrams.
Kellein, Thomas. 1995. *Fluxus*. New York: Thames and Hudson.
Crow, Thomas. 1996. *Rise of the Sixties*. New York: Harry N. Abrams.
Munroe, Alexandra and Jon Hendricks. 2000. *Yes: Yoko Ono*. New York: Harry N. Abrams.

Times change and as an agent of deconstruction time is changing what it is that we view as art. Sensibilities shift, and what was at one time non-art can be transformed into art through little more than the passing of years. Once determined, examples of visual art are preserved, kept safe in frames, on plinths, flattened behind glass and protected even from flash photography. We add value onto value. We choose what to keep and in choosing we determine, and not least for others what it is that is not only 'art', but also 'good' or 'important' art. In keeping only that which we decide is worthy of preservation, we encourage an increase in value according to uniqueness that is often determined by forces other than those imposed by the artist. In this way a mass-produced print is worth no more than the paper it is printed on, until such time as all other copies have faded away. Then and only then does the once mass-produced achieve (or have ascribed to it) the status of art. Because a print may be of as fine a quality as an original, we know that the quality of reproduction is not an issue. The issue is one of reproduction itself.

The 20th century saw a number of artists and art movements rebelling against this idea of the uniqueness of the art object. What happened, perversely, was that in striving to destroy the uniqueness of art, the artists themselves became celebrated in entirely new and different ways. In turning their backs on the idea of alchemy artists became alchemists like never before. Lauding Leonardo da Vinci's *Mona Lisa* was one thing, proclaiming Marcel Duchamp's *L.H.O.O.Q* (a print of the *Mona Lisa*, on which Duchamp had drawn a goatee beard and moustache) as an art object in itself was something else entirely. When Andy Warhol and later Jeff Koons made kitsch copies, which were worth more than the originals on which they were based, the art world stepped out, off the edge of previously held notions of definition. As artists whose medium had hitherto been the creation of permanent objects began to crave the ephemerality of performance, distinctions between 'art' and non-art' became even more difficult to determine. The difficulty now was one of immediacy. Because the work could not be preserved, judgements had to be as of the moment as the work itself.

There is insufficient room within this introduction, chapter-length though it is, to arrive at anything like an even quasi-history of the ways in which art of the last century *segued* into performance; these ideas will form the thrust of Chapter 1. It is imperative, however, that we begin to focus upon key post-World War II activities in order to record an emergent focus on the performative body and its subsequent impact on performance writing. The aftermath of 1945 saw a seismic shift that did much to shatter the boundaries between action, performance and fine art. Where these boundaries were not rendered indistinguishable, they became seemingly irrelevant. The dropping of The Bomb triggered a shift in global consciousness. In the face of such emphatic proof that life was fragile the body in art became central. Actions undertaken with the aim of producing objects, such as Jackson Pollock's action paintings and Yves Klein's *Anthropometries* made way for art where the intention was the creative process rather than the creation of marketable artefacts. With Pollock and Klein a key shift had taken place in painting. Prior to this artists almost without exception had worked hard to conceal the evidence of their creative processes. When Pollock and Klein sought to focus the attention of the viewer on the performative aspects of painting, one of their successes was the transformation of art into action.

There is a clear enough line between Pollock and the Viennese Actionists, just as a line exists between Herman Nitsch, Gunter Brus and Franko B. The step from the artist's studio to the performance space was for many a short one indeed. In 1952, at Black Mountain College, John Cage presented his *Concerted Action*, which was later known as *Theater Piece No.1*. The action included David Tudor's piano music, Robert Rauschenberg's Paintings, poetry from atop a ladder and the reading of a lecture. Cage's seminal *4′33″* of the same year was heavily influenced by Rauschenberg's *White Paintings* and the steps became shorter still. In focusing spectatorial attention away from the artwork (a silent composition) an engagement was made with the processes that led to the work. All that remained were the intending artist and the receiving spectator, with little that was demanding of applause in between. Allan Kaprow's *18 Happenings in 6 Parts* took place at New York's Reuben Gallery, and the frequent location of subsequent Happenings in art galleries served to emphasise the fact that their origins lay primarily in visual art. In much the same way that installations of today are often drawn to the aspirational neutrality of galleries rather than to the metaphorical potency of theatres.

The art of the 20th and 21st centuries has become the realisation of Jean Malaquais' dictum that once there were enough artists in the world the artists would become their own works of art. In collapsing distinctions between the maker and the made, we have slid into a post-Duchampian world where, true to Kurt Schwitters' beliefs, anything an artist spits is art. In 1961, the Italian artist Piero Manzoni went further than Schwitters by canning his own faeces and labeling it *Merda d'artista* ('Artist's Shit'). This may be fine and good, but what makes Schwitter's spitter an artist in the first place? What makes one human being an 'artist' and another not? The difficulty stems from the shift away from immediately discernible quality. We recognise a four-minute miler as an athlete and a plodding jogger as not because we make considered and relatively common judgements as to what constitutes athletics. The jogger on a racetrack is a non-athlete engaged in athletic pursuits, whereas the miler remains an athlete no matter how slowed down the pace may become. The distinction is clear. Even when debates range as to whether, for example, the throwing of darts at a board should be regarded as an Olympic sport, we are not regarding darts players as athletes anymore than we would use the term to describe snooker or chess players. An athlete is defined by a degree of physical achievement aligned to potential. They can do that which the rest of us cannot (or could not, under similar circumstances) and, crucially, they are able to demonstrate this ability often enough to impress the distinction upon us.

Because actors act and playwrights write plays, we are able to locate and make assessment of their abilities within a relatively secure contextualising frame. We can ask how Treat Williams' Stanley Kowalski compares to Marlon Brando's. We can ask how Henrik Ibsen's work compares to Arthur Miller's. We can and do compare like with like even when we know that the comparison is flawed, when we know that like is not very much like like at all. We are able to do so because whilst so much else has changed, ideas of imitation and otherness have remained relatively constant. We can compare the art of Rembrandt to that of Francis Bacon, whereas to attempt the same with Francisco Goya and Damien Hirst would be an act of diminishing reward. Despite the variety of its manifestations, imitative art seeks that suspension of disbelief that is the staple of dramatic writing and dramatic performance. Rebecca Schneider's position is that 'We still function largely under the auspices of naturalism today as, in a direct lineage, the major tenets of mainstream Hollywood cinema generate a "slice of life," "as if" that life were not under observation – as if actors, far more than in previous styles of theatrical representation, did not know that they were being watched' (Schneider 1997: 194). If anything approaching a gulf between 'theatre' and 'performance' exists, it emerges in attitude rather than form or content. There are two points of view: one locates the written script as the mainstay and basis for the performance, while the other regards the performance as an autonomous event. Martin sees this as symptomatic of the fact that 'The 20th century has witnessed a revolution in the structure and form of dramatic literature, as compared with the Aristotelian approach, and the director has assumed more control rivalling the playwright as author of the staged work' (Martin 1994: 17).

Historically, art and theatre have been reliant upon a small number of subjects being treated in a small number of ways. Still lives, nudes, racehorses, landscapes and portraits of the rich on the one hand, tales of kings and queens, royal intrigue, battles and betrayal on the other. Furthermore, dramatic presentation is reliant upon certainty. The certainty that what we see is not for real: the whiskey in the tumbler is no more than cold tea, the sword point is blunted off and passed painlessly under the arm, and the blood that stains is a harmless dye. The seeming once only is part of an ongoing season of repertory fare. These certainties shift beneath us with performance.

Bruce Wilshire suggests that 'Because there is an element of performance in all human skills and professions, the performers who are most vital will tend to push out the limits of their performances into borderline areas in order to test for increasing ability in the outlying actual world: to test, confirm and constitute their very selves' (Wilshire 1990: 169). This idea of the 'actual', 'real' and 'unreal' worlds of life and performance is central to any debate, for if performance is able to overlap at will with everyday behaviour, then the imposition of defining terms is inevitably suspect. Conversely, if we choose to embrace an idea premised on total inclusion, then the study of performance *at the edges* drifts away and back on nothing other than whim. If one is able to frame everyday behaviour as art, merely by dint of one's saying so, then we are thrown back on ideas of quality as the only supposedly sound barometer of art.

And yet if art has no rules of reception-as-definition, not even rules of dismissal, then everything is placed in the hands of the artists. So that anyone can say that any object is art, any moment performance and any text performative, whilst no one can say with any confidence that anything is not. For those of us in search of some kind of authority to cling to, no matter how flimsy it might be, this is something to avoid rather than engage with. As Schwitters returns to release or enslave us, it is small wonder that we feel ourselves stumbling in either the darkness of confusion or the false light of certainty.

We can see that the opening up of theatre into performance takes us on journeys to the very edges of possibility. The only limit that remains is our own ingrained sense of what it is that constitutes performance. Whether we like it or not, we in the West are living at a time when our daily lives – from the cars we drive and the designer clothes we wear, through to the interior design of our homes, our iPods, mobile phones and body ornamentation – have come to resemble and even at times be indistinguishable from art. The reverse is also true in that performance has come not only to resemble life, but also to be no more than a frame around the everyday, the commonplace and the banal. In conversation, John Cage and Richard Schechner argued for 'definitions that won't exclude ... simply that theatre is something which engages both the eye and the ear, so one could view everyday life itself as theatre' (Schechner 1985: 248).

Writing for new performance is what new-performance writers do. Very little defines the work. What does provide a link is a sense of writing in a way that is in itself performative: inasmuch as the approach taken tends towards the transgressive, the fluid and the questioning, rather than the reassurance of (relatively) stable characterisation, plot, structure and denouement. If dramatic plays occupy a space where we feel we know something of the rules of engagement, writing for performance is located within a landscape where only uncertainty reigns. We are not always sure what behaviour the writing will induce in either performer or spectator. Occupying a space that is neither blueprint nor act, somewhere between the ephemerality of performance and the permanence of print, between the fixed and the malleable ... it is what Clifford Geertz describes as 'the inscription of action' (Geertz 1983: 31). Conversely, Worthen reminds us that 'From the "literary" perspective, the meaning, and so the authority of performance is a function of how fully it expresses the meanings, gestures, themes located ineffably in the structures of the work, which is taken both as the ground and origin of performance and as the embodiment of cultural intention. ... Though performances may discover meanings or nuances not immediately available through "readings" or "criticism", these meanings are nevertheless seen as latent potentialities located in the words on the page, the traces of the authorial work' (Worthen and Holland 2004: 12).

Texts for performance are rarely regarded as literary and are seldom seen as stand-alone objects, forming as they do one part of a continuum of process. This is not a qualitative exclusion: the monologues of Holly Hughes, alongside the pained poetry of Tim Etchells' *Club of No Regrets* and Deborah Levy's *The B-File* are clearly demonstrative of writing that can be enjoyed and admired for rhythm and cadence. But unlike a play by Miller or Mamet, Shakespeare or Shaw, a text for performance is unlikely to reveal much in the reading of a subsequent performance. The text, like a map where nothing is ever quite to scale, is that, which it is also not.

One of Sigmund Freud's most telling observations was that every denial was 50 per cent affirmation. *Mea culpa.* Towards the start of this introduction, I denied the setting up of a binary between modernism and postmodernism, and now, as we near its end, I am disclaiming the setting up of some adversarial oppositionality between 'text' and 'play'. If that is half a falsehood, it is also half a truth. The work of Sarah Kane certainly communicates no easy *French's Acting Edition* sense of privileged directorial approach without losing its status as 'play'. Distinction joins the list of other unstables, as practices leak from one category to another at no more than the mood of the moment. And yet the idea of theatre as the realisation of a scripted play and of performance as something 'other' is the axis on which this book will begin to swing. And the force of the argument's swing may be all that defines the difference. It says much in fact for our cultural need for the establishment of hierarchies that the umbrella term 'performance' is seen as a sub-section of 'theatre', rather than vice versa. Historically, narrative is joined at the hip to theatre. That is where we went for the fix we get now from a diverse array of sources: from cinema, from television, from the Internet, from literature. That we are at the end of our cultural love affair with theatre, like a couple with nothing much to say to one another and fearing the finality of divorce, is not the result of dumbing down so much as wising-up. What we once needed we need still, we just do not necessarily need to sit still in theatres to receive it. Narrative order becomes the first sacrifice of new performance.

Performance consists of a series of recognisable conventions and conventions are the stuff of tradition. Inasmuch as progressive practitioners attempt to free themselves and their work from the shackles of tradition, from convention as the conventional, they do so by locating their own approaches within the world of similarly minded artists. This results in one set of traditions being exchanged for another, making radical, surprisingly original developments the rarest commodity in theatre. Some writers, such as Sarah Kane, engage in a dialogue with the past that is so shocking as to lead to a genuine unfixing of spectatorial and critical expectation.

CASE STUDY 1.6 :   SARAH KANE

Sarah Kane (1971–99) was born to parents who were each journalists and each devoutly religious. She studied Drama at Bristol University, graduating with first class honours, before taking an MA at Birmingham University. Kane suffered from depression throughout her life, leading to intermittent spells in hospital. A suicide attempt in early 1999, using sleeping pills, was unsuccessful, but on 20 February in the hospital where she was being treated, she hunged herself.

Kane was the author of several plays, notably *Cleansed* and *Blasted*, which were regarded as distorted, repellent, obscene and brilliant. They address almost all the taboos of modern society in a provocative 'in-your-face' form, and for many, including hardened theatre-goers and critics, the work was almost unbearably violent and bleak, with British theatre critic Jack Tinker regarding her play *Blasted* as 'this disgusting feast of filth'. In fact Kane's plays dealt uncompromisingly with themes of love, and every act of cruelty, pain and torture they contain is characterised by a highly individualised poetic intensity and a rich affirmation of love in all its forms. Kane's use of powerful and disturbingly violent imagery, which includes the sucking out of eyes and the barbecuing of genitals, is used to cut across and fragment the narrative of her plays, giving

$\rightarrow$

→

something of the experience of a life torn up by its roots. Harold Pinter, an early supporter of Kane's writing, said of *Blasted* that Kane was presenting theatre audiences with 'something actual and true and ugly and painful'.

Kane always denied that the violence in her plays was gratuitous. Relating her work to her upbringing, she claimed that the ultimate source of her inspiration was the Bible. In her teens she had lived a very intense form of Christianity, one that was strongly Biblically based, at least within the context of her family. For Kane the Bible was nothing if not a rape and mutilation-filled book, with incredible outrages seemingly sanctioned, and at times initiated by God. Compared to the Bible, Kane regarded her own work as tame and bloodless.

Chronology:
Blasted (1995)
Phaedra's Love (1996)
Skin (1997)
Cleansed (1998)
Crave (1998)
4.48 Psychosis (2000)

Recommended Reading:

Invirne, James. 1997. *Jack Tinker: A Life in Review*. Ottowa: Oberon.

Stephenson, Heidi and Natasha Langridge. 1997. *Rage and Reason: Women Playwrights on Playwiting*. London: Methuen.

Eyre, Richard. 2001. *Changing Stages: A View of British Theatre in the Twentieth Century*. London: Bloomsbury.

Buse, Peter. 2001. *Drama + Theory: Critical Approaches to Modern British Drama*. Manchester: Manchester University Press.

Kane, Sarah. 2001. *Sarah Kane: Complete Plays*. London: London: Methuen.

Sierz, Alex. 2001. *In-Yer-Face Theatre: British Drama Today*. London: Faber & Faber.

→

→

Unwin, Stephen and Carole Woddis. 2001. *A Pocket Guide to 20th Century Drama*. London: Faber & Faber.
Dromgoole, Dominic. 2002. *The Full Room: An A–Z of Contemporary Playwriting*. London: Methuen.
Saunders, Graham. 2002. *Love Me or Kill Me: Sarah Kane and the Theatre of Extremes*. Manchester: Manchester University Press.
Rabey, David Ian. 2003. *English Drama Since 1940*. Harlow: Pearson.

Performance strives always for change. For Gómez-Peña, 'the performance arts world is merciless. Since it defines itself always in opposition to its immediate past and it is always inevitably and acritically looking at the future, you are forced to redefine yourself constantly if you want to remain seated at the table of debates in the field. Otherwise you are out … gone. The speed at which the field changes is vertiginous, unlike any other field, and a performance artist nowadays has a very hard task, which is that of constantly reinventing him or herself and developing new and surprising strategies in order to remain alive and current' (Gómez-Peña 2000: 194). Contradictory though it may seem, to know the now that Gómez-Peña seeks, we must go back to the start of the last century – a century, let us in no way forget, that was defined from first to last by its consistent striving for newness: in art, in warfare, in travel and technology. We must go back to great century of change: to Dada, Surrealism and the Futurists, to the manifestos-as-performance of Marinetti, Arp and Breton.

1
Nothing Dates like the Nearly New: Futurism, Dada, Surrealism and a Century of Change

The beginning of the 20th century can be regarded as the start of a fascination with the subversion of previously accepted art, literary and performance codes, of a near-obsession with the possibilities of interdisciplinarity, hybridity and assemblage. Despite these obvious connections, using the past to make sense of where we are is a complicated endeavour. History, lest we forget, is always only what the historian makes it out to be. Nowhere is this idea truer than with the history of live performance, where the work denies all but a reliance on selective memory and borrowed influence. What is allocated to the archive and what is erased or disregarded is a question that haunts all who seek to make sense of the past, and this question permeates the pages of this book.

Whilst this chapter will provide an historical framework within which recent developments in performance making and writing can be better understood, it is not intended to function as an authoritative historical document *per se*. What follows is a condensed view of performance from the early 1900s and includes work that seems *to this writer* and *at this particular time* to be of significance to present-day performance and performance-writing practices. In telling one story, we neglect to tell another. In adopting a reading of the recent past that prioritises movements from a visual arts history, rather than, for example, opting to trace links back through the work of Meyerhold and the Russian Constructivists, I am at the same time writing out a huge and hugely influential part of theatre's lineage, which is also the lineage of performance. In acknowledging this, I am aware that the history of theatre is a history of smoke and mirrors in more ways than one and that we have to peer hard to see what is hidden.

With this caveat we can at least agree with David Zinder that the first half of the 20th century saw its avant-garde practitioners pursuing 'a wholesale revision of artistic, cultural and even political values. It was this avant-garde attack on traditions and conventions that caused its adherents to adopt the political designation of "schools"' (Zinder 1980: 1). From a mainstream perspective the 20th-century European and American understanding of theatre could be said to have begun with the Moscow Arts Theatre, with the naturalistic plays of Chekhov and (elsewhere) Ibsen aligned to Stanislavski's directorial insistence on that which has been passed down to us, a quasi-photographic attention to imitative detail. This approach was an attack on prevailing sensibilities. The commonplace nature of that which passes for naturalistic theatre today has numbed us to the fact that the work based on naturalism was regarded by many at the time as rebellious in the extreme. Nevertheless, for the purposes of performance writing as distinct from playwriting *per se* and for the purposes of this book, we look to Futurism rather than Naturalism as the birth of the performative new.

The founder of Futurism was Filippo Tommaso Marinetti. A man of the arts with a grounding in performance rather than painting or sculpture, Marinetti came to Futurism from a background as a playwright. Accusations of Fascism have always clung to the Futurists: Marinetti dedicated a great many Futurist works to Mussolini, as well as declaring that war was nature's truest and most honourable form of hygiene. Fascism notwithstanding, the Futurists set the scene for a century of innovative and subversive performance, and their influence, not least in terms of approaches to and use of text, needs to be noted here.

Futurism began around 1909, when Marinetti published his first manifesto in the Paris newspaper *Le Figaro* before moving Futurists into the realm of performance with poetry and manifesto readings. Where poetry had been hitherto regarded as something solemn and even sacred, the Futurists used poems as an incendiary prelude to public disturbance and a series of high-profile riots. In this way, the influence of Alfred Jarry's provocative work of some 15 years earlier was clear, not least because Jarry's play *Ubu Roi* had created such violent outrage when it opened in 1896. However, the confrontational style of the Futurists took the baiting of audiences to a new dimension. The Futurists' first theatrical event occurred at the *Politeama Rosetti*, the Municipal Theatre of Trieste, on 12 January 1910, where the spectators were instructed 'not to applaud but to boo us off the stage' (Martin 2005: 9). The performance comprised a direct and unashamed incitement to chaos and disorder, which the spectators appeared largely unprepared for.

One month later, after intense publicity in the Italian press, spectators at public performances were more than equal to the Futurists' requests, and fights broke out in the theatre and spilled out into the streets.

For the main part, and whether through empathy or anger, spectators at Futurist events played their own roles with gusto, with vegetables and rotten fruit being purchased beforehand and subsequently hurled onto the stage and at the performers. Umbro Apollonio reports an exchange between Futurist performers and spectators: 'A vase, several saucers and five and ten centesimi pieces were hurled at the actors and the leading lady received a severe blow over the eye from an unripe tomato. The occupants of the orchestra stalls suffered considerably from tomato juice and beans. And the performance came to a premature end when the actors themselves began to hurl vegetables and fruit back at the audience' (Apollonio 1973: 22).

The Futurists' deliberately provocative and confrontational relationship with their spectators would be taken up some half-century later by the Austrian writer Peter Handke with his 1966 play *Offending the Audience*.

Although Futurism was around in one form or another until the mid-1940s, its momentum had begun to show signs of slowing long before that, when its emphasis on simultaneity, dynamism, anarchy and violence through art had, not least in the wake of the First World War, begun to pale. Marinetti's publication in 1924 of *Futurism and Fascism* was of considerably more interest politically than it ever was artistically, and the movement had lost a great deal of its force. The 'roaring machines' that Marinetti, Boccioni and Balla had embraced as the great future of mankind had killed too many people, and spectatorial attention was shifting away from the diatribe of Futurist hostility towards the Dadaists' good-humoured sense of play.

For the Futurists, art and performance needed to become functions of life, something as necessary to existence as breath, and its practitioners saw no distinction between one's daily life and, as Eugenio Barba would come to describe it, the 'extra-daily technique' of performance (Barba and Savarese 1991: 36). This, above all else, is the legacy of Futurism and the foundation of the performance practice subsequently undertaken by the likes of Linda Montano, Marina Abramović, Vito Acconci and Elizabeth LeCompte.

During the First World War, Zurich became the European centre for disaffected artists and left-wing intellectuals alike. Separated from their respective cultures and brought together by a shared contempt for bourgeois morality, this collection of artists was motivated by outrage at what they perceived to be corrupt, war-mongering politicians. This outrage was the platform on which Dada was built. From its now-seminal origins in the Cabaret Voltaire at Zurich's No. 1 Spiegelgasse of 1916, to its dissolution in the Paris of the early 1920s, Dada enjoyed the type of wide international support that had been denied to the more overtly aggressive ('Burn down the Louvre!') Futurists. In December 1919, Dada was defined as 'nothing at all, in other words everything' (Eiger 2004: 6). This contradiction, of an anti-art art movement, lay at the heart of Dada. The number of manifestos the unashamedly internationalist Dadaists produced was impressive, yet the movement failed to cohere into a particularly organised and tightly focused group. This had little impact on its effectiveness, however, as Dada events in 1919 Berlin played to audiences as large as 2000 at a time.

If indeed 'the manner of playwriting is inseparable from the kind of theatre it is written for' (Styan 1981: x), Dada clearly sought to mirror the peculiar dynamics of its age. In this Dada was always as much about attitude as art. Whilst the word 'Dada' means hobby horse in French, the name itself (so one of the many versions of the story goes) was chosen from a dictionary page opened at random by Tristan Tzara, Hans Arp and Raoul Hausmann in 1916; its usefulness to Dada lying precisely in its banality and lack of meaning as an art-descriptive term. Accordingly, the name for its founders was without significance, whilst its method of selection was symptomatic of all that Dada would come to represent. Tzara's cry that 'DADA DOES NOT MEAN ANYTHING' (Tzara 1981: 21) is echoed through the Dadaists' perverse and obsessive creation of manifestos at the same time as they proclaimed themselves to be thoroughly against manifestos of all kinds. Their manifestos stood, thus, as anti-manifestos, just as their art at the time was widely regarded, not least by the Dadaists themselves, as being anti-art. With prescience of Piero Manzoni's *Merda d'artista* (1961) and Marc Quinn's *Shit Head* (1997), Dada, in partial homage to the opening line 'Merdre' of Jarry's *Ubu Roi*, operated under the banner slogan 'Art is shit', and the consistent element of Dada manifestos was their pouring of scorn on the idea of art as it was being customarily practised in the European academies and *conservatoires*. As ironically functional responses to a seemingly dysfunctional world, it is hard to consider Dada as anything other than a complete art of its time. And the time was one of dissonance, which Dada responded to by calling for state prayers to be replaced by simultaneous poetry and for sexual intercourse to be regularised by the Central Dada Sex Office. It was a time when Berlin Dadaists held races between the writer Walter Mehring seated on a typewriter and the artist Georg Grosz atop a sewing machine, whilst cabaret performances provided a blend of political satire, striptease and sexual licence, washed down with copious amounts of alcohol.

Marcel Duchamp's famous, and to some minds infamous, 1917 urinal, entitled *Fountain,* signed R. Mutt and entered unsuccessfully into a New York exhibition organised by the Society for Independent Artists stands as a paradigm for more than the Dadaist's so-called ready-mades that followed. Subsequent defence of the object's artistic legitimacy was based on claims that 'Whether [the artist] with his own hands made the *Fountain* or not has no importance. He CHOSE it. He took an ordinary article of life, placed it so that its useful significance disappeared under the new title and point of view – created a new thought for that object' (Mink 1995: 67) and, succinctly, that 'This work by Marcel Duchamp revolutionized art like almost no other' (Eiger 2004: 80). In creating a climate of acceptance for the idea that art might be anything an artist chooses to call art, so too was the idea accepted, albeit on a more gradual basis, that performance was able to accommodate everyday behaviour. Through this, the great postmodern preoccupation with context takes root, leading to serious consideration of the belief that what matters is not *what* is art so much as *when* is art.

Even though 'since Duchamp' has become a commonplace of art and performance history, a notoriously cheap and easy shorthand for change and the all-too-often-used paragraph-opener of many an academic paper (it should be acknowledged here that this is a shorthand I have never been slow to employ), Duchamp's influence continues to be significant in our understanding of current and recent practices. It is there in Andy Warhol's screen prints and Jeff Koons' millionaire-kitsch copies of cheap-kitsch originals, in the Living Sculptures of Gilbert and George, and in Joseph Beuys' *I Like America and America Likes Me*, in Carolee Schneemann's *Eye Body* and Spalding Gray's monologues, in Kira O'Reilly's *Succour* and Abramović and Ulay's *Nightsea Crossing*. In death, Duchamp has become that which he resisted in life. He has been made to stand, like the fiercely guarded stage directions to Samuel Beckett's plays, for something rigid and fixed, as an epoch-definer, rather than as one whose life and work was eclectic, eccentric and restless, one tirelessly committed to change.

CASE STUDY 1.7:   MARCEL DUCHAMP

Marcel Duchamp (1887–1968) was born in Normandy. Trained as a painter, in 1911 Duchamp exhibited his last recognisably Cubist work *Nude Descending a Staircase*. From this point on Duchamp's work was always on the periphery of styles

→

→

and movements. At various points, he was regarded as a Surrealist or Dadaist, but these terms meant little to him. The artist William de Kooning's description of Duchamp as a 'one man movement' is apt.

Duchamp produced probably his most famous work, the ready-made *Fountain* in 1917. The work consisted of a urinal signed R. Mutt, and this established his reputation as one of the few ground-breaking artists who were able to successfully challenge the accepted notion of what comprised a work of art. In 2004, a survey among the 500 'most powerful people in the British art world', artists, dealers, critics and the curators, resulted in *Fountain* being named the most influential artwork of all time, with 64 per cent of the vote. In 2006, in an act that we can imagine Duchamp would have acknowledged, albeit reluctantly, as art, *Fountain* was attacked with a hammer, causing its surface to become chipped. The sculpture was being displayed as part of a major Dada exhibition at the Pompidou Centre in Paris. The attacker was subsequently identified as a 76-year-old performance artist from the Provence region of France named Pierre Pinoncelli, who had urinated on the sculpture when it had been displayed in Nimes in 1993. Pinoncelli was not the only person to vandalise Duchamp's work. In 2000, two Chinese artists, Yuan Cai and Jian Jun Xi Lanjun, urinated on *Fountain*, claiming that they were honouring Duchamp's belief that only artists defined art. In the previous year the pair had jumped on and into Tracey Emin's gallery-installed *Bed*.

Duchamp remains one of art's most iconoclastic figures, one who spent a lifetime deriding the pretensions of art at the same time as he was relentlessly exploring its possibilities. He is regarded by many as the godfather of modern art, predicting movements such as Conceptualism, Minimalism and even Pop Art and Postmodernism.

Chronology (Selected):
Nude Descending a Staircase (1911)
Nude Descending a Staircase No.2 (1912)

→

→
Bicycle Wheel (1913)
3 Standard Stoppages (1913–14)
The Bride Stripped Bare by Her Bachelors, Even (The Large Glass) (1915–23)
Fountain (1917)
L.H.O.O.Q. (1920)

Recommended Reading:

Jones, Amelia. 1995. *Postmodernism and the En-Gendering of Marcel Duchamp*. Cambridge: Cambridge University Press.
Mink, Janis. 1995. *Duchamp*. Koln: Taschen.
Cabanne, Pierre. 1997. *Duchamp & Co*. Paris: Editions Terrail SA.
Naumann, Francis M. 1999. *Marcel Duchamp*. New York: Harry N. Abrams Inc.
Eiger, Dietmar. 2004. *Dadaism*. Koln: Taschen.

If world politics could not be easily overhauled, then the Dadaists would commence at least with an overhaul of poetry, art and performance. Dadaist poetry, for example, was predicated upon the idea of placing cut-out words from newspaper articles in a bag, giving the bag a vigorous shake and then constructing text according to the order in which each word was removed, an embracing of the random that would have a significant impact on 20th-century art, not least through Tristan Tzara's declaration that the subsequent poem would create an exact image of the poet (Tzara 1981: 17). When Tzara's second manifesto determined that 'the chief purpose of a dada exhibition was to bring about the utmost degree of misunderstanding between the performer and his audience' (Ibid.: 51), it was nothing if not a prediction of the ambiguous interior landscapes that would be encountered by spectators in the late 20th-century 'found text' work of Robert Wilson.

The Dadaists were clearly successful in their undermining, and even ridiculing, of mainstream art sensibilities, and yet in doing this as systematically as they did, they also and inevitably included their own work. Without the afterlife provided, perhaps even *demanded*, by published dramatic material, Dada suffered from its own ephemerality. Dada was never able to cohere into a legitimate practice of opposition precisely because of its avowed distrust of legitimacy. With demonstrable indifference to the setting up of standardised categories for performance, Dada's scepticism meant that 'Scandal for scandal's sake ... proved to be as redundant and as ineffective as the art for art's sake which [Dada] had set out to undermine. ... Dada was a remarkable ferment which, more or less in spite of itself, enabled new and more powerful forces of subversion to gain time, to gather energy, to prepare themselves' (Rosemont 1998: 18–19).

Art precedes analysis, and developments in art take place before they are born theoretically. As Hal Foster describes it, art criticism often fails to address performance directly; rather, it seeks (and not always knowingly) 'to see how historical shifts may be registered in theoretical texts ... which will thus serve as both objects and instruments of history' (Foster 1996: 208). Despite this, the disorientation that Tzara and the Dadaists called for was never as nihilistic as it at first appeared and it sowed seeds that would be brought to fruition through the more aesthetically refined and ideologi-cally defined Surrealism: a movement made up of artists and thinkers who were about to unleash an approach to art and performance that would develop into the greatest innovation of their century and of any other.

Twelve years before the publication of André Breton's 1924 manifesto, the term 'Surrealism' had been used by Guillaume Apollinaire to describe the collaboration between Jean Cocteau, Erik Satie, Leonide Massine and Pablo Picasso that led to the ballet *Parade*, which was premiered on 18 May 1917, at the Théâtre du Chatelet in Paris. The programme notes read: '... until now stage sets and costumes on one side and choreography on the other had only a sham bond between them, there has come about, in Parade, a kind of super-realism (sur-réalisme) in which I see the starting point of a series of manifestations of this new spirit (esprit nouveau)' (Tzara 1981: 22).

Whilst conceptually related to Dada, from which many of its initial members came, Surrealism was significantly broader in scope. If Dada was a response to the First World War that came to be regarded as little more than a joke without legible codes, Surrealism possessed a more positive and positively avant-gardist view that the world could be changed for the better through art.

Breton had been shaped in this European intellectual avant-garde envi-ronment. As a student of medicine, he had come into contact with Freud's ideas, and it was Freud's therapeutic use of free association that directly influenced the development of what Breton and his fellow Surrealists came to describe and define as automatic writing. In complete political contrast to the association of the Futurists with Fascism, Surrealism enjoyed links, certainly between 1927 and 1933, with the French Communist Party. Social change *through* art was the Surrealists' aim, and in this they embraced Karl Marx's belief that 'It is not the consciousness of men that determines their existence, but their social existence that determines their consciousness' (Marx 1995: 34).

Breton's Surrealist Manifesto of 1924 and the publication of the magazine *La Revolution Surrealiste* marked the beginning of the movement as a major force for public agitation. In his manifesto, Breton defined Surrealism as 'pure psychic automatism in its pure state, by which one proposes to express – verbally, by means of the written word, or in any other manner – the actual functioning of thought. Dictated by the thought, in the absence of any control exercised by reason, exempt from any aesthetic or moral concern' (Breton 1972: 14). For Breton, automatism meant spontaneous creative production without conscious moral or aesthetic self-censorship. By his admission, however, as well as by the subsequent development of the movement, this was a definition capable of considerable expansion.

The manifesto included numerous examples of the applications of Surrealism to poetry and literature, as well as making it clear that its tenets were capable of application in any circumstance of life and were not to be restricted to the world of art. The importance of dreams as a deep reservoir of Surrealist inspiration was also highlighted, and it was this striving for a type of dream-state subconsciousness that came to define the movement in the popular imagination.

Breton had discussed his initial encounter with the surreal in a famous description of a hypnogogic state that he had experienced, in which a strange phrase inexplicably appeared in his mind: 'There is a man cut in two by the window' (Breton 1972: 103). This phrase echoes Breton's ideal of Surrealism as the juxtaposition of two distant realities brought together to create a new, wonderful and hitherto unimaginable union. Hypnogogia, a term coined by the 19th-century French psychologist Alfred Maury, is the name of an experience one can go through when falling asleep. In a hypnogogic state a person can have lifelike auditory, visual or tactile hallucinations, which are sometimes accompanied by full body paralysis. The individual is aware that these are hallucinations, whilst being unable to physically react to them. One of the stumbling blocks for Surrealism was that whilst hypnogogia was a reasonable and admirable aim for immersive art, the reproduction of such was no more than realism in another name: no more, ultimately, than Aristotle's imitation of an action dressed in borrowed robes. We shall see when we move through forthcoming chapters that performative attempts at the recreation of natural and primitive impulses create as many problems as they aim to solve.

For Breton, Surrealism was automatism. He defined automatic writing as the absence of critical intervention in the creation of text. Automatic writing was thus able to proceed not on the basis of narrative sequence or systematic description, but rather in accordance with the random interplay of word and image associations. The etymology of automaton is 'chance', and the working of chance is of essential importance for Breton's notion of automatic writing. In his instructions for the production of automatic texts, Breton urged writers to write randomly and without any specific intentions; this would lead to monologues 'spoken as rapidly as possible without any intervention on the part of the critical faculties, a monologue consequently unencumbered by the slightest inhibition and which was, as closely as possible, akin to *spoken thought* (Grace, Sherrill and Wasserman 2006: 76). In reflecting on work undertaken with The Chameleons Group in 1996, Steve Dixon pares automatic writing to the bone in his description of the processes involved: 'The technique is essentially simple. One sits down, empties the mind, and then writes as quickly as possible without pausing or trying to consciously interfere with the stream of consciousness' (Dixon 1998: 67).

Through automatic writing, or so at least thought Breton, the unknown depths of the subconscious would be brought to the fore, leading to intellectually impossible connections being made quite literally by chance. As the Surrealists' primitivism would be to Artaud, so their notions of chance would, some quarter of a century later, have a huge and lasting impact on John Cage and his collaborators at the Black Mountain College.

The shift from Tzara's cutting up and rearranging of pre-existing text into text for the new author and on towards Breton's appeal to the subconscious to draw out what is already there is significant. The Surrealists were committed to the release of hitherto unconscious material and to harnessing the power of dream logic, to the power of associative correspondence between previously unconnected ideas and images, words and actions. For Breton, through text, as with the drawings made by André Masson between 1927 and 1934, the intention was to put the artist in direct contact with her/his subconscious thoughts and desires. Breton linked this directly to Freud when he wrote that it was there, in the unfathomable depths of one's mind, that 'there prevails, according to Freud, a total absence of contradiction, a release from the emotional fetters of repression, a lack of temporality, and the substitution of external reality by psychic reality obedient to the pleasure principle and no other. Automatism leads directly to these regions' (Breton 1965: 73).

Surrealism can be linked as much to style as to system. Rimbaud's appeal to the systematic derangement of the senses was the fuel that fed Masson's deliberate implementation of disorientation as process through a blend of sleeplessness and starvation, aligned to the consumption of alcohol and narcotics. These attempts to subvert traditional notions of competence and polite artistic behaviour would be developed through the decades of endurance-based performance work that would begin in the 1960s and would include such projects as Abramović and Ulay's walking the Wall of China for *The Lovers, The Great Walk* (1990), Teching Hsieh's *Thirteen-Year Performance* (1986–99) and Stelarc's *Sitting/Swaying: Event for Rock Suspension* (1980). These would co-exist alongside mind and body-state alterations such as Abramović's swallowing of medication for depression and schizophrenia in her 1973 performance *Rhythm 2*, Gina Pane's blood-infused climbing of a razor-stepped ladder in *Escalade Sanglante* (1971) and Bruce Gilchrist's sleeping mindscape-as-performance *A Way of Asking for Reasons* (1994). The Wooster Group's fabled use of hallucinogenic drugs as part of their rehearsal for the 1984 performance of *LSD (... Just the High Points ...)* amounted to the strategic incorporation of disorientation within a production, which gave the illusion of random behaviour at the same time as it was at its most precise. This approach, which was not so much automatism, or its performative twin *improvisation*, as it was a form of imitative behaviour so rigorous and deliberately rehearsed as to read as the real, is paradigmatic of postmodern performance.

The mainstream concept of chance in ancient times, at least up until around the end of the 18th century, had been connected to a premise of chaos, to a lack of order and an absence of design. Since Aristotle had referred to chance as an indefinite cause, very few people, at least up until 1800, had really challenged that view. Only when Pierre Simon Laplace at the beginning of the 19th century discovered the Central Limit Theorem did the atmosphere begin to exhibit signs of change. Laplace arrived at this theorem as a consequence of his observations that errors of measurement tend to be normally distributed. For that reason the Central Limit Theorem was often referred to as the Law of Frequency of Errors. At the end of the 19th century the whole concept of chance had changed to the extent that Francis Galton was able to write: 'I know of scarcely anything so apt to impress the imagination as the wonderful form of cosmic order expressed by the Law of Frequency of Error' (Ross 1988: 399).

It was not just in abstract theory that this new concept of chance emerged. Charles Darwin's massively influential work on *The Origin of the Species* (1859) related chance to his revolutionary concept of random selection. As Darwin had it, in any given species over time, random and arbitrary changes occur. These random changes can turn out to be either successful or unsuccessful. If the changes are successful it means that that part of the species will survive. If changes are unsuccessful that part of the species dies out. Chance then becomes the New God and, in direct opposition to the psychological underpinning of every action, arbitrariness becomes the New Order. Influenced as he was by Darwin, Sigmund Freud developed a theory of free association to uncover hitherto inaccessible memories and cognitive structures. Again, the free or random associations were believed to reveal certain deeper structures, ones that lay hidden behind apparent chaos. For his own part Breton was conscientious in his citing of Freud as one of the inspirations for his concept of automatic writing.

The Surrealist approach to the creation of text was a strategy designed explicitly to displace conventional notions of text generation. The Surrealist text, deliberately written without effort, plan, or calculated symbolic inclusions and through the utilisation of radical dream-like associations, displaced the literary aspirations of dramatic text, altering the language of performance to the point where it no longer corresponded to familiar conventions. Conte de Lautreamont's definition of Surrealism as the chance meeting of a sewing machine and an umbrella on an operating table led in 1925 to Man Ray, Joan Miró, Max Morise and Yves Tanguy combining to create a drawing in ink, pencil and coloured crayon. They used the children's drawing game of 'Heads, Bodies and Tails', or 'Consequences', to create a bizarrely skewed and analogical depiction of a creature with an ass's head, a snail's body, female legs and tennis racket feet, opting to label the work *Cadavre Exquise* (*Exquisite Corpse*), after the phrase arising from a Breton-instigated game where five people wrote a word or phrase each on folded paper: 'The exquisite ... corpse ... shall drink ... the young ... wine'. Whether the manifestation was visual or textual, these activities were intended to undermine the idea of individual invention as a measure of artistic value at the same time as the possibility of collective reality was given form and artistic legitimacy.

Rather than regarding the automatic as something completely random or arbitrary, we might from a performance-writing perspective view it more usefully as a synonym for spontaneity. When created material is considered the product at once of nature and of intelligence, the act of representing the unconscious can only (logically) be regarded as a conscious act. In this way automatism emerges as a form of ideologically motivated and applied technique, rather than the purely random act proposed by Breton.

As envisaged by Breton, automatic writing was the key means of access to the creator's subconscious. This idea, however, involves a very specific interpretation of automatism, and the concept might be better served by regarding it as an approach that is controlled at least as much by human physiological associations such as phonetic resemblance, as it is by the human subconscious. Breton acknowledged as much in his second manifesto, where he warned readers that automatic writing could also lead to the production of clichés, instead of becoming a wholly original picture of the subconscious mind. Breton tried to repair this shortcoming by the practice of what he called *dedoublement*, or detachment (Breton 1965: 28). By this Breton meant the detachment of the mind from the body. In practice this would function as a conscious intervening of the will of the writer, the opposite, in fact, of Breton's earlier views on automatism. *Dedoublement* would be the guarantee that automatic writing would reveal the hidden order of the writer's subconscious.

The theory of automatic writing is always already in conflict with itself due to its conscious urging for unconscious writing. The incompatible dualism between the writer's role as the generator of an undirected text and the continuous concentration of the mind on its own activity to submit to the principle of writing automatically is immediately apparent. The result of this is that Breton's *dedoublement* occupies an uncomfortable place within the writing process. In functioning as a conscious and clearly deliberate parallel check-up of the mind as it is involved in automatic writing, it cannot be other than in and of the mind itself. In order to work in this way, and to work appropriately, the writer's mind would have to be conscious and unconscious, active and receptive, at one and the same time. From a theoretical perspective one could argue with relative ease that this results in the failure to establish a coherent methodology for automatism-in-art. From the perspective of the artist, however, the fact that the methodology does not live up to its theoretical claims is no hindrance to practice. Indeed, whilst theory is an undoubtedly invaluable tool for unpicking performance, it is rarely a useful way into performance itself. Lyotard cut to the heart of things for practitioners when he wrote that all theories of art are encapsulated in the question: 'Why does something happen rather than nothing?' (Lyotard 1979: 17). Arguing for a reappraisal of theory within performance, Susan Melrose goes as far as to say that 'theory may, indeed, be counter-productive in the context of effective performance making' (Melrose 1999: 41).

When the Surrealists pursued the representation of subjective internal experience rather than objective external reality, it followed logically that anything that could be imagined would immediately assume the validity of 'art'. This demanded a receptive shift on the part of spectators, requiring like-minded receivers to decode the work. And perhaps this was destined never to be fully achieved in the moment, the definition of a theatrical masterpiece as a work 'that achieves a sort of internal purposiveness, setting up demands which it continually satisfies within its own structure' (Pepper 1949: 73) destined never to be realised. Since its earliest ritual acts theatre has generally been unified and defined by a limited number of basic elements: a person (performer) communicates something (a text, an action, an event) to somebody else (spectator). As Eric Bentley puts it, Person *A* represents Person *B*, whilst Person *C* watches (Bentley 1965: 64). This has held true from Aeschylus to Ayckbourn. Even if/when we accept the idea that the only witness to the certain act is the performer, theatre is always in some way about the to-be-seen and the to-be-heard.

In practice (or perhaps in less practised hands) Surrealist techniques often led to a series of clichéd determinations, which in turn created traps for the very subconscious creativity that Surrealism sought to release. Notwithstanding Breton's acknowledgement in his second manifesto that there were a significant number of problematic aspects relating to automatic writing, which he tried to alleviate by the introduction of a certain detachment of the mind, there was, within his own theoretical framework, little or no space for a concept like *dedoublement* to adequately flourish. Caught between the rock of rigour and the hard place of liberty, between conscious manipulation and unconscious free association, automatic writing began to feel like a spent force. In *The Creative Unconsciousness*, Hans Sachs urges caution when it comes to the idea of applying the logic of dreams to art: 'Daydreaming is by the daydreamer, for the daydreamer and of the daydreamer. ... The daydream is thoroughly asocial, it does not build a bond of mutual understanding between individuals, nor does it propagate intellectual or moral communion, nor transfuses emotion from one person to another' (Sachs 1942: 14). Spectators of the day may have been sympathetic to the stimulus for the work they saw at the same time as they found themselves at some considerable remove from the subconscious source of the writers involved. To put this briefly, the self of the artist was beginning to become more important than the selves of spectators, whilst the same spectators, to use Barthes' terminology, were invited to become *writers* of meaning into the work they experienced rather than *readers* in the sense of functioning as relatively passive recipients of predetermined information (Barthes 1977a: 142–48).

Writers select from a wide range of experiences and ideas, determining from these aspects a point of investigation and attack. Theoretically at least, if not always in practice, this creates a unified imaginative focus, which is subsequently shaped and made concrete through the circular process of writing, reflecting and rewriting. Without disregarding or undermining the types of deconstructionist activities described and embraced in later chapters of this book, we are almost always able to say that the writer writes that which s/he intends the spectator to receive (Bauman 1978: 229). Where some writers will choose to control the spectators' experience and compel their perception towards an antecendently prescribed course, others, such as Apollinaire, Aragon and Jarry, were to be less concerned with persuasion and control. 'Freedom', as Breton was to say, 'is the only word that excites' (Breton 1972: 155).

In whichever way we choose to approach it, writing cannot escape knowledge of its own activity. Radical attempts to do so, such as those undertaken by Breton, alongside their relative failure, only confirm this fact. The Surrealists needed to *identify* distinctions between the banal and the beautiful – between Marcel Duchamp's pen stroke and Leonardo da Vinci's brushwork – in order to expose the illogicality of their juxtaposed togetherness. Late 20th- and early 21st-century postmodern practitioners conversely, demonstrate rather less inclination towards acknowledging the *appropriateness* of one image or phrase over another. Robert Wilson's utilisation of Christopher Knowles' autistically generated texts as elements of major performances has little or nothing to do with satisfying external ideas of either appropriateness or juxtaposition. They are simply aspects he chooses to use. No more than this and no less. As with his at-will borrowing of Eastern forms, where Wilson is happy to tear techniques from their cultural roots, so with Knowles is he willing to use what he feels works for no greater reason than this. The surface then is the depth, and what we see is what we get. Anything else is a product of spectatorial projection rather than the laying of directorial clues. Charles Jencks has it that postmodern-ism has created spectators who are 'lobotomized mass-media illiterates' (Jencks 1987: 12), but it might be more accurate to acknowledge that we are in fact substituting one form of literacy for another and that academic study, alongside performance practice, is reflecting this. Perhaps Umberto Eco is correct when he wryly and self-deprecatingly suggests that 'All the professors of theory and communication, trained by the texts of twenty years ago should be pensioned off' (Eco 1986: 149).

Robert Wilson is regarded as the adoptive son and rightful heir of Surrealism. After seeing Wilson's *Deafman Glance* in Paris, Louis Aragon wrote an open letter to Breton claiming that the production was what those who had fathered Surrealism had dreamed it might become after the initial movement had died out. Wilson had initially studied as an architect, designer and painter, yet he was drawn, as were a number of artists of his generation, towards the greater scope of three-dimensional space, simulta-neity and montage that could only be found in the time-based medium of performance. By 1970, after five years of making theatre with children, Wilson had formed a company of trained and untrained performers (the Byrd Hoffman School of Byrds) who were to add the physical and aural elements to the hypnotic dreamscape of *Deafman Glance*. Wilson's own programme notes to the production give a clear indication of the work's indebtedness to Surrealism:

> It was two years ago September. The child threw a brick thru a window as I was going to an ART class in Summit on my way I saw the judge about to hit him as the mother pressed her hand against his head I crawl on his back to relieve the pain he was ten years old September. The line out my window leads to the Sun, the ox, the child and to all of us becoming worms. At Pratt I wrote my thesis on designing an imaginary cathedral or a fewture city perhaps. Then there was a murder, a murder in the eyes at the top of the cathedral two years ago September as the red dog howled into the moon light son notta wink! Only the bones can tell. … There are 14 cows out my window. Only their heads move. Jerry wrote me of a beautiful dream. The lion's leader leads to the Sun, the East, the son, the child. The broken arched windowed woman's house sinks as the deaf child sings an onion sliced in two (his) particulars. a don't a men.
>
> *Wilson 1970*

For Wilson, 'the dream is *uninterpretable*. Life is a language without denotation (and) symbols mean nothing' (Brecht 1978: 50); performers move with somnambulistic grace and abstract deliberation, granting spectators vast interpretative scope at the same time as making them aware that none of the clues that they read in the work will take them any closer to a conventional idea of 'understanding'. A practitioner who feels that something is missing when everything's explained, Wilson has described his textual concern as being primarily fuelled by a theatrical response to 'the sounds and the way the words look on the page' (Marranca 1979: 15). This results in a series of exaggerated and repetitive verbal phrases, which in their own turn form a complementary counterpoint to the cool, ultra-stylised metronomy of the movements carried out by his performers, along with a disturbance to the 'ordinary' function of language. But to state things in this way is not to agree with the suggestion, made by some, that Wilson's approach to performance plays down the spoken word to the point of extinction. On the contrary, the multi-linearity, found text and rhythmic cadences regularly adopted by Wilson lead to a sensibility that is in many ways as aural as it is visual. This allows him to transpose his inner vision into theatrical terms, and to avoid the sometimes-crippling conventions of dramatic presentation. For Wilson, these conventions lead to ping-pong dialogue and banal televisual delivery. The spoken word is not then excised from theatre and performance so much as it is relocated as one element in a non-hierarchical performance of space, personnel, sounds, words, light and movement.

The absence of any clear hierarchical relationship is an unbalancing act. Theatre tradition in the West is also the history of the literary text: the history of the play. Non-verbal theatrical and performance forms or those that have treated the spoken word differently, such as *commedia dell' arte*, street theatre, carnival, music hall and eponymous live art and installation-driven work, have until recently been largely sidelined academically and critically, as though their immediacy and ephemerality have led to the denial of legitimate retrieval and so to a form of scholarly dismissal. Theatre remains joined at the hip to the idea of actors being led by directors towards the realisation of previously (and almost exclusively *privately*) scripted dramatic matter. Richard Schechner described the 20th century as 'the history of the avant-garde, which can be seen as wave after wave of anti-bourgeois, mostly left-leaning, angry yet visionary artists pouring themselves out onto a hostile shore' (Schechner 1982: 15). The shore remains hostile to this day, despite the fact that a century of performance texts have signalled a move away from interpretations and towards creations.

The majority of textual practices with which this book is concerned have been created with no real sense of any literary or even performative afterlife. What we see from a growing number of contemporary writers are scores for performance, texts that are created specifically, maybe even exclusively, for the original performers. Of an often equal importance are aspects of diverse source material, autobiography and media interventions, shopping lists and private letters, recipes and interrogation, all being utilised as grist for the mill of text production. Performance texts are no longer necessarily concerned with providing evidence of an *a priori* concern with the words spoken in performance. Central to this shift is the idea that performance is not about the imitative duplication of human behaviour as much as it is about focussing on aspects of behaviour in ways that 'everyday life' may disguise. This makes theatre 'not a simulation of life outside, any more than football is, or the circus, or a game of chess, but an activity in itself, neither less nor more real than any other activity; its artificiality consists only in the fact that it is deliberately condensed to fit a particular time and place' (Fletcher & Spurling 1972: 20).

As Futurism, Dada and Surrealism embraced innovative and process-driven approaches to writing and performance, we can say that the performance making and writing focussed on in this book have roots in the disruptions wrought on art at the start of the last century. We may indeed go further than this and argue that (almost) all of the elements we now regard as central to our most advanced experiments in performance stem in principle from the avant-garde practices of 1910–30s Europe, not least those of Surrealism, which has emerged as the most significant of the three named approaches, if for no more telling reason than that the involvement of artists such as Dalí, Magritte and Tanguy has resulted in a painterly permanence denied to the temporality of the more event-driven output of Dada and the Futurists. Time has taught us (to distil Robert Hughes' extraordinary work *The Shock of the New* to one sentence) that historical periods and styles do not break clean; rather they splinter, feeding into and out of their neighbours (Hughes 1980). The terms we might use at this point in the 21st century are more watery – slippage, leakage, fluidity – yet the meaning remains the same; and this meaning is that nothing exists in isolation. Despite their differences, it is the similarities between these three radical approaches to art and performance that matter the most. They sum up a time, and in showing us something of what happened then, they provide a contextualising frame through which to view the now.

To summarise, Surrealism, Dada and Futurism:

- Broke down the barriers of conceptual language.
- Argued that the direct outpouring of the individual subconscious was a valid form of art.
- Experimented with an over-loading of sensory circuits through a multi-media barrage of sensations, in order to arrive at a new form of perception.
- Encouraged an emphasis on context as the defining principle of art.
- Involved the audience in three-dimensional environmental events that forced spectators to participate in communication by the (f)act of entering the theatre space.
- Led to a generation of theatre makers, including but not limited to Artaud, Beck, Brook, Mnouchkine, Grotowski and Wilson, whose concerns were with improvisational flow, space, movement, light, sound, abstraction and a resistance to linear narrative.

The combined belief in the cult of self augured against precisely that type of directorial intervention which was becoming prevalent in a Europe gripped by naturalistic fervour. For if the intention was to create an untrammelled exploration of the inner (dreaming) self, it followed that directorial involvement could only ever amount to a form of dilution. Subversive theatre at this time signalled a disinterest in the imitation of external reality exemplified in the plays of Ibsen and Chekhov, opting instead for the exploration of personal experience, alongside and through freedom for the artist to create without any concessions to general comprehension. Because theatre is a perishable commodity of time, it is in constant opposition to permanence; accordingly, historians will often look to film as the best barometer of Surrealist performance.

As one of history's happy accidents this is no bad thing. Surrealism is inextricably linked to film inasmuch as the passing of illuminated images across the screen is akin to the feeling one might have of watching somebody else's dream. It does not end quite there: in dreams we journey in jump cuts and montage; we shift perspective at irregular intervals; we witness and perform impossible tasks; we change identity, location and shape. Our dreams function as a means of transforming fantasy into narrative and narrative into fantasy. And dreams, in the early 20th century, were a genuine and permissible part of the European cultural, social and scientific landscape. It was no accident therefore that Surrealism allied itself to Freud's interest in dreams as the providers of parallel realities. Freud was not alone in his location of art and performance in a realm almost beyond reality, in a world not bound by historical time and social events. Surrealism's love affair with film was born of the logic of abrupt shifts in ways of seeing, wherein the disruption of normally perceived ideas of narrative structure and linearity was sacrificed to apparently random associations and occurrences.

Cinema is named after the Greek word *kinema*; if the word denotes 'motion' we can say that the connotation is also with 'emotion'. Theatre (like theory) has its etymology in *theatron*, meaning, 'where you view'. Terms such as theatre *audience* and cinema *viewers* steer us away from another equally valid reading, which is that theatre is always about looking, whereas cinema is about movement and transport: the transporting to somewhere else via emotion. Perhaps the closest word we can find for this phenomenon is the Italian *trasporto*, which encompasses the attraction of humans to one another. It is about a going from and a coming to. This is the reason why love in the movies is about cinematic space and movement and emotion, both on the screen and in the viewer. It is in this way that film moves us as it moves. It is a geography of light and shade, of memory and hope, of community and loneliness. We care about the cinema because, as the Surrealists well knew, it is a medium with the capacity to transport us to someplace else: to a new world to view. The particles of light shone at 24 frames per second transform the flatness of the screen into a type of fantasy as fact where stillness is always an impossible dream.

The Latin root of the word 'emotion' stems from *emovere*, an active verb composed of *movere* ('to move') and *e* ('out'). It speaks of a moving force. Emotion then is about a moving out, the transferring from one place or one state to another, from what we feel to what we see and from what we see to what we feel, and Surrealism exposed this state like no approach before. The word 'feel' is possessed of currency that is at once emotional and tactile, and feelings affect us physically, just as physical feelings affect our emotions. Because emotion is of the heart and of the mind and of the body, passive watching is as oxymoronic as passive loving, and it is impossible to watch a film such as Buñuel and Dalí's *Un Chien Andalou* of 1928 without some form of active engagement.

Un Chien Andalou, described by Raymond Durgnat as 'Seventeen minutes of pure, scandalous dream-imagery' (Durgnat 1998: 7) ran in the cinemas of Paris for eight months, gaining a critical legitimacy so unexpected and unwanted by its authors that it prompted Buñuel to describe the film, in full anarchic vein, as a desperate and impassioned call to murder. The narrative content of the film, such as a sense of narrative could be said to exist, roams across time and space, from Buñuel's slitting of the heroine's eyeball as a cloud cuts through the moon, through ants emerging from a bloodlessly punctured hand, gunshots, hit-and-run deaths, a body in a field and a mouthless man, before concluding with a glaringly pre-Beckettian image of two people buried up to their chests in sand.

The film dislocates itself from its own narrative flow even as its story unfolds. Neither Dalí nor Buñuel sought links between successive scenes, and it is true that there are no logical links from scene to scene, leading to the fact that an almost limitless number of interpretations can be drawn from the images shown. A usual and initial response is to feel that each section is random and unconnected, although Buñuel includes elements and items which are present throughout. Rather than providing the security of common ground, the repeated sightings of these things in situations and places where they should not necessarily be (à la Lautreamont) only adds to the feeling of general confusion. The eternal themes of life, death, lust and love are thrown up at various points, although there is no logical framework to which viewers can easily attach these emotions. Despite Buñuel and Dalí's energetic rejections of any rational meaning in the film, *Un Chien Andalou* exists as an exploration of desire and the obstacles in the path of instinctual passion. As an example of Surrealist film and Surrealist performance *per se*, it is without parallel.

The impact of Surrealism on performance writing was vast. As we have seen, the voracious openness of Surrealism led to an absence of fixed meaning, to the extent that the nature of art itself was brought into question: if nothing had meaning then art had no function left other than as liberation. This is the point at which the idea of 'art for art's sake' took hold, the idea of art as a space for exploration without avowed intention, of art for the sake of the artist. There is an obvious indulging of the self here, which is not necessarily the same thing as self-indulgence, and which prepared the ground for much of the autobiographical, or alibiographical, performance writings of Linda Montano, Spalding Gray and Vito Acconci that emerged as the century grew. Similarly, Marinetti's claim that the stage was no more the life it represented than the wheel was the leg signalled an of-the-moment caveat to the very suspension of disbelief that Stanislavski's Moscow Arts Theatre was calling for through the psychologically imitative works of Chekhov. This is significant inasmuch as the concept of realism as a form, as a stylistic device, was already, at the start of the 20th century, being tightened into a stranglehold on European culture. The invitation from writers, directors, actors and critics to suspend our collective disbelief calcified almost immediately into theatre's truest absurdity. What, after all, could be more absurd than to buy so whole-heartedly into the on-stage illusions of *Uncle Vanya* or *Hedda Gabbler*, to the crying of real spectatorial tears in response to false actorly behaviour?

Marinetti's 1918 *Berlin Dada Manifesto* had claimed that the highest art imaginable would be that which presented the thousandfold problems of the day, which acknowledged, alongside the likes of Duchamp, that the world was so full of interesting objects, sounds and events that the artist need not add to them, that the mere act of selection was a valid act of creation and that dropping scraps of paper and pasting them in the random order in which they fell, like drawing chance words from a bag, was a legitimate form of writing. In 1920 Kurt Schwitters developed his *Palette of Objects*, drawn from the detritus of cities; in 1923 he began the process of transforming his house into an installation, which he called a *Cathedral of Erotic Misery*, predicated on the notion that anything and anybody could be seen as art. An unbroken and easily traced line can be drawn from Marinetti, Duchamp and Schwitters, through Warhol, Koons, Manzoni and Quinn, through John Cage and Tracey Emin. It is also a line that connects Antonin Artaud and Chris Burden, Ron Athey and Tim Etchells, Robert Wilson and Elizabeth LeCompte. It is a line that runs through innovative performance making and writing of the last 100 years, and it is this line that will determine the trajectory of this book's chapters as they move through the 20th century and on into the 21st.

Whilst time has stripped the early 20th-century manifestos of much of their currency, what has remained is a poetics of indeterminacy, aligned to a calculus of probabilities and possibilities: of the potential for art to transcend the boundaries of the known. The legacy of interventionist art of the early 20th century is the legacy of doubt, where art functions as a springboard into an array of potential readings. For when the resonance generated by art is no longer grounded in a coherent and recognisable discourse, it becomes impossible to decide which associative elements of the work are relevant and which are not. This uncertainty paved the way for the postmodern performance strategies of the latter part of the century. As Nicholas Zurbrugg puts it: 'Whereas a rainy day or cloudy seascape could delight … modernist writers like Joyce and Marcel Proust, pioneer postmodernists ... transform the harmonies of modernist discourse into their own peculiarly solipsistic and apocalyptic evocations of incoherence and desolation' (Zurbrugg 2000: 49).

Zurbrugg's words could be used as a description of the kinds of performance texts we recognise now as part of our cultural fabric, of a 'schizophrenic experience of isolated, disconnected, discontinuous material signifiers which fail to link up into a coherent sequence' (Foster 1983: 119), of being faced with a 'pure and random play of signifiers ... which no longer produce monumental works of the modernist type, but blocks of older cultural and social production, in some new and heightened bricolage; metabooks which cannibalize other books, metatexts which collate bits of other texts' (Jameson 1987: 223). It is to works such as these – to the ways that they are created and the ways in which they are opened up to multiple readings – that the principal address of this book's remaining chapters lean. It is what links much of the compositional practice that makes up our highly complex and ever-shifting contemporary performance world.

2

Writing the Space

Writing the space, or writing for particular spaces embraces ideas of intervention, indeterminacy and adscititious engagement. Adscititious is a rarely used term referring to the imposition of critical perspectives that are alien to the subject,[1] to alter what is viewed in the act of viewing. The act of viewing is always to a degree adscititious, and where we view from – no less than what we view – is determinant in this.

And what are the places from which we view and how neutral can they ever be? Ric Knowles notes that theatre spaces are inevitably 'full of histories, ghosts, pressures, opportunities, and constraints, of course, but most frequently they are full of ideology – the taken-for-granteds of a culture, that don't need to be remarked upon but which are all the more powerful for being invisible' (Knowles 2004: 63). These 'taken-for-granteds' are geographical, social, cultural, spatial and gendered; they are inevitably and markedly determined and impacted upon by one's age, sexuality, mood, relative comfort or discomfort, state of fatigue or alertness, relationship to the surroundings, relationship to other spectators and relationship to performers. And these examples are by no means exhaustive. Perhaps more significant than any of these determinants is the question of whether or not the spectator is inside or outside of the 'rules' – as Savran (1985) would have it – inside or outside of the protocols, practices and procedures of making and of making known.

This relates to Susan Melrose's description of the sometimes-gulf and sometimes-bridge between performer knowledge and spectator knowledge. In Melrose's view, 'it is rare to find practitioner expertise. ... It is rare, even in the case of those writers who consistently engage with expert practices and practitioners from their own position as expert spectator' (Melrose 2005). This is exasperated by the on-the-ground situation in which few

---

[1] See Peter Harrop's elegant 1996 usage.

academics will admit to an absence of performer knowledge, as though directing an end-of-year play immediately doubled one's status. The practitioner expertise Melrose is commenting upon has less to do with experience than with empathy: it's about a mind set that is as distinct from normative academic analysis as the vocabulary of making is from the vocabulary of taking apart.

Notwithstanding the belief in some quarters that we are no longer able to make comfortable distinctions between those who do and those who watch (Allain & Harvie 2006: 9), this chapter is predicated upon the idea that those readers who regularly attend to a variety of performance modes watch differently to those who do not. They do so because they know that the easy-to-show is not necessarily the easy-to-make, that performance making is as much about stripping away as layering on, as much about attrition as addition. They know that the 'My Story' of autoperformance is as much about alibiography as autobiography, as much about interrogation as illustration, that the seeming truth is in many ways no more than a well-told lie. This is not about elitism. Those who make performances watch with a still different concentration. When the viewers are also performance makers, the act of watching is likely to be filled with moments of generative impulse recognition: the work makes practitioners think about their own performance practices, and in these moments of hither and thither spectators, 'return' to the work they are watching with their own always-adscititiously-arrived-at agendas.

According to Grotowski's pre-paratheatrical statements, we can 'define the theatre as "what takes place between spectator and actor". All other things are supplementary – perhaps necessary, but nevertheless supplementary' (Grotowski 1969: 32–3). In whichever ways it might be defined, performance then becomes, essentially, the dialogue between one who does and one who sees. In this sense performance remains as committed to communication as it ever was, but the idea of a prescribed text as something to be communicated has been replaced by the idea of text as something which implicates its spectators in crucial ways. The written word is no longer the default determinant in theatrical performance. Where the words in a performance were at one time regarded as the messenger and the message, today they have shifted to their new role as the constituent element of mountainous critique, where it sometimes seems as if a text is not a text until it is written about elsewhere.

In Gay McAuley's neo-Grotowskian terms, theatre is 'essentially a relationship between performers and spectators, and ... it seems to me that both are somewhat at risk. Spectators sitting in their serried ranks in the darkness, discouraged from all but the most stage-managed interactions with one another or with the performers ... are disempowered' (McAuley1999: 281). McAuley extends this position by suggesting that things will only improve when the 'performance space is designed and ordered in such a way that genuine exchange can take place between the human beings on the stage and those in the auditorium' (Ibid.: 282). We can further these ideas through an increased strategic negation of the distinction between spectators and performers. Negation is a more useful term for our purposes than 'denial', because negation allows for the possibility of differing views being simultaneously held. In this way the postmodern invitation for spectators to read performed events as inhabiting the realm of the real – or more accurately the peculiarly real/not-real – can function alongside the centuries-old tradition that strips performed events of common social consequence. Aristotle's notion of theatre as the imitation of an action does little to prepare contemporary spectators for the sight of Ron Athey's crown of syringes or Kira O'Reilly slicing into herself with a surgical scalpel, much less for the invitation to spectators to make their own cuts in her flesh. And yet Athey and O'Reilly's work is theatrical in the extreme, as well as functioning as examples of the type of practice that is discussed in this book's next chapter.

In concentrating on the differing ways in which spectators receive what they see, this chapter moves between live performance, visual art and cinema. Along the way the text will explore something of the ways in which memory is linked to cinema, in contradiction to theatrical performance, which, it will be suggested, is in increasing danger of being arrested by its own past. In part the following paragraphs create a peg on which to hang a series of often-subjective notions of performance, ranging from installation to links with the subsequent chapter's concentration on body art. In so doing, the preoccupation with the live body in the late 20th century performance emerges as the sole referent capable of being pinned down in an otherwise unstable and fragmented age of theatrical art and identity. Some well rehearsed links and ruptures between modernism and postmodernism are revisited here. These are used to read the ways in which mid to late 20th-century installation art betrayed the intentions of its own modernist makers, creating a postmodern site of subjective spectatorship.

This chapter is about ways in which we write the body, memory and space. Those elements that begin separately coalesce as the chapter develops. As with every other section of this book, this chapter comes with a warning. The notion of 'writing as we watch' is riddled with undecidability and the gulf between the spectator-theory of watching and the practitioner-theory that comes with creative writing is as wide as it is deep. As Melrose has described it, the performance practitioner tends to engage with performance-making problems, which are fundamentally incompatible with the academic theorist's attempts to infer creative cause from perceived effects (Melrose 2005). If at times it seems as though the job of academics is to try to prove themselves (ourselves) smarter than the artists who make the work, then this book treads a precarious step through certainty and doubt. And so by implication does the reader.

Performance makers and writers engage in conscious and experiential attempts at addressing their own 'participation in processes' (Kaye 1994: 10), creating in turn a literal play on the constitution of time and place, of matter and event. Critical commentators on performance on the other hand are more inclined towards a discursive and distanced form of speculation. The artist, so Pierre Bordieu tells us, does more than s/he knows (Bordieu 1977), whilst it is the fate of the critic to always know more than s/he does. The two forms of knowing are not the same and the oppositional methods of communication only add to the gap. Performances which are intrinsically unstable, ephemeral and multi-modal contain within them knowledge which, when transposed into print on the page, only confirms Lyotard's concern that performative mobility is misremembered by critics into new and artificial fabrications (Lyotard 1989: 24).

Whilst the binary of lies and truth is no longer one which we have any uncomplicated, critical and cultural faith in, the very impermanent nature of the relationship nevertheless continues to make sense. The wheel allows us to travel faster and further than the leg, without being 'true' to the essence of legs. It is an imitative lie that tells the truth of movement. Cubism is a lie inasmuch as the images it offers can only exist as art. Until such time – that is as one sees from the sky, the cities below as flattened out cubist landscapes or the outside/inside, front, back and sides of an x-ray photograph – the lie becomes another type of truth. In a similar way text for performance is a lie that seeks to bridge the gap between the 'as if' of writerly construction and the 'is now' of reconstruction through performance.

Guilio Camillo's 16th century *Memory Theatre* with its radical intention of presenting performatively that which would otherwise remain unseen was a precursor to the films of Wim Wenders as much as to the theatre work of the likes of Tadeusz Kantor, for it is cinema that most emphatically articulates our need to link the present with the past. If the connection here is obvious, inasmuch as the film we view is almost always of the gone, the done, the dead and the remembered, it is also more obliquely linked to the notion of the ways in which memory works. As the revolutionary Soviet film director Dziga Vertov explained, and as we saw in Chapter 1, cinema, like memory, serves to free us from the boundaries of time and space, enabling the coordination of any and all points of view to be posited in any way one chooses. Vertov's take on film was that it led towards the creation of a fresh perception … of the explanation in a new way of a world that would otherwise remain unseen and unknown. If the invention of the camera emphatically changed the ways in which the world was viewed, it did so in ways that already existed in dreams and recall.

The acute sense of cultural displacement many of us currently feel is a central aspect of contemporary art and performance; and be it zenith or nadir, this displacement has found a home in the marriage of film and live theatre. As film emerged historically from theatre, so does theatre now seem, in many ways, to aspire to film. The employment of film, video and more recently digitalised computer technology in the work of the Wooster Group – not least their 2002 production *To You, the Birdie* (*Phedre*) – has its antecedents in Piscator's 1927 production of Yvan Goll's *Methusalem*, and in its own way it extends the potential of live performance at the same time as it continues to tamper, ground-shiftingly, with those Aristotelian ideas of unity that modernism, for all of its innovation and inventiveness, seemed always to return to. Walter Benjamin understood film as a medium much more akin to surgery than alchemy, as something with the potential to reveal an optical unconscious. Benjamin's ideas were posited between on the one hand, a view of film as being governed by psychoanalysis and on the other, the more overtly political idea of film revealing that which is otherwise concealed in the social order of things. In this way, film can be said to occupy the space between Artaud's faith in embodied actions working through sensation on the bodily perception of the spectator and Brecht's famed use of montage as a strategy for revealing the inner workings of a given situation. When Brecht deployed montage in order to focus spectatorial attention upon the dialectical tension between the narrative thrust of a scene and its structure, his relationship to the cinema of Eisenstein was immediately apparent. And so one of the seminal bridges between modernist theatre and modernist film was revealed.

Memory is the cartography of experience and the borders of memory are the edges of our internal screen's ability to resurrect the past. In 1934 Benjamin wrote that he had for years considered the idea of setting out the sphere of his life graphically, on a map. In a similar vein Jorge Luis Borges once wrote a poem in which all of the journeys made during a person's lifetime mapped the lines of his protagonist's own face. As far back as 1654, Madeline de Scudery had published a fictional map as part of her novel *Clelie*. She called this map a 'Carte du pays de Tendre', a topography of the land of tenderness. The emotional material of the novel was given a visual identity, inasmuch as the exterior landscape was used to depict the interior world of the characters. Like Camillo before her, de Scudery aimed to imbue the unseen and the emotional with legible form. Through the

Lake of Indifference, the Dangerous Sea and a town called Negligence the visual – the optic – and the sensory – the haptic – were brought together. It is hard to regard de Scudery's work now as anything other than a paradigm for the ways in which performance art is approached and understood.

As it is with our comprehension of the fictional protagonist of *Clelie*, so it is that we come to make sense of the internal world of art through our visual comprehension of that which the artist elects to make shown. The geography of art leads us to the core of our selves. But this is an awkward geography and an elusive self. When Alex Kelly, from the European performance collective Third Angel, writes that the company makes 'work that strays into the grey area between the truth and fiction, memory and imagination ... work that incorporates documentary detail and fiction but doesn't bother to point out which is which' (Kelly 2003: 49), he articulates the absence of fixity in both the navigator and the route that turns the art of performance into an act of detection.

Geography is the site where emotion meets memory. In the 1st century AD, Quintilian wrote of memories as architecture, with image-filled rooms of the mind triggering thoughts. In order to move our minds from room to room, these images need to be affectively and emotionally charged. We need to care enough to take the time to make the trip. Like these invented rooms, actual spaces and places are loaded with the emotive power to make us recollect. And as memory (like film) is never still and never at rest, so is the case with the remembered and the act of remembering, the trigger and the triggered overlap and build and deepen. What we remember, we change it in the act of remembrance: the room of the imagination stays the same. It is we who visit who have always changed. And if these rooms have an optic quality, then that quality is also always haptic. Haptic in this context refers to being able to come into contact with, and in this it is art's form, function and reception no less than it is a function of memory.

Like *The English Patient* out of Michael Ondaatje and Anthony Minghella we drift between memories and dreams as seamlessly as wrinkled sand dunes seen from the sky melt into love-crumpled sheets, as effortlessly as a mountain range becomes a lover's back. Haptic articulates a sensory function: a function that is as much of the body as it is of the mind. Haptic can also be related to kinesthesia, to the innate ability our bodies have to sense their own movement in space. When we live we move and the less we move the more we want the eye to flicker. Gallery-goers can gaze forever at the dried out stillness of paint precisely because the movement they crave is in their own hands and in their own feet. In the gallery we stop, we shuffle, we step closer and we then step back. Accordingly, ideas of elsewhere are always in our gift. We walk away when we feel like doing so and if we are so inclined then we return. 'Elsewhere' in the theatre, that necessary need for visual movement, is too often the function of clumsy and outmoded metaphor. The limits of the stage become the limits of our seeing world. Sight lines hem us in, forcing our gaze down channels no wider than the wooden boards. If what we see is what we get then theatre-based performance rarely gives us as much as we need.

As the chorus of Greek theatre has been replaced by the gossip mongering of characters from small-box soap operas, where the venomous asides provide a running commentary on the action, so is our narrative performance fix provided by television and cinema. And it does so at the mainstream theatre's expense. At this point in history, we no longer need the story lines of Chekhov played out à la Stanislavski for dramatic contemplation, anymore than we are drawn to the theatre as a space for education and enlightenment. More fundamental than this, however, is the possibility that in the memory game of art, theatre is being left behind, and by some considerable distance.

This is no mere wordplay. The legacy of postmodernism seems at times as though the only future we can look forward to is the past that has already been lived. As postmodernism grips us in its rigor mortis vice of selective eclecticism, the temptation to withdraw into modernism is strong, and pervasively so.

Modernism carried with it, or was carried by, a claim that non-interpretative judgement could be applied to art, and that judgement could thus be universal. As interpretation is innately prejudicial, modernist art, and not least performance, had at its core the entirely honourable idea of emancipation; because understanding would not be reliant upon the privileging of certain interpretative methodologies over others, the work would be open and accessible to all. Or so at least went the argument.

More than this, the work would contain no vestige whatsoever of concealed dimensions that could only be uncovered by specific and specifically privileged interpretative processes. In this way, the work is what the work is. The art does not require differing forms of completion, rather, it exists as the thing itself and the thing unto itself. This was the hoary old 'art is art is art is art' argument advocated by Ad Reinhardt, exemplifying the modernist ideal in which the art object or event was seen to possess an apparent placelessness, which in reality meant the place of the gallery, the museum or the theatre. The disturbing of these prescribed sites for art was born of a substantial and wide-ranging opposition to modernism, even before that opposition was being formally articulated. In so doing, site-specificity and installation 'unveiled the material system (modernism) obscured – by its refusal of circulatory mobility, its belonging-ness to a *specific* site' (Crimp 1993: 17). The performance space is not architecturally defined as a precondition of performance so much as it is regenerated and re-imagined by the work and the spectators inhabiting it.

What we, the spectators, bring to an installation is no longer the gaze that rests upon the perpetually present aspects of the work: that which Michael Fried – suggesting that the perceptual experience of the work is inseparable from the work itself – referred to as the 'grace of presentness' (Fried 1998: 147). The only grace of presentness is provided by the spectator. This dislocation and relocation of presence was developed and subsequently challenged through ostensibly modernist installations, more than through theatrical and theatrically placed performances, and even more so than through the more expected form of painting. When Chris Burden, Vito Acconci and Marina Abramović created those installations such as *Five-Day Locker Piece*, *Seedbed* and *Nightsea Crossing*, which have since become iconic, the object/event was collapsed into the space in a way that was fundamental.[2] The location became an absolutely central part of the event even when, or *particularly when*, these locations were not fixed. Contextualising her own practice, Cathy Turner takes a view of site-specific performance as that which is 'freer to renegotiate relationships with audiences than performance within traditional spaces' (Wrights and Sites 2000: 39). Simon Persighetti reinforces this when he writes that 'In site-specific work the artifice of acting is exposed when the site reminds the audience of their own presence in a particular time and space', arguing that site-specificity 'suggests a different approach to performance' (Ibid.: 9).

Theatres continue to operate 'with their conventional partition of scenic and spectatorial space, the (seemingly) public and (darkling) private, onstage and backstage, the seen and unseen ... preserving at least a minimal difference between actor and audience, object and observer' (Blau 2002: 9). The current modes of site-orientated installation practices are being mapped out here upon a genealogy of performance art. It is useful to consider Vito Acconci's comments on performance as an ultimately contract-based practice: 'On the one hand, performance imposed the unsaleable onto the store that the gallery is. On the other hand, performance built that store up and confirmed the market system: it increased the gallery's sales by acting as window dressing and by providing publicity ... There was one way I loved to say the word "performance", one meaning of the word "performance" I was committed to: "Performance" in the sense of performing a contract – you promised you would do something, now you have to carry that promise out, bring that

---

[2] See Abramović, A. & Ulay. 1997. *Performances 1976–1988*. Eindhoven: Stededijk Van Abbamuseum; Linker, Kate. 1994. *Vito Acconci*. New York: Rizzoli; and Burden, Chris. 1996. *Beyond the Limits*. New York: DAP/Distributed Art Publishers.

promise through to completion' (Acconci 1993: 29). Acconci's completion of his promise is matched in part by an equally spectatorial contract to attend to. His views are echoed by Margaret Morse, for whom installation and interactive performance is defined by its approach to the idea of subject: 'Performance, even where it has installation-like sets, differs from installation, because the artist occupies the position of the subject within the installation world. Interactive work differs in yet another way. Room is made for the visitor to play with the parameters of a posited world, thus taking on a virtual role of "artist/installer" if not the role of artist as declarer and inventor of that world' (Morse 1998: 163).

Allan Kaprow saw the word 'Performance' as an ultimately poor surrogate for happenings, events or activities, which were some of the terms used in the 1950s and 1960s to indicate a number of somewhat tangentially related series of real time and real space events. Kaprow's belief was that what we call an installation today is the child of that which used to be called, before the first happening in 1959, an environment. For Kaprow, the words, installation and performance, serve to mark the attitudinal shift toward a rejection or sense of abandonment of an experimental, modernist position. From Kaprow's perspective this is a fair point, but the bracketing of modernism with experimentation implies an end to experimentation *per se*, rather than acknowledging, as Kaprow did in 1966 when he declared installations as dead, that whilst time is always in progress, terms offer only calcification.

For the purposes of this chapter, the installation work of interest is about spectators (and usually performers) coming face-to-face with sound, image, activity and architecture in a non-theatre space which is nevertheless theatricalised by virtue of the events taking place there. Culturally interesting though they might be, Tracy Emin's bed, Christo and Jean-Claude's wrappings and Damien Hirst's formaldehyde-soaked shark are not part of this focus, neither is the sometimes extravagant reconfiguring of space in extant theatre buildings. To this end, Schechner's elaborations with The Performance Group and Elizabeth LeCompte's subsequent work with the Wooster Group on the space that is New York's Performing Garage, based in no small part on their radical rethinking of the possibilities within that interior/exterior space, do not turn their performances into installations. A flexible theatre is still a theatre and its space in this context will always lack the peculiar dynamic of performance in non-performance sites.

Whilst installations are often theatrical, it remains a one-way street, and theatres are never installations. Theatres are designed as metaphorical sites where here is almost always made to stand for there. This sets up a difficult, not to say impossible, set of conventional spectatorial expectations to shift.

It is the business of theatres to install performers, spectators and material inside a space that is always at least relatively flexible: accordingly, the term 'installation' when applied to theatres takes on a meaning so ubiquitous as to lose all currency. If installations demand nothing else, they demand a relationship with the spaces they occupy. This relationship might be unique, inasmuch as the work can exist in one site only, or the relationship might be such that the work is portable. What installation rarely is is simply an arrangement of objects or actions in a space. In these instances space becomes a surrogate for either the gallery or the theatre. There is a reasonable expectation that actions, images, events and text will feed off the existing environment in ways that would resonate entirely differently in a building specifically designed and built to host performance.

The temporary nature of an installation provides a telling mirror to performance. When the work is done the space reverts to its prior usage, albeit one that bears the traces of performance. Space as much as time defines performance, and a thing done is always a thing done somewhere, some place, some space. Whatever we choose to view is viewed within the frame, and this is not defined by black drapes, wooden rostra and painted flats, so much as by the limits of one's gaze, so that *'anything that happens in the theater during the performance time is part of the performance'* (Schechner 1973: 84).

'Most performing arts events still take place in structures that originally emerged in the seventeenth to eighteenth centuries: the playhouse, the concert hall' (de Wend Fenton and Neal 2005: 151). In the second half of the 19th century, Wagner began a re-conceptualisation of theatrical space at Bayreuth. This, with its fan-shaped auditorium, removal of boxes and concealment of the orchestra pit, was an attempt at creating a 'mystic chasm' between the 'real' world of the audience and the 'idealised' world of performance (Brockett 1995: 426). It was also the first time in the history of Western theatre that the spectators were systematically placed in darkness. In the early part of the 20th century, Georg Fuchs – with his idea of theatre as something communal and ritualistic, as a space for shared encounters – removed scenic arches and curtains, placing his spectators on three sides of the playing space. Pre-dating the idea of phenomenology by several years, Fuchs regarded performance as incomplete until the moment of its realisation in the vision of the spectator. Accordingly, spectators were positioned in ways that made them central to the action. In 1909 Adolphe Appia created his own ideal theatre space on the outskirts of Dresden. In this instance the theatre comprised a large open hall that enclosed performers and spectators alike. With no raised stage and no scenic arch, this was a space defined by little other than the performance work itself, and Appia's theatre was almost certainly the first open performance space since the Renaissance. These examples aside, it is little wonder that the spectatorial reconfigurations in the second part of the 20th century by, amongst others, Grotowski and Schechner were deemed as radical as they were considered to be.

What we do is where we do it. The expectations we bring to the Performing Garage are different to those we take with us to the Royal Shakespeare Theatre. Different spaces carry with them their own protocols, which impact on the ways in which performance work can be presented. Protocols determine what is and what is not acceptable within the space; they suggest the mechanisms that govern the actions and words to be performed and also the ways in which they are received. Protocols are expressed through the performance codes adopted. These codes encompass, primarily, the use of language, the role of narrative and the relationship of performer to her or his role. Protocols orient the spectator to the work. That is to say that protocols invite, even integrate the spectator into the world of the performance, rather than assuming an automatically external and 'passive' act of looking on the spectator's behalf. Protocols are never final, never fixed. Nevertheless, the conventional theatre space will usually function as a metaphor for elsewhere: a battlefield, a garden in Moscow, the chambers of a dying king ... the actors endeavour to make us buy into illusion via false beards, costumes and learned lines. (This is something of a given: Spalding Gray's plaid shirt is every bit as much a costume as Uncle Vanya's frock coat or Hamlet's black suit). Representation is problematised by theatrical performances that rely on a disturbed performative presence, to be sure. But the fact remains that the position articulated succinctly by Peter Brook that 'In everyday life "if" is a fiction ... In everyday life "if" is an evasion, in the theatre "if" is the truth' (Brook 1968: 157) is still the axis on which mainstream theatre spins.

And it is hard to disagree with Brook. Mainstream theatre is all about ifs, all about artifice, all about lies ... albeit lies in pursuit of a greater truth; for with all the good will in the world, the 'if' is never also the 'as'. It is for this reason that Lacan reminded us that 'The effect of mimicry is camouflage' (Lacan 1977: 99). Milly Barranger's chapter on 'Theatre Language' in her book *Theatre: A Way of Seeing* includes analyses of writers as diverse as Shakespeare, Shepard, Weiss and Mamet, and yet she is able to summarise by writing that 'All contribute to the overall illusion that life is taking place before us' (Barranger 1995: 217). Barranger offers a number of dramatic conventions that are commonly used by playwrights: stage directions, exposition, point of attack, complication, crisis, resolution, simultaneous plotting and the use of dramatic versus actual time.

These conventions have remained broadly constant from the time of Aristotle. And since that time, theatre has pursued nothing so much as notions of unity, coherence and consistency. Like the well-practiced liar that it is, it knows that one slip will lead to disaster: one misremembered line, and the fourth wall it has so painstakingly constructed will tumble into the stalls. This is not to suggest that all Western theatre conforms to the Stanislavskian ideal of fourth wall realism. However, the *idea* of the fourth wall has become such a given of theatre that when it does not 'appear', we tend to speak about its absence. That 'breaking the fourth wall' is as commonplace a term in theatre as it is shows just how prevalent the practice of performing to a supposedly unseen other has become.

Unlike a conventional script for drama, performance writing is more able to concentrate on exploring ways of disturbing and destabilising presence. It is free to do this precisely because the presence of s/he who performs is not necessarily illusory in the same regard as s/he who acts. Performers stand before us in space, and they are first and foremost themselves. The situations they speak of are their own. They present a performatised presence, but not a performatised and fictional 'other'. This was not always the case. According to Josette Feral, 'Where performance art in the seventies was simply refusing the representation of a real it tried to attain in its immediacy ... performance art in the nineties has renounced the play of illusion. It has chosen to return to the real as a construction of the political, and to show the real as necessarily bound to the individual' (Feral 1992: 154).

This is not about 'truth', and it is certainly not about making a claim for the integrity of one approach at the expense of another. Rather than elevating performance to an expression of who the performer *is*, we might more accurately regard performance as one event that is written across the performer's self. Viewed in this way, the performer becomes a manuscript that has been written on repeatedly, with the previous lines incompletely erased and often still legible. Postmodern performance writing – or writing for postmodern performance – is more likely to acknowledge and challenge the nature of performance in and through its own practice than a dramatic text is. As Paul Rae says: 'One of the aims [of traditional theatre] has been to render itself invisible, to make it look as if everybody is not really reciting written words, or moving in ways pre-ordained by directors, but rather that everything is happening spontaneously. ... This apparent spontaneity is called 'presence'. Conventional theatrical performance erases the mechanics of its appearance in inverse proportion to the degree of presence it seeks to achieve' (Rae 1997).

Adrian Heathfield reminds us that 'Ever since artists in the late 1960s and early 1970s broke from the gallery-bound constraints of their immediate predecessors into other locales of creative practice, performance art has run a consistently close course with site-specific art in its investigation of the matter, conception and perception of space' (Heathfield 2004: 10). Notions of boundary shifting in art are normally metaphorical. With installation and site-specific performance, the shift is literal and concrete. The locating of performance product within temporary spaces, often with the atmospheric residue of pre-existing functionality, creates tensions and dialogues beyond those existing in texts that were written for theatre buildings, no matter how unconventional and experimental those buildings may be.

'Far from being neutral, place itself is seen by many Live artists as a restrictive force to be opened and resisted' (Ibid.). Theatrical space thus has significance beyond its architectural (and occasionally natural) construction. The differences between on-stage and off-stage are mutable and are often subject to challenge, intervention and subversion. Theatre in the round, for example, places its spectators firmly in the sight of each other, but lights and costumes notwithstanding, we tune in almost automatically to the different levels of implied significance between fellow spectators and performers. On- and off-stage are not so much defined by sight lines as by the particular awareness we bring to the people we view. Performers in a play by Brecht may well be asking to be read as 'off-stage' at the same time as they are still highly visible and, on a literal level, clearly 'on-stage.' The same might be true of performers in a piece by Robert Wilson, Forced Entertainment or Richard Foreman. Culturally conditioned as we are, we assume a conceptual frame that allows us to watch and listen with particular focus to those events, sounds and actions that we regard as appropriately 'on-stage.' Interventionist performance of the last 100 years, however, has shown us that notions of 'on' and 'off' stage are as complicated as notions of performance itself. In a 1965 interview with Richard Schechner, John Cage suggested that 'one could view everyday life as theatre' (Schechner 1985: 248), that performance can occur 'without any knowledge on the part of the "performers" that they are performing' (Ibid.: 249). As soon as this becomes even a possible blueprint for performance, notions of 'on' and 'off' stage are given over entirely to the decision making of spectators. The peculiar self-awareness of performers' intentionality, which has always been a staple of even the most radically experimental work since Marinetti, shifts to active intentionality on the part of the viewers, and the 'to be seen' element of Bentley's A, B and C example falls apart.

The Greeks and the Romans had their specifically designed and designated theatre spaces, yet from the Middle Ages through to the early reign of Elizabeth I, theatre in Britain had to find its own sites. The Mystery Plays, with their temporary adoption of the city's cathedral and its adjacent grounds were installations in every modern sense of the word. The socio-cultural, religious, financial and iconographic significance of the space, along with the knowledge the spectators had that within a brief period of time, the site would return to its prior and *designated* function as a grand and formal place of worship cannot have failed to impact upon the way the work was seen. The Mystery Plays of Coventry, York and Chester continue the tradition to this day. Carnivals, fairs and the varying forms of street theatre repeatedly blur the boundaries between designated and appropriated usage. A visitor to Stratford-upon-Avon during the periods when the relatively rarefied High Street is taken over by the Royal Charter protected funfair will see customers for Marks and Spencer and Café Nero negotiating crowds queuing noisily for their spin on the Waltzers and their turn on the Dodgems. This visitor is seeing a different but no lesser type of performance to whatever the Royal Shakespeare Company happens to be playing at their theatre some 200 yards distant. Equally, anyone who has visited Edinburgh during its International and Fringe Festival has no choice but to see the city itself as a reconstructed performance site that has an existence way beyond the number of its designed and adapted venues. Spectators thus become an integral part of the performance they are witnessing. And, with at least a nod towards Cage, spectators become the prime-determining agents in deciding what to view and what not to view as 'significant'.

The proscenium arch, the apron and thrust stages help to define and set the slippery distinctions between theatre and life, between the theatricalised and the everyday, between the to-be-seen and the simply-being-done. It is inevitable that performance, which bills itself in one way or another as 'radical', will seek to reconfigure the established rules of theatrical space. This resulted in a challenge from two directions. For whilst theatre practitioners were attempting to free their own work from the boundaries and expectations that came with making work in and for theatre buildings, so were fine artists from the 1960s drawn towards the time-based nature of performance as a means of challenging what they, in substantial numbers, had come to regard as the commodification of the object.

What emerged was that which we now call installations. Installation-based discussions will often concentrate on the architectural and the visual, on what is seen, on the where and how, and this is at the expense of language. There is a historical rationale to this: performance work of the 1970s tended to prioritise the visual; in the 1980s performance embraced emergent technology, and in the 1990s, the politics of representation. And now, at the start of the 21st century, we are witnessing a re-evaluation of the importance of the word. A type of textual harassment that is cognisant of difference. Furthermore, this recognition of difference is not so much a philosophical and academic imagining as one of the givens of daily existence.

Louise Bourgeois told us that 'The relation of one person to his surroundings is a continuing preoccupation. It can be casual or blunt. It can be painful or pleasant. Most of all it can be real or imaginary' (Swindells 1995: 35). Whatever it is, it is increasingly clear that it cannot be ignored. With the gift of understanding via hindsight, we can see that this was one of the points on which modernism impaled itself. Art events could no longer be seen to transcend interpretation by virtue of the grace of their being or taking place when the very act of installation subverted and exposed the relationship between presence and spectatorship. In one fell swoop, certain key structures of receptivity were disrupted. As the space that the work was presented in was central, so too was the internal and interpretative space the viewers carried with them. One could not be important without the other. This proved to be central to modernism's falling away from favour, as the inclusion of the relationship between art and space, to the relations between art and its conditions of display, ran counter to the assumed authenticity of the work in and of itself. That which we once felt comfortable referring to as the real is always in key ways absent. Our engagement is real enough, but the event itself is always a phenomenon that is constituted in abeyance, something out of our reach no matter how closely we attend.

We can say that it is the spectator who becomes more 'real' than the event as s/he is made subject to the gaze of other spectators. The spectator's relation to other spectators as well as to performers becomes as much the subject of installation as the created artwork, as it is implicated in the very event that the usual protocols inherent in theatre buildings keep separate and discrete. The merging of spectator as object with performer as subject denies the necessary distance for gazing upon, which is the predication of galleries and theatres, and forces the watcher (whether s/he recognises it or not) into a relationship with the seeing self.

What is contained within the work is in this way no less relevant than it ever was or than it was ever thought to be, but a shift took place that showed the perception of the artwork could not be accurately predetermined. Rather, perception came into being through a haphazard and never entirely predictable combination of memory and anticipation, location, duration, activity and experience. We could not then, as we cannot now, approach any work on its own terms precisely because our own terms work so emphatically as agents of determination. The only terms we can ever understand are our own, and it is this that leads to adscititious engagement, an engagement that is always the imposition of a critical perspective that is alien to the phenomenon under inspection.

The very nature of installation-driven performance works on the implication that what is being presented is just one part of an environmental totality. This serves to remind us that what is at the centre of the perceptual frame is not necessarily at the centre of importance. The perceptual experience of spectators becomes inseparable from the relation of the event and its location, and also from the movements that spectators may be making around and through the space. By collapsing many of the seemingly clean distinctions between the presence of space and the (re)presentation of events, installations deny the faux-purity of performance. This is to say that we generally regard theatrical purity as something at once supposedly neutral at the same time as we know that it is massively loaded. A conventional theatre building is a case in point: 'The [theatre] space is, of course, not an empty container but an active agent; it shapes what goes on within it, emits signals about it to the community at large' (McAuley 1999: 41); theatres thus offer a massive number of indications as to the product they are inclined to accommodate. The inclusion in installation performance of a prime consideration of the work's relationship to its (non-theatre) location is an exercise in resistance to the notion of authenticity as something that resides exclusively in the created event. Rather than being prescribed and pre-determined in rehearsal, spectatorial perception emerges as a result of the tension between the haptic and the optic, the located-in-space and the space itself, the adscititious and the accidental.

The work is present, as is the space and as is the spectator, and text for installation is not about the evaporation of presence so much as its re-evaluation. The notion of 'presence' is shifted away from something that is ascribed to the performer acting 'in the moment' and 'in the light'. It is in turn relocated in the interplay between the watchers, the watched and their negotiation of the type of space they occupy, and also to the manner of that occupation. The only thing that is not present is that then which was never actually there as other than a romantic ideal, and that is the belief that the metaphorical truth of theatres could ever be anything other than a literal lie. In inviting us to look beyond the borders that have been cultivated into expectations and to step away from the conventional separations of spectator and spectacle, installations open doors into an intrinsically postmodern negotiation of bourgeois aesthetics. One that takes a resistant line to the regime of representation that is always at work in the theatre.

There seems little reason to go to the trouble of creating an artificial environment when environments exist around us all the time. As areas within these ready made locations, installations make aspects of space conspicuous in particular ways. This is utilisation in place of fabrication, and it is through this negation of conventional theatrical structures that the dissolution of the event and spectator occurs, leaving in its place an unstable and yet ultimately more holistic sense of being inside the work one is seeing. A play in a theatre is usually set directly in front of its spectators, overtly sharing its space, and yet as spectators we are always separated from the performers by a series of invisible signs that tell spectators not to touch, not to change position, not to look or walk away, and in effect, to engage with the work *only* in a specific, stylised and highly regimented manner. Installations shift the focus of concern away from these modernist preoccupations with theatrical 'thereness' to questions about the constitution of the event and the ways in which it implicates, the spectator in the 'hereness' of place and event, in the shared space of the work. The installation artist's intention, such as it is, is rarely equated with the meaning of the work. What we find in its place is that the radical decentring of authorial intention opens the field up to the (almost) anything goes of inexpressionism. In this way installations are able to connote experiences, which the spectator can only be aware of as a result of an interaction with other individuals in a shared space. The idealistic blank slate theatre space of dominant modernism has been roundly subverted by the impure space of the everyday. This subversion is also through the foregrounding of the physical presence of the spectating subject amid the sensory immediacy of spatial extension and temporal duration. If plays are still generally designed to be read through an act of disembodied spectatorial epiphany, installations demand a relationship between work, site and spectator. Without these elements the work remains incomplete.

Lyotard had it that 'The postmodern [art] denies itself the solace of good forms, the consensus of taste' (Lyotard 1984: 55). Likewise, Donald Judd wrote that art need not be demonstrative of 'taste' so much as that it needed to be 'interesting' (Judd 1975: 75). The interest that stems from surprise occurs when our autobiographical receptors are confronted with art events that resist or develop our expectations. Indeed, there can be no element of surprise without this trade off between anticipation and realisation. When modernists made their claims that art works could be perceived in ways that were at once authentic and immediate, they were in denial as to the experiential subjectivity of s/he who is doing the observing. Art may confront and alter experience, but the experience that is confronted can never be pure and can never be fixed. The canvas may be blank, or as Peter Brook famously suggested, the performance space may be 'empty' (Brook 1968: 11), but the spectator is always already filled with histories, estimations, preconceptions and prejudices, with life histories which collide and collude with the work on display.

We can see that as modernism has given ground to the postmodern, so the art of installation has shifted from a focus on the object on display to an exploration of the elasticity of site. Where, after all, is the 'object' in Stelarc's keyboard-generated impulse that is *Fractal Flesh*? And where, come to that, is the site?

CASE STUDY 1.8:   STELARC

Stelarc (1946–) is a Cyprus-born, Australian artist who has created work based on the idea that the human body has become obsolete, or 'biologically inadequate'. From the late 1960s he began working with the idea that the human body is a limited being, rapidly approaching obsolescence. Through kinetic body attachments and Internet-body connectivity, Stelarc has set out to explore and redefine the nature of the human body and modify it to the level of technological advancement we find elsewhere in our world.

From his 1980s work on suspensions, with his body hanging from hooks above gallery floors, city streets and the sea, Stelarc's idiosyncratic performances have increasingly involved robotic technology integrated in key ways with his body. He has performed with a robotic third hand, a robotic third arm, and a pneumatic spider-like six-legged walking machine, the Exoskeleton, which sits Stelarc in the centre of the legs and allows him to control the machine through a series of arm gestures.

Stelarc continues to problematise the notion of space through works such as 'Movatar'. He introduces the concept behind the work thus: 'Motion Capture allows a physical body to animate a 3D computer-generated virtual body to perform in comparative space or cyberspace. This is done by markers on the body, which are tracked by cameras, their motions analyzed by a computer and mapped onto the virtual actor. Or it can be done using electromagnetic sensors ... which indicate position/orientation of limbs and head. Consider, though, a virtual body or an avatar that can access a physical body, actuating its performance in the real world. If the avatar is imbued with an artificial intelligence, becoming increasingly autonomous and unpredictable, then it would become

→

$\rightarrow$
more an AL (Artificial Life) entity performing within a human body in physical space' http://www.stelarc.va.com.au/.

Chronology (Selected):
Microfilm Footage of Stomach Interior (1973)
Third Hand Project (1976)
Sitting/Swaying Event (1980)
Seaside Suspension (1981)
Multiple Arms (1982)
City Suspension (1985)
Stretched Skin/Third Hand (1988)
Stomach Sculpture (1993)
Ping Body (1996)
Parasite (1999)

Recommended Reading:

Stelarc and James D. Paffrath (eds) 1984. *Obsolete Body/ Suspensions/Stelarc*. Davis, CA.: JP Publications.

Carr, Cindy. 1993. *On Edge: Performance Art at the End of the Twentieth Century*. Hanover: Wesleyan University Press.

Dery, Mark. 1996. *Escape Velocity: Cyberculture at the End of the Century*. New York: Grove Press.

Birringer, Johannes. 1998. *Media and Performance*. Baltimore: Johns Hopkins University Press.

Bell, David and Barbara M. Kennedy (eds) 2000. *The Cybercultures Reader*. London: Routledge.

Smith, Marquard (ed.) 2005. *Stelarc: The Monograph*. Cambridge, Massachusetts: MIT Press.

Dixon, Steve. 2007. *Digital Performance: A History of New Media in Theatre, Dance, Performance Art and Installation*. Cambridge, Massachusetts: MIT Press.

John Cage sought to dissolve a number of distinctions between music, sound and silence. In part we can regard Cage's explorations as an invitation to listen without prejudice. And yet without prejudice, we would not be able to hear, let alone listen. In fact the legacy of Cage is, like that of Cézanne, Cunningham, Beckett and Picasso, that his work seduced us into looking above and beyond the borders of our expectations and assumptions. In so doing, a number of the conventional divisions we impose on experience begin to fall away, and they've been falling ever since. This is the simple reason why works of the past, revisited or restaged, can never affect us in the ways that they initially did. Brecht's approaches to theatre, for example, have become such a recognisable part of our understanding of performance that we now expect and assume those same strategies for estrangement and distance that were once surprising. Brecht, as one would expect, was aware of this in advance.

The gulf between modernism and postmodernism is not so wide as we might at first imagine. Where modernism spoke of and for the universal, postmodernism's engagement is with relativism. The gulf is not wide between the two because each approach is of its time. As postmodern performance (whether it identifies itself as such or not) is constituted out of a rejection of a number of universalising worldviews, so too is contemporary life, no matter how nostalgic the aims of our age may appear. Despite their similarities, the shift from modernism to postmodernism can be seen as the site of oppositional views. A key idea is that whilst the former regarded the written script as a map that should be followed in order to arrive at performance, the latter tends to regard performance as its own independent event. Where the 20th century saw a gradual shift in power from the writer to the director, with directors assuming an increasing control over the ultimate interpretation of the text, postmodernism has heralded a reconfiguration of the once-sacrosanct split between roles. The writer *is* the director and the written *is* the done. The experience of specta-tors is as sensory as it is cognitive and the distinctions between the two, like the distinctions between director and writer, are being challenged by contemporary work. Heiner Müller described his own work as 'psychic polyphony' (Müller 1994: 181), a statement that chimes with Vito Acconci's belief that performance uses language as a means 'to cover a space rather than to uncover a meaning' (Linker 1994: 12).

That there are no absolutes in our world has become quite possibly the sole absolute of 21st-century life. Truth, authenticity and beauty created the triangular frame that was used to encompass and identify much art of the past, and this frame is now up for grabs. And it is proving just a little too slippery to hold on to. Baudrillard's simulacrum is writ large in Koons' million dollar copies of worthless originals, while 'beauty' has emerged as an unstable and increasingly suspect category for the identification and valuation of art. 'Beautiful' might be used to describe a particular staging by Robert Wilson, or even of the way that Ron Athey's punctured skin is bathed in light, but the term is unlikely to be possessed of such currency when applied to the work of Blast Theory, Orlan or La Fura dels Baus. To search for beauty is, we often find, to miss the point. We do well to remember, however, that there are distinctions between a concentration on beauty and a consideration of aesthetics. Wherever and whenever decisions are taken about the ways in which an artwork is presented, we witness an aesthetic articulation, albeit one that is used as a means to an end rather than as an end in itself.

Where modernist beauty has come to stand for many as a type of complacency, as a potentially facile exercise, a postmodern sense of aesthetics remains central to the way we negotiate a response to art. One could argue that the more work moves from the excesses of theatricality towards the minimalism-as-naiveté of 'is it performance or isn't it?', the more important a sense of aesthetic arrangement becomes in distinguishing art and art making from general behaviour.[3] Performance is always spectatorial, even when the only spectator is the artist in the act of making or when the spectator imposes art-ness on what it is that s/he sees, because the activity of art making will always involve a consideration of aesthetics. Deciding not to care how something looks, quite apart from being an aesthetic decision in itself, is art's falsest claim, and it goes hand-in-glove with the idea of 'art for art's sake' as some sort of cultural cancer, as a wholly negative act of self-contemplation and consumption.

For the postmodernist, no less than the modernist, 'art for art's sake' is shorthand for the deterioration of art into meaninglessness. But the term also suggests that art has moved beyond the point of having to shroud itself in justification. Art is intrinsically independent and its values are not reliant upon the patronage of external scrutiny, even as artists seek endlessly to make themselves subject to it. Art for art's sake is no more damning as a concept than pleasure for the sake of pleasure. Pleasure, like art, brings its own rewards, and one person's pleasure is another person's pain.

If modernism in art stressed feeling over understanding, perhaps all that has really changed through postmodernism is that we are more ready to accept that feeling is understanding. Attending to the work is knowledge

---

[3] Distinctions between 'art' and 'general behaviour' are not fixed, and perhaps not even desirable. The days when performance could be defined as Person *A* representing Person *B* whilst Person *C* watches on have long gone. As the likes of Duchamp, Koons and Hirst have brought notions of the 'readymade' into art, so too have a number of practitioners sought to collapse the distinctions between the performative and the everyday. See Zarrilli, Phillip B. 1997. *From Acting to Performance*. London & New York: Routledge; Schneider, Rebecca. 1997. *The Explicit Body in Performance*. London & New York: Routledge; and Jones, Amelia and Andrew Stephenson. 1999. *Performing the Body, Performing the Text*. London & New York: Routledge.

enough. Art can no longer make the demands it once did on the spectator's attention. In our multi-media world of mass-communication, we have more to look at now. Accordingly we look at art if we so choose, and if and when we choose not to, then we look away. In dropping its guise as an instrument of political change, art has empowered us all. As Barba and Boal invite us to join in and become spectactors, so too can we choose to walk away. Where Brecht *showed* us contradiction theatrically, Boal *exposes* us to it through theatre. In turning spectators into spectactors, Boal gives us the choice to stay or go, to join in and play or to remain passive. The decision becomes ours and remains in our gift. Performance is integrated into life, and the illusionist praxis of traditional (modernist) theatre is further challenged.

The segue from modernism to postmodernism is contained in these attitudinal shifts, and they date back some 40 years. The blank and neutral objects created by artists such as Donald Judd and Robert Morris, mirrored by the seen/unseen aspects of Acconci and Burden's installations stimulated an awareness of the physical presence of the work and beyond this to a consideration of the art/spectator relationship in the *real* spaces of art and performance. Up against this type of concrete reality, the artifice of theatre as metaphor for other has never really recovered. Baudrillard's ideas of simulacrum notwithstanding, we know that once the real breaks through the frame, the act shows the simulation as its shadow, as the shape without substance.

Artists make their work in the here and now. Because of this, all art is contemporary. The harder an artist seeks to recapture the past, whether through revival or imitation, the more powerfully the present pulls through. The interests of the artist, or art maker, however, are rarely compatible with those of the academic. As art making is in the here and now, the analysis of art tends towards the there and then, and it can sometimes feel as though every visit to the theatre or rehearsal space is little more than an invitation to engage in the conveyor belt of documentation. Gómez-Peña questions the workings of this relationship outright when he asks, 'what are the scholar's ethical responsibilities towards us? When ... they just sit in the back row once every decade with a jaded and aloof gaze, or else they rent one of our performance videos and go home to write a dissertation ... crucifying us ... to oblivion with convoluted phrases meant to impress colleagues in their own field' (Gómez-Peña 2000: 265). Gómez-Peña makes a fair point, but there is another side to the coin. Amelia Jones argues that 'Having direct physical contact with an artist who pulls a scroll from her vaginal canal does not ensure "knowledge" of her [as an individual and/or artist and/or work of art] any more than does looking at a film or picture of this activity, or looking at a painting that was made as a result of such an action' (Jones 1998: 33–4). Something of the relationship between scholarship and performance is addressed in Chapter 4; perhaps the dispiriting truth is that, despite relative goodwill on both sides, a type of disharmony between critical performance and performance criticism will always exist.

Scholarship seeks to locate art within a continuum, to make and show connections between what was and what is. Artists make art, academics pick art apart. Like the midwife and the coroner we view the same phenomena from widely differing and mutually incompatible perspectives. No small surprise then that most discourses on art and performance have less contact with the complexities of their subject than with the relative simplicities of well-rehearsed thesis and antithesis. Academic books are at their most interesting, primarily because they tell us something about how the particular academic wishes the subject to be seen. They (we/I) seek to define work through a type of literary depiction that glories most often in its own erudition. Fine and well, but when the role of academics is to prove themselves cleverer and more culturally vital than the artists whose work they explore, art emerges as the casualty. If for no more reason than that a coroner is redundant without a corpse.

There is considerable evidence that the act or even the intended act of analysis does much to alter the ways that we view. As soon as we know that we will be called upon to defend our choices in a reasoned, articulate and intelligent fashion, we start to make choices as to what we like based in no small part on what those choices have to say about us and on what we can find to say about our subject (Wilson and Schooler 1991). We may well like what we see less than we like the things we have plenty to say about. It follows in this sense that the larger the platform from which we speak, the greater the subconscious temptation to project images of ourselves through public reflection on certain types of work (Gladwell 2005: 181). This is the nature of the academic beast. Academic honesty, like any other form of honesty, can only exist within consciously controlled frames, which is not the same thing as saying that things are true because we believe them to be. For Sartre, the conscious being is defined by the capability for conscious and subconscious acts of self-deception. Inasmuch as 'self-deception consists in pretending to be something' (Sartre 1990: 27), we describe ourselves (and our interests) to others *and to ourselves* in ways that are loaded with the potential for misdescription. After Wittgenstein, Charles Taylor locates language itself as a game that never quite reveals the truth: 'Language is not merely the external clothing of thought, nor a simple instrument which ought, in principle, to be fully in our control. It is more like a medium in which we are plunged, and which we can cannot fully plumb' (Taylor 1985: 235).

The idea of truth in art has always had a doubled status. On the one hand, we crave the certainty that the signature and the artwork amount to a truth, on the other, we accept that art is (for the most part) no more than a representation of the external truth it seeks to depict. And (for the most part) this seems reasonable enough. The British art critic Clive Bell insisted that art should have nothing to do with life. His contemporary, Edward Bullough, wrote that 'Explicit references to organic affections, to the material existence of the body, especially to sexual matters, lie normally below the Distance-limit, and can be touched on by Art only with special precautions' (Bullough 1912: 100). At these statements a large part of Euro-American society breathed a sigh of collective relief that all was in order. Everyone, however, did not share Bell's and Bullough's views. At the same time as they were making their claims for art's lofty and exclusive purpose, and as Chapter 1 of this book has reminded us, Marinetti was publishing his Manifesto of Futurism, the Dadaists were waiting in the wings and Duchamp was attempting to exhibit his urinal as a Readymade. The First World War was about to turn the wrath of machinery on its inventors, and art was set to sacrifice its sense of certainty.

We live in an age where nothing much is certain. And yet it is becoming increasingly difficult, for this writer at least, to avoid the feeling that if theatre had not been long invented, we would not be inventing it now. Lost in a world of Reality Television and Quick-Fix Celebrity Stardom, our collective memories have reinvented theatre as something other than what it is. In this retro age of repackaged nostalgia, nothing is more nostalgic than our willingness to sit silently in darkened auditoria whilst pretending to suspend a disbelief we long since learned to control. Rooted to the spot, we root ourselves too firmly in theatre's golden past, remembering what we think we should and choosing to forget that theatre has become a medicine with all of the taste and very little of the cure.

Seeing is believing, but that is not the only order in which the words work. Possessing *a priori* belief in theatre only blinds us to the truth of our gaze. Blinds us to the fact that in all but the rarest of cases, live theatre has been dead for a long time. All too often all that remains are the actors acting, the watchers watching and the spotlights taking a century to fade away to black.

That is too bleak a position to sustain. In the stark black and white of print, sentiments such as these become more dogmatic than provocative. In engaging with this book, up to this point at least, readers have demonstrated a commitment to the subject of performance and performance writing that is unlikely to be deterred by the belief, shared it must be said by a growing number of critical commentators, that beyond the veneer of the West End and Broadway, all is not quite well. Terms such as 'Theatre in Crisis' have after all become part of our everyday vocabulary, and a case can be made that it is only through acknowledging concerns that we can begin to make moves towards positive change.[4] It is in pursuit of this positive change that issues of space and text come together.

As it is with theatrical space, so have words for performance been stretched to their near-limits. Robert Wilson's operatic treatment of text, as ruthless as it is rhythmic and which sees words torn from their linguistic denotation, is a paradigm for the ways in which performance language, like the concept of performance, is being stripped of its meaning and conventional usage at the same time as it is imbued with new signification. At one time it was the norm for the completed script to be delivered to the actors, designers and director before rehearsals commenced. The script carried within its form its own coded messages of pace, action, denouement and drive, which it was the actors' and/or directors' task to then translate into theatre. Increasingly, texts are as likely now to be devised in situation, in relation to space, personnel and the particular rhythmical, structural and ideological concerns of the making process. Furthermore, texts are no longer automatically assumed to be constructed in ways that lend themselves to the intrinsically performative.

Vito Acconci's tryptychal performance event that took place at New York's Sonnabend Gallery in 1972 utilised spoken language, which became performance material by simple dint of its location within a mutually agreed frame of performance. Specifically, it functioned as 'a prime example of the artist's use of his person or voice to induce a power field, exerting influence over the space through which people passed' (Linker 1994: 44). Forced Entertainment's text for their 2000 performance *Quizoola* consists in its durational entirety of numerous scripted questions ranging from 'What is Love?' and 'What stories would you tell a person who had lost their child?' to 'Can you see tiny shapes and colours moving in the corners?' The answers are 'unscripted and may be true, false, long, short, confessional, abstract or otherwise', dependent upon the performers' decisions taken in the moment (Heathfield 2004: 101). As the company describes it, this durational approach to text results in a disconnectedness, which is followed by hysteria and a losing of control: a type of unpreparedness that leads to 'something priceless – a sensitivity and concentration in the actual moment … so very close simply to being and doing' (Ibid.: 101). In this, an environmental and disruptive line runs four decades from Schechner's

---

[4]   See Delgado, Maria M. and Caridad Svich. 2002. *Theatre in Crisis?* Manchester: Manchester University Press.

1970 *Commune* to the near present. A feature of *Commune* was the nightly selection of fifteen spectators who were invited to leave their seats and enter a circle within the framed performance space. The spectators were given this information: 'You people have the following choices. First, you can come into the circle, and the performance will continue; second, you can go to anyone else in the room and ask them to take your place, and if they do, the performance will continue; third, you can stay where you are, and the performance will remain stopped; or fourth, you can go home, and the performance will continue in your absence' (Schechner 1973: 49). Schechner speaks of a particular occasion when the performance of *Commune* was delayed by three hours. And yet, it was precisely during this extended pause in the play that the nature of the performance event shifted into a new focus. *Commune*, the play, was interrupted and in this interruption, *Commune*, the performance, emerged. For Spalding Gray, a performer in the piece, a transformative moment occurred, which saw him 'as the performer and not the role the performer was playing'. Accordingly, 'there was no need to pretend that [his] actions took place anywhere else than in this theater at this time' (Ibid.: 54). The influence of this moment on Gray's subsequent transformation from actor/performer to actor/performer/auto-monologist leads us into Chapter 3's concerns with the writing and performing of the autobiographical self.

We have seen how texts that are no longer assumed to contain either instructions for actions or speech can empower performers to respond in ways that are otherwise associative, to create work which does not defer to the authority of the written word or indeed to the author. In short, to approach text as something that serves performance rather than assuming that performance is designed intrinsically to serve the text. Additionally, and crucially, a growing number of texts are being constructed for particular locations and performers. This shift away from the ubiquity of the published play towards texts that are permanently wedded to the psyche of specific authors – and sometimes also to their bodies – forms the focus of Chapter 3.

3
Writing the Body, Writing the Self

We use body art as a term for work that locates the body as subject, object, focus and site. The body has been utilised by a steadily growing number of significant contemporary artists. We saw this development particularly in the 1960s and 70s, where the body was used as form and site of protest, and we see it now in the 21st century, when the body is articulated as the battleground for extremity and a declared opposition to those ideological constraints imposed by the dominant culture. This is evidenced in the work of practitioners such as Stelarc, Orlan and Franko B, as it was 30 years ago by the likes of Carolee Schneemann, Chris Burden and Vito Acconci. The body has not become outmoded or obsolete simply because it has been used by earlier generations of artists. 21st-century practitioners come from different cultures and they work in different ways to those who came before, just as visual artists, writers and musicians are working differently to those who came before them. In this way the body can be regarded as the canvas on which ideas are given form and also as the form itself. As the page, the ink and the writer; as the instrument, the sound and the musician.

On 31 December 1999, on his 49th birthday, Tehching Hsieh concluded a 13-year performance that was never presented to the public. Like his April–April *One Year Performance* of 1980–1, all that the art 'contained' was the body of the artist. Our trust in the artist's integrity is what separates art from artifice: not a suspension of disbelief on our part so much as an act of belief. In body art the self is problematised. It is often doubled, idealised, made subject to acts of transgression and obsession, transformation and duration. The artists' bodies are regarded as matter, as the raw material of their work. This raw matter is in some way transformed, made strange. The body strives for articulation through exhibition, even when this is the exhibition of absence; it strives for difference, even when this distinction reframes the humdrum and the everyday.

Art that has a focus on the body often runs counter to issues of morality. The British visual artist Damien Hirst has it that his work is neither moral nor immoral so much as it is an invitation to the viewer to take a holiday from morality. This brings specific challenge to those of us who make art under the auspices of a university or similar educational environment, and the ability to recognise that morality amounts to no more or less than a shared and subsequently imposed set of conventions is a feature of most body arts. The question of who owns the body is no less pertinent today than it was in 1971, when Chris Burden made himself a target to be shot at.

CASE STUDY 1.9:   CHRIS BURDEN

Chris Burden (1946–) gained international attention in the 1970s as an influential and often controversial figure in the West Coast body art, performance and conceptual art movements. Investigating the psychological experience of personal danger and physical risk, he used his own body as an art object in outrageous, sometimes shocking acts, aggressively confronting the artist/audience relationship and the processes of performance making. David Hughes, editor of *Live Art Magazine* and a leading authority on contemporary performance practices, writes that 'Chris Burden is perhaps best known for ... performance art of the early 1970s. For example, Shoot (1971), in which a friend famously shot him in the arm. The move of "fine" artists, such as Burden, into the realm of time-based activities through the use of their own bodies was, of course, a defining moment of Live Art' (Hughes 2002: 2). In 1974 Burden began a drift away from body-art practice, working increasingly with video, which he used as an integral component of his performances, as well as for the documentation of his works and in the production of a series of conceptual 'commercials' for American television.

Towards the end of the 1970s, Burden began producing sculptural objects, installations and technological or mechanical inventions. In these extensions of his conceptual works Burden sought to address the artist's relationship to an

→

$\rightarrow$

increasingly industrialised and technological society. Burden is the recipient of numerous awards, including grants from the National Endowment for the Arts and a Guggenheim Fellowship. Having famously stated that 'students cannot make art', Burden taught at the University of California, Los Angeles from 1978, where he was Professor of New Genres in the Department of Art. In 2005 Burden resigned from this position following controversy over a postgraduate student's performance piece involving a loaded gun in a reworking of Burden's earlier work. Ironically, in light of his own back catalogue of transgressive performance, Burden's resignation was a response to UCLA's reluctance to immediately suspend the student involved.

Chronology (Selected):
Five Day Locker Piece (1971)
220 (1971)
You'll Never See My Face in Kansas City (1971)
Shoot (1971)
T.V. Hijack (1972)
Bed Piece (1972)
Deadman (1972)
Trans-fixed (1974)
Velvet Water (1974)
White Light/White Heat (1975)
Death Valley Run (1976)
Chris Burden Promo (1976)
Merry Christmas from Chris Burden (1976)
The Citadel (1978)
Send Me Your Money (1979)
Show the Hole (1980)
The Big Wheel (1980)
War Games (1982)
Beam Drop (1982)
Samson (19
Mini Video Circus (1994)
Endurance (1995)

$\rightarrow$

→
After Hiroshima (1995)
Beyond the Limits (1996)
Ghost Ship (2005)

Recommended Reading:
Searle, Adrian (ed.) 1993. *Talking Art 1.* London: ICA.
Noever, Peter, (ed.) 1996. *Chris Burden: Beyond the Limits.*
Vienna: Museum of Applied Arts.
Morris, Frances, Chris Burden, Nicholas Serota and Tom
Horton. 1999. *Chris Burden: When Robots Rule – The Two
Minute Airplane Factory.* London: Tate Gallery Publishing.
Burden, Chris, Fred Hoffman and Paul Schimmel. 2000. *Chris
Burden.* New York: Distributed Art Publishers Inc.

Body art tends towards the presentational rather than the representational. In this, the artist is likely to function as both story and character – as subject and object. The artist is positioned as object since s/he is conscious of the processes in which s/he is involved. This is a tendency, not a rule. The things that distinguish body art, or live art, or performance art from 'theatre' are tendencies, drifts. Of equal significance are overlaps.

What gets used? Memory, invention, trivia, traces of experience, documentation, photographs, sounds, technology, nature, space, identity, ideas of ownership and authorship, of originality and reproduction, love, loss, death, life, the scars on a body, chance, prediction, predictability, dreams, desires, relationships, isolation, duration: time stretched, time condensed and real time, sex, sexuality, gender, innocence, travel, geography, archaeology, science, displacement. The private made public ... the telling of secrets to strangers.

Any and all things can function as stimulus, focus or departure point. In one sense, one's own life – or that which we might regard as the proof of one's existence – is the library from which all art is drawn. Anything can be used and anywhere can be used. Every space is a potential art space, every action a potential event, and this disturbs conventional distinctions between 'theatre' and 'life' and spectatorship and observation. When a Ukrainian man climbed into a lions' enclosure at a zoo in Kiev on June 4, 2006, shouting 'God will save me', before removing his shoes and subsequently being mauled to death, the people witnessing this act were what? Spectators, observers? Who can say with any authority? It is clear that the act of faith (misguided though it plainly was) required an audience of sorts, but what sort of audience? Observation generally assumes a calm indifference, as opposed to spectatorship's more passionate engagement, but these edges blur and fuse like all other elements of performance. Like it or not and understand it or not, we watch Stelarc's hooked-up body hanging overhead in the same way we watch a jumper on a car-park roof, a high-wire act without a net or a shoeless Christian throwing himself to the lions. We watch with a morbid fascination: part fear, part hope, part horror.

In *Essays on the Blurring of Art & Life*, Allan Kaprow offered a distinction between 'artlike art' and 'lifelike art' (Kaprow 1993: 104). For Kaprow, lifelike art rarely fits within traditional ideas as to what art is: lifelike art can be about moving furniture around a house, dressing or undressing, arranging plants in a garden, leaning against a wall. In the 1960s Kaprow wrote, 'once the task of the artist was to make good art; now it is to avoid making art of any kind' (Ibid.: 101). In the 1990s he said, 'The experimental artist of today is the un-artist' (Ibid.: 111). For Kaprow – consistently – the point of any art is to discover art where nobody knew that it was. This is not dissimilar to Duchamp's statement that art is what happens when an object is taken out of context and given a new thought (Tomkins 1997: 176). It is echoed in Oliviero Toscani's belief that whilst 'Any idiot can see the beauty in something beautiful. ... The thing is to see beauty elsewhere. There is beauty everywhere if you are an artist' (ten Cate 1996: 78) and Richard Foreman's argument that anything, even a jar rolling across a stage, could be afforded the status of 'theatre'.

Performance is about seeing something differently, and this has as much to do with the gaze as with that which is gazed upon. Kaprow speaks of a student who was asked to do the stupidest thing he could think of, followed by the smartest. For the stupid act the student hung pickles to cook under electric lights, for the smartest he repeated the activity (Kaprow 1993: 110).

CASE STUDY 1.10:   ALLAN KAPROW

Allan Kaprow (1927–2006) helped to develop the phenomenon of Happenings in the late 1950s and 1960s. By 1966 Kaprow had described Happenings as a 'dead form', a sentiment that was in keeping with his ideas of newness and work being always in process. Kaprow was instrumental in the development of techniques designed to prompt a creative

$\rightarrow$

→

response from spectators, encouraging those present at performance events to make their own connections between ideas. Committed to the idea of art as a provocative means of enhancing awareness of life, Kaprow's concentration on the spectator as a unique agent in the realisation of art's intentionality placed him at the vanguard of mid-20th-century post-avant-garde thinking. John Cage made a hugely influential impact on Kaprow. Whilst Kaprow's main endeavour up until 1958 was the creation of assemblages and constructed paintings, the fact that he was also studying musical composition with Cage at the New School for Social Research in Manhattan altered his thinking from that point on. The notions of chance and indeterminacy as a vital means of aesthetic organisation (and disorganisation), which Cage advocated, alongside the disintegration of formal categories of practice, were instrumental to Kaprow's subsequent thinking and artistic activity.

   As one of the most influential art and performance makers of his or any other time, Kaprow's events, teachings and writings transformed the nature of performance/art making. Kaprow was Professor Emeritus in the Department of Visual Arts at the University of California, San Diego.

Chronology (Selected):
Grandma's Boy (1956)
18 Happenings in 6 Parts (1959)
Apple Shrine (1960)
Coca Cola, Shirley Cannonball? (1960)
A Spring Happening (1961)
Yard (1961)
A Service for the Dead (1962)
Words (1962)
Eat (1964)
Sweet Wall (1970)

Recommended Reading:
Kirby, Michael. 1965. *Happenings: An Illustrated Anthology*. New York: Dutton.

→

→

Kaprow, Allan. 1993. *Essays on the Blurring of Art and Life.* California: University of California Press.

Sandford, Mariellen. R. (ed.) 1995. *Happenings and Other Acts.* London & New York: Routledge.

Kaprow, Allan. 1996. *Assemblage, Environments & Happenings.* New York: H.N. Abrams.

Reiss, Julie. H. 1999. *From Margin to Center: The Spaces of Installation Art, 1969-1996.* Cambridge, Mass.: MIT Press.

Buchloh, Benjamin. H. D., Judith F. Rodenbeck & Robert Haywood. 2000. *Experiments in the Everyday: Allan Kaprow & Robert Watts.* California: Miriam & Ira D. Wallach Art Gallery.

Kelley, Jeff. 2004. *Childsplay: The Art of Allan Kaprow.* California: University of California Press.

Artaud told us that he desired a close relationship with every possibility for self-knowledge that originated from or through the body. From a performance perspective Artaud's legacy is significant. Claude Schumacher's words (and we can substitute here 'art' for 'theatre') show Artaud and Kaprow sharing similar ideals: 'For most people, there is everyday life and there is theatre, a fictional world animated by actors at predetermined times, in a special building where actors and spectators arrange to meet on either side of the footlights or the proscenium arch. It is precisely this division, based on the notion of 'spectacle', of 'mimesis', of 'imitation of life *outside* life' that Artaud rejects. He assigns to the theatre no less a mission than to renew life itself' (Schumacher 1989: xxiv).

It is important that we do not misremember Artaud and assume that life – like suffering – is automatically transformed into either mysticism or art. We need to guard against this, as we need to avoid a situation where Duchamp is revisited as an excuse … as a rationale for serving up tired, once-revolutionary ideas. As ever, the balance between influence and regurgitation is a difficult one to achieve.

It may be that it is only through an acute consideration of self that we are able to understand others. Catharsis – inasmuch as we can find a use for the term – exists as much within the domain of the artist as the spectator. When in the 1960s Bruce Naumann made sound and video recordings of his body his work was part of an identifiable cultural shift that encompassed events such as Tom Marioni's *The Act of Drinking Beer with Friends is the Highest Form of Art*, alongside Chris Burden's *Five-Day Locker Piece* and Vito

Acconci's masturbation-as-art that resulted in *Seedbed*. It was clear then, as now, that the self – one's biology, no less than one's psychology – has currency as art. And this currency is the currency of tangibility. The body as real, the body as non-illusion, the body as evidence of its own being. Erika Fischer-Lichte articulates something of the relationship between theatre and life when she suggests that 'in theatre as well as in every day life we construct our own reality, proceeding from our perception of more or less the same kind of material. In any case, reality is the product of a subjectively conditioned and performed process of construction' (Fischer-Lichte 1996: 103). So far so good, but Fischer-Lichte recognises the fact that our processes of construction are based on our levels of awareness. 'Whereas in everyday life we construct reality without being aware of it and without reflecting on it ... in the theatre the focus of our attention shifts to the very process of construction and the conditions underlying it' (Ibid.: 104).

Performers and body artists stand before us in space and they are (usually) first and foremost themselves. The situations they speak of and the bodies they deploy are (usually) their own. They present a performatised presence but not an automatically performatised 'other'. Body art thus inscribes its text in space and sound, rather than producing it as a separate entity, as something to which an entire production will be subsequently subsumed. Body art is wedded to the process of performance making; it is not separated from it in the way that much dramatic writing is constructed.

We can say that the performing of oneself is a feature of performance, even something central to it, whereas the submergence of self into character is a defining trait of acting, a phenomenon that Auslander describes as 'The blending of real and fabricated personae and situations that occur when performance personae assume the same functions as "real"' (Auslander 1994: 78). We can also say that – as theatre is the place for the well-told lie – so performance may now be the place for revelations of truth. In this context, body art and performance allow for the possibility of performers revealing themselves without the consequences such truths would lead to in their daily lives. Performers, no less than the rest of us, can tell secrets to strangers because it doesn't really matter what those strangers think.

Theatre and dramatic writing aspire to imitation. But what is it that they seek to imitate? Earlier imitations? For if, after Baudrillard, no originals exist, or could *ever* exist, then all things are already imitations (intimations) of representations; photocopies of photocopies, blinding us to the fact of their own core of emptiness; pictures of pictures; shadows of shadows. Traces of that which is only ever the trace of something never even there.

In 1989 the Ayatollah Khomeni issued a fatwa that sentenced the British writer Salman Rushdie to death for apostasy and blasphemy against the faith of Islam. In response Rushdie gave a television interview where he said, 'Doubt ... is the central condition of a human being in the 20th century. One of the things that has happened to us is to learn how certainty crumbles in our hands' (BBC News, 14-02-1998). The further from our hands that certainty slips, the greater is our desire to fashion it anew. A photograph is no more evidence of something having taken place than a novel is evidence of an author's beliefs, and yet we cleave to this idea of truth through representational imaging as and when it suits us. Tierney Gearon's 1999 exhibition *I Am a Camera* at the Saatchi Gallery, London was raided by police officers, attempting – under the Obscene Publications Act – to seize photographs of Gearon's naked children. Police action followed outcry in the popular press that the exhibition was an example of child pornography. John Stathos, writing in the *Tate* magazine commented that 'Children are undoubtedly in their own way sexual beings, but the social contract we live by insists, for good and adequate reason, that their sexuality should not be manipulated by adults. The violation of this taboo, one of the strongest and most deeply rooted of all, in the name of artistic production could be seen as significant evidence of disorder' (Stathos 1999: 40). The question of Gearon's innocence or guilt in this matter is not at issue here. What is is the extent to which images rather than actions are taboo. There are a great many historical precedents for this. Following Michelangelo's death, his *Last Judgment* had forty sets of genitalia covered with newly painted loincloths and a number of fornicating background figures painted over entirely.

Be it the apparent truth of the represented image, the visceral truth of the body that bleeds or the gaze that meets our own, for good or for ill, it is truth that we crave, in performance no less than in politics, in life no less than in law and in art no less than in love.

Chapter 2's documentation of the shift from representations of elsewhere in the theatre to re-presentations of hereness in installations coincided with a parallel shift in the relationship a number of performers were beginning to have with issues of self/other in performance. The readymade art object quickly segued into the readymade art event, with performers like Schneemann blurring the boundaries between private and public acts, collapsing the divisions between present experience, first person narrative, emotional engagement and spectatorial distance. Schneemann's performances continue to address spectators (and viewers when the work is filmed) in ways that are demanding of the taking of positions. There is no audience as such in work like this, only a series of distinct and different spectators, each being nudged away from neutrality, away from the comfort zone of assumed objectivity. Schneemann's work is in this way demonstrably linked to a vast swathe of practitioners, Adrian Piper, Orlan, Ron Athey, Franko B,

Karen Finley et al. These are the usual suspects of any paper on body-based performance, and yet their seemingly interchangeable aspects should not create a smokescreen that blinds us to the radical impact these live artists have had on performance and performance writing since the 1960s.

CASE STUDY 1.11:   CAROLEE SCHNEEMANN

Trained initially as a painter, Carolee Schneemann's work cuts across disciplines, encompassing painting, performance, film and video. Her early investigations into themes of gender and sexuality, identity and subjectivity, as well as the cultural biases of art history, laid the foundations for a great deal of post-1960s' feminist performance work. Schneemann's work has consistently challenged taboos and attempted to redefine notions of the naked female body as the erotic, the passive and the to-be-seen. Her work creates a formal address and radical confrontation of the social construction of the female body, and Schneemann's seminal perform-ances of the 1970s were both transgressive and influential in their interrogation of the exclusivity of traditional western thinking about performance and the body. The strength and significance of Schneemann's work has resulted in the transformation of art and performance definitions, notably with regard to discourses concerning the body, sexuality, and gender.

Schneemann continues making provocative and testing work in diverse media, including performance, writings and installations.

Schneemann (1939–) has taught at many institutions including New York University, California Institute of the Arts, Bard College, and the School of the Art Institute of Chicago. She was the recipient in 1999 of an Art Pace International Artist Residency at San Antonio, Texas, as well as receiving a Pollock-Krasner Foundation Grant, a Guggenheim Fellowship, Gottlieb Foundation Grant and a National Endowment for the Arts Fellowship. Schneemann received an Honorary Doctor of Fine Arts from Maine College of Art, Portland and a Lifetime Achievement Award from the College Art Association in 2000.

→

→

Chronology (Selected):
Labyrinths (1960)
Newspaper Event (1962)
Eye Body (1963)
Meat Joy (1964)
Noise Bodies (1965)
Body Collage (1967)
Naked Action Lecture (1968)
Rainbow Blaze (1971)
Up To and Including Her Limits (1973)
Interior Scroll (1975)
Homerunmuse (1977)
Mother Lexicon (1982)
Dream Death (1985)
Dirty Pictures (1987)
Cat Scan (1988)
Out to Lunch with Carolee Schneemann (1993)
An Evening with Carolee Schneemann (1995)
Made/Enacted (1995)
Enter ... Vulva (1997)
Your Dog My Cat or Delirious Arousal of Destruction (1998)

Recommended Reading:
Schneemann, Carolee. 1979. *More than Meat Joy: Complete Performance Works and Selected Writings*. New York: McPherson & Company.
Lippard, Lucy. 1984. *Overlay: Contemporary Art & the Art of Prehistory*. New York: Pantheon Books.
Schneider, Rebecca. 1997. *The Explicit Body in Performance*. London & New York: Routledge.
Jones, Amelia and Andrew Stephenson. 1999. *Performing the Body/Performing the Text*. London & New York: Routledge.
Schneemann, Carolee. 2002. *Carolee Schneemann: Imaging Her Erotics: Interviews, Projects*. Cambridge, Mass.: MIT Press.
Smith, Sidonie and Julia Watson. 2002. *Interfaces – Women/Autobiography/Image/Performance*. Ann Arbor: University of Michigan Press.

It is difficult to consider live art as a genre. It is, in essence, a field of unbounded practice, ideas and attitude, throwing up work that shatters the expectations and assumptions of spectators and critics. This constant shift is in no way limited to live art. In 1956, at the same time as John Osborne and the Royal Court were initiating their redefinitions of British notions of theatre, others were arguing a persuasive case against closure: 'Aesthetic theory – all of it – is wrong in principle in thinking that a correct theory and definition of art is possible. ... What I am arguing then, is that the very expansive, adventurous character of art, its ever-present changes and novel creations, make it logically impossible to ensure any set of defining properties' (Margolis 1978: 122). We identify this ability to transcend expected boundaries as one of live art's generic features. The collapsing of conventions assumes certain pre-knowledge on the part of the spectator; accordingly, ideas of elitism are often embedded in the practice, creating work which can appear so highly codified as to alienate 'regular' theatre-goers. The generic qualities we apply to performance art are those of transgression and combination, and these invoke their own frameworks of recognition and expectation, which allow us to identify the work for what it is. Crucially, this act of recognition occurs through a series of 'not quites': we see that the work is not quite that which we assume to be theatre and not quite that which we assume to be art; It is not quite theatre (or art) cabaret, street theatre, performance poetry, community arts or drama therapy; performance drops off the edges of these known quantities, and we identify the way and place it lands as live art. Guillermo Gómez-Peña's one-man performance of 1992, *a performance chronicle of the rediscovery of America/by/'The Warrior for Gringostroika' aka Guillermo Gómez-Peña* contains a line that encapsulates this: 'my art is undescribable therefore I'm a performance artist' (Levy 1992: 127). The closer we look the more we see that live/performance art is more of a strategy than a practice. It is in this conceptual relationship with the unfinished, the unpolished and the hybrid, this nudging at the edges of the possible, that the work is revealed to us as something that passes for genre.

The word 'genre' is ambiguous, and relatively new, only coming into its modern usage towards the end of the 19th century. It stands for similarities of form, style or purpose, and each of these are open to spectatorial interpretation. Spalding Gray's monologues suggest to this author/spectator ideas of performance and *theatre*, whereas Annie Sprinkle's verbal and no less theatrical work suggests performance and *art*. Another spectator might argue for different definitions. It is in the nature of the work that we are always kept slightly off our guard, always a little uneasy, unsure and undecided. In this sense, being undecided about what to call the work emerges as a logical response. Deirdre Heddon reminds us that 'Performers have the ability to move in and out of classifications' (Heddon 1998: 49), and this ability requires boundaries, which are 'neither permanent nor immutable, but are subject to social, historical, political and economic forces' (Ibid.). In the introductory notes to *Theatre Praxis*, Christopher McCullough is happy to use the seemingly separate terms 'Drama' (to do) and 'Theatre' (to see) loosely and to regard them as eminently flexible. 'As long as we are aware of the interchangeable aspects of the two terms through common usage I see no point in labouring precise definitions'(McCullough 1998: 9). Marvin Carlson's assertion that 'performance is an essentially contested concept' (Carlson 1996: 1) further reinforces the idea that work is no longer easily pinned down into discrete categories.

The creation of performance text is an act of metaphor. Emotional connections are sought through the selecting and ordering of words so that information has the potential to be recognisable and resonant beyond the sum of their constituent and linguistic parts. As a general rule, text is considered to be at its most valuable when it can be made to function as something greater than the representational and descriptive arrangement of the words that go to make it up. This is Barthes' 'grain of the voice': the traces of 'the body in the voice as it sings, the hand as it writes, the limb as it performs' (Barthes 1977b: 188). It is this centrality of the performer behind and within the performed that is important to notions of performance writing, which take as their subject, the indivisibility of writing and performing.

This indivisibility runs counter to the traditional idea of text as something created by a writer in order for a series of possibly unknown others to realise the words in subsequent enactions. The relationship between autobiography and performance is one that is rarely mediated by distinctions between writing and doing. The roles of writer, director and performer may be radically different, but with autobiographical performance they likely to be adopted by the same person. There is logic here. A disempowered subject seeking a platform for her or his voice does not necessarily want that voice diluted by difference: be this through the macro of gender, race, sexuality, nationality or culture, or the micro that comes with subtle variations. Far from remaining in the domain of the rich and famous, autobiography has been developed into the chosen form for members of minority and marginalised groups, with the deployment often incorporating complex critiques of identity construction, alongside evidence of the performative self. Bonney sees contemporary culture as the era of self, a 'product and reflection of a century that has given rise to the hedonism of the twenties, the radical individualism and activism of the sixties and the so-called "me decade" of the eighties. The nineties finally made room for the previously marginalized, diverse voices of this society, and the solo [performance] form has tracked these developments' (Bonney 2000: xiv).

Autobiography carries within it claims for truth. It builds on the idea of stable identities without disunification, and yet the act of autobiography is always concerned with the creation rather than description of self. As identities are innately contingent so the attempt to base performance around autobiographical material is no more than the most public of a series of Goffmanesque representational acts.

CASE STUDY 1.12:　ERVING GOFFMAN

Erving Goffman (1922–82) was assistant professor at the University of California, Berkeley, 1958–9, associate professor, 1959–62 and professor of sociology, 1962–8. Between 1968 and 1982 he was the Benjamin Franklin Professor of Anthropology and Sociology at the University of Pennsylvania. A sociologist who was known for his analyses of human inter-action, Goffman relied less on formal scientific method than on his own observations to explain contemporary life. He wrote extensively and persuasively on the ways in which people behave in public, effectively creating and performing a complex series of roles for themselves. The impact of Goffman's thinking on contemporary performance is consider-able and it functions as a useful bridge between theatre, life, reality and artifice.

Goffman saw all forms of social interaction as phenomena to be viewed in performance terms, as relationships shaped at all times by one's environment and audience, constructed and endlessly modified to provide others with impressions of a complete and coherent 'self'. For Goffman this is consistent with the desired goals of the actor, and it is for this reason that Goffman makes the use that he does of a terminology which, prior to his work, was rarely employed outside of the theatre.

We can see Goffman as something of an ethnographer of the self. As an analyst of ordinary people in everyday life, Goffman's focus was on circumstances in which our combined efforts to create and sustain creditable selves are largely

→

→
successful and, when successful, go relatively unnoticed and
unremarked.

Recommended Reading:
Goffman, Erving. 1959. *The Presentation of Self in Everyday Life*. New York: Doubleday.
Ditton, Jason (ed.) 1980. *The View from Goffman*. New York: St. Martin's Press.
Riggins, Stephen Harold. 1990. *Beyond Goffman: Studies on Communication, Institution, and Social Interaction*. New York: Mouton de Gruyter.
Burns, Tom. 1992. *Erving Goffman*. London & New York: Routledge.
Manning, Philip. 1992. *Erving Goffman and Modern Sociology*. Cambridge: Polity Press.

Autobiography, or autoperformance, does more than provide artists with the opportunity to make themselves subjects to be seen by spectators; it allows them to see themselves in the process of being seen. Lacan described a state wherein 'the visible me is determined by the look that is outside me' (Lacan 1977: 49). For Barthes, 'You are the only one who can never see yourself except as an image; you can never see your eyes unless they are dulled by the gaze they rest upon the mirror or the lens' (Barthes 1977b: 31). A questioning of self through self's construction, the self as subject does not, we see, amount to the self as given. Autoperformative identity is under constant challenge from selective memory and an oscillation between self-mirroring, self-questioning and self-inventing and there are distinctions between the terms 'identity', 'person', 'self' and 'autobiography'. Mary Warnock reminds us that the idea of a person is not a scientific so much as a superficial concept (Warnock 1987: 53). The word 'person' is suggestive of constancy, inasmuch as one might assume a binding reference to the past, so that I remain the same *person* I ever was, regardless of changes in situation. One's identity is constructed from labels in ways that one's person is not. For Sartre, self is defined by memory: 'The past is characterized as the past of something or somebody; one *has* a past' (Sartre 1990: 112). The self's ability to reflect on one's past allows for the possibility of determining what it is that one will become. Conversely, we can say that a postmodern take on the narrative past suggests that it has lost a great deal of its authenticating power.

We can go so far as to say that the narrative of one's past has inauthenticity as its defining feature. Autobiographical performances are ultimately authorised fictions. All that we can know as authentic is the here and now, and no art form trades on the here-and-now like performance.

The here and now suggest solidity, two givens that join at the hip to make performance. But borders are crossed in performance as often as they are reinforced, and the here-and-now of performance can be employed as a means of exploring transience and liminality. The work of Gómez-Peña trades on a destabilisation of culturally stereotyped expectations, often by adopting an exaggerated sense of otherness within the work. Accordingly, what we see in the work is often no more than our own mirrored expectations, and the labels we use to describe it say much about our own spectatorial desires and fears.

CASE STUDY 1.13:   GUILLERMO GÓMEZ-PEÑA

The creator of 'Chicano Cyber-Punk Performances', Guillermo Gómez-Peña (1955–) was born in Mexico City and moved to the United States in 1978. Since then he has been exploring cross-cultural issues with the use of performance, multilingual poetry, journalism, video, radio, and installation art. His performance work and critical writings have helped develop debates on cultural diversity, identity and relations between the US and Mexico.

Gómez-Peña, Nola Mariano and Roberto Sifuentes founded La Pocha Nostra in Los Angeles in 1993, moving to San Francisco some two years later. The artists' collective poses questions for which they have no easy answers. These questions, such as 'Where are the new borders we must cross?' 'What do words like "radical", "transgressive", "rebellious", and "oppositional" mean after 9/11?' and 'What is our new place, our role as performance artists in the new century?' cut to the heart of the matter. The question of what performance might address and how and to what end informs a great deal of contemporary work but it is rarely articulated with as much passion as we see here. Referring to La Pocha Nostra as a conceptual laboratory, Gómez-Peña sees the group as a

→

→

diverse collection of rebel artists linked by a desire to shatter false boundaries between the performer and spectator, art theory and art practice, art and politics. 'I see the ever changing performance art world as a moving laboratory in which to develop and test radical ideas, images and actions, a conceptual territory that grants us special freedoms (aesthetic, political and sexual) often denied to us in other realms such as academia, political activism, grassroots organizations and certainly the media' (Gómez-Peña 2000: 62).

From 1984 to 1990 Gómez-Peña founded and participated in the bi-national collective Border Arts Workshop/Taller de Arte Fronterizo and contributed to the national radio programme *Crossroads*. He is one of the editors of the magazine *High Performance*, as well as *The Drama Review*. He has received, amongst other awards, the Prix de la Parole at the International Theatre Festival of the Americas (1989), the Bessie prize in New York (1989) and a MacArthur Fellowship (1991).

Chronology (Selected):
The End of the Line (1986)
Sons of Border Crisis (1990)
Border Brujo (1990)
A Performance Chronicle (The Rediscovery of America by the Warrior for Gringostroika) (1991)
Temple of Confessions (1994)
Cruci-Fiction Project (1994)
El Mexterminator (1995)
Returning to America (1997)
Friendly Cannibals (1997)
Ellis Island Y Que? (1998)
Border Brujo (1998)
Borderstasis (1998)
The New World Border (1999)
The Great Mojado Invasion (1999)
BORDERscape (2000)

→

→

Recommended Reading:
Gómez-Peña, Guillermo. 1997. *New World Border*. California: City Lights.
Gómez-Peña, Guillermo. 2000. *Dangerous Border Crossers: The Artist Talks Back*. London & New York: Routledge
Gómez-Peña, Guillermo. 2005. *Ethno-Techno: Writings on Performance, Activism and Pedagogy*. London & New York: Routledge.

Spalding Gray's celebrated monologues, such as *Swimming to Cambodia* and *Monster in a Box* traded on the spectatorial and oftentimes critical misnomer that what was being participated in was an intimate and to some eyes *honest* encounter between the watchers and the watched. Gray's carefully crafted texts are a type of heightened, poeticised faux-diary of the writer's own experiences, filtered through his assiduously acted East-Coast neurosis. And the work is *acted*, rehearsed, refined and played out (minimally) to maximum effect. Like the 10,000 year-old Jericho Skull – a human head dressed in death with sea-shell eyes and lime plaster flesh by a Neolithic artist – Gray gives us something that is the genuine article and an aestheticised vision at one and the same time, upsetting in its deceptively gentle lyricism our preconceptions about art and identity. Gray's performance writing, like his acting, is at once continuous and fractured, discrete and incremental, revealing the changes in Gray's life at the same time as it takes as its subject, the subject of self. Richard Coe believes that if the writer's self is to be made the subject, then it needs to be 'transmuted into something durably significant, it needs to possess a vitality and originality which is very far from common; and it needs further to be spurred on by the imperious urge to impart a message or to impart a truth which may not be allowed to vanish, or else by a dose of vanity so strong that never, for one instant, can the author doubt that his own existence, in all its intimate and unmomentous detail, is supremely meaningful to the world at large' (Coe 1985: 26). Diary-like though it may at first appear, Gray's writing differs in that diarists write in the moment, without foresight. Gray's texts, whilst often utilising the present tense are written, reflected upon and edited after the event, with the description of events having a more complex relationship with that which might or might not have occurred than Gray's delivery would lead us to assume. Nothing that is framed as performance can ever speak for itself, and yet theatre's greatest conjuring trick has been to seduce us away from this fact.

Gray's life experiences were the stimulus for his writings, but professional performance was the peg on which they hung, and his work was always tailored towards this end. Autobiographical performance functions around the 'I' on the page and the 'I' on the stage: one is a paper construct, the other is personal and neither can be regarded as wholly true. The forms deny truthful communication precisely because their methods are so innately artificial. We can read this in the light of the distinction Barthes made between the self who writes, the self who was and the self who is. Barthes' challenge to the popular idea of a stable, real and essential self reveals in its place a fabrication, a fictive truth.

In conversation, Gray wondered, 'Could I stop acting, and what was it I actually did when I acted? Was I, in fact, acting all the time, and was my acting in the theatre the surface showing of that? Was my theatre acting a confession of my constant state of feeling my life as an act? ... Now there was the new space between the timeless poetic me (the me in quotes, the self as poem) and the real-time self in the world (the time-bound, mortal self; the self as prose). The ongoing 'play' became a play about theatrical transcendence' (Callens 2004: 118–19). Gray's musings here are important to our understanding of the role of self and art, because, as Gray acknowledges, his work is about the space between a knowingly constructed performance self and a 'real time' self which, Goffman notwithstanding, is less poetically made. In fact, Goffman was always careful to stress that we put on acts, *whether we are aware that we are doing this or not*, and it is this phenomenon of playing roles without any knowledge of doing so that distinguishes the self in (performance) quotes from the self (or selves) of one's daily life. What we saw with Gray's work was the representation of experiences offered up in ways that invited empathy, engagement and *belief* at the same time, as we were never quite sure about what the performance persona revealed or obscured. Gray's performances were forged in such a way that we were seduced into believing that the work reflected his 'everyday life, the quotidian experiences that make up his autobiography' (Grace and Wasserman 2006: 35).

In constructing his texts for performance, Gray first relied on recollection, trusting to his memory of events. These memories were spoken onto tape and then, before his words were transcribed, Gray would, as he described it, 'listen to a tape of what I said and wonder how I can make it a little more dramatic and funny by juxtaposing a little hyperbole here and play with it a little bit there' (Schechner 2002: 163). This act of reflection and revision continued through early work-in-progress versions of his monologues, which Gray would make audio recordings of in order to develop material in line with spectators' responses.

Gray's morphing of self into storytelling chimes with Peggy Phelan's reading of the real and the performative. For Phelan, performance is likely to take place 'in the suspension between the "real" physical matter of "the performing body" and the psychic experience of what it is to be em-bodied' (Phelan 1993: 167). Stopping some way short of the school of thought that sees reality itself as a fiction, Phelan goes on to say that the real clearly exists, but that it can never be captured or contained in performance (Ibid.: 192). Gray's work, like Phelan's words, reminds us of the need to remain aware of the distinction between one's identity, which is constantly shifting and ever elusive, and the characters one chooses to perform, which are at least relatively stable. In Gray's case, the character he adopted in his monologue work was one for whom the construction of identity was a prime trait, perhaps even an obsession, but the effective reading of Gray-in-Performance does not equate to an understanding of the 'real-time' Gray. Despite our best efforts to pin identities down into something we can recognise and fix, the very act of living makes such efforts an always-impossible dream. So much so that we continue to be as fascinated as we are with autobiographical performance, to the extent where the form has 'acquired a position of unprecedented importance over the past thirty years' (Grace and Wasserman 2006: 13) because the work relies for its effectiveness upon a unique pact between performers and spectators. 'When we sign on to this pact we expect to be told the truth about someone's life, we believe that the people we encounter are *real*, that they live outside the text and go to the bank and grocery store as we do, and we bring this expectation to autobiography … *despite our realization that we are engaged with art, not life*' (Ibid.: 16). Gray's work implied the real beyond the frame, even as everything about it – an actor, costumed, made up and lit, speaking crafted lines to paying spectators, seated in the dark in a series of theatre buildings – wore its theatricality so emphatically upon its red plaid sleeve.

CASE STUDY 1.14:   SPALDING GRAY

Despite his film career and work with the Wooster Group, Spalding Gray (1942–2004) is probably best known and most fondly remembered for ruthlessly blurring the line between

$\rightarrow$

→

life and art during his celebrated monologues. Since 1979 he wrote and performed confessional autobiographical material that plumbed his own life-experiences for all their irony, absurdity, and humour. A magnet for stories, text for Gray, no matter how precisely it might be written in advance, was always at least partly created in front of the audience. Gray made numerous references to the fact that the words he performed were not always pre-written, rather, he said, he would draw on key words, composing his words in the moment as a form of oral writing. The life-art continuum, however, runs both ways, making it impossible to determine the exact truth of Gray's claim.

Gray's ultimate legacy is that he opened the door for performers to make live events out of their own experiences; his own work lent a type of credibility to the small-scale theatre projects of Holly Hughes, Eric Bogosian, Tim Etchells, Mike Pearson and many others. Gray's performance was a theatre of identity, of a personal politics premised on the unearthing of stories that had hitherto seemed too lacking in significance to be told to paying strangers.

Gray had spent the two and a half years prior to his suicide recuperating from a car accident in Ireland, in June 2001. Gray, who had always battled with depression, sustained a fractured skull and a badly broken hip, leaving his right leg almost immobilised. In just under two years, Gray underwent six operations and was a patient at 12 hospitals. During this period Gray made notes for *Life Interrupted*, the work that would become his last, never fully completed monologue.

Chronology (Selected):
Commune (1971)
The Tooth of Crime (1972)
Sakonnet Point (1975)
Mother Courage and Her Children (1975)
Nayatt School (1978)
The Balcony (1979)
Sex and Death to the Age 14 (1979)

→

→

Booze, Cars and College Girls (1980)
Interviewing the Audience (1980)
47 Beds (1982)
Swimming to Cambodia (1987)
Our Town (1988)
Terrors of Pleasure (1989)
Monster in a Box (1992)
Gray's Anatomy (1991)
It's a Slippery Slope (1996)
Morning, Noon and Night (1998)
Life Interrupted (2001)

Recommended Reading:

Savran, David. 1986. *Breaking the Rules*. UMI Research Press.
Callens, Johan (ed.) 2004, *The Wooster Group and its Traditions*. Brussels: Peter Lang.
Gray, Spalding. 1994. *Gray's Anatomy*. New York: Picador.
Gray, Spalding. 2005. *Swimming to Cambodia*. New York: Theatre Communications Group.
Gray, Spalding. 2006. *Life Interrupted*. New York: Crown.

Where autobiographical text for performance and the diary overlap is that each is always a description, one that at best serves only as an approximation of a life lived. And there the overlap ends. In all but the most exceptional cases a diary is written primarily for self-perusal. The writing may be no less partial, subjective and manipulative than any other kind, but it is distinguished by its absence of any aspirations towards an external readership. There is no sense of considering 'How will I be seen?' because there is no intended other out there to do the seeing. The diary writer may be writing the self, may even be writing the self as other, but by definition the writer of a diary is not writing for us. A self that is overtly written for public consumption is Orlan's. Orlan's work radicalises notions of self and self-image to a considerable degree. In deconstructing her own face through a series of highly theatricalised acts of plastic surgery, Orlan deviates from standardised notions of 'improvement', of beautification according to the pursuance of some supposed Western ideal. For Miglietti the images of Orlan 'whether they are photographic or on video, are always extremely powerful and shocking. The body opens up, blood spurts out of it, which the artist uses to make drawings, the scalpel penetrates, cuts, modifies the formal structure of the face. The impact is unquestionably disturbing and shakes up an audience anaesthetised by the generalised spectacularisation that characterises the contemporary world' (Miglietti 2003: 173). Engaging in a complex process of identity-mutation, Orlan transforms her face into an artwork that she has no choice but to carry with her beyond the conventional time and place frames of performance. And what we see is a series of layers, a series of fictions that will ultimately mislead. 'Skin is deceptive', Orlan tells us during her 1991 performance of *Operation Reussie*, and 'a person is never what they have. I have the skin of an angel, but I am a hyena, I have the skin of a crocodile but I am a puppy, I have black skin but I am white, I have the skin of a woman but I am a man; I never have the skin of what I am.'

For Orlan, that which is seen exists alongside that which is heard. Each of her performance works commence with readings from philosophical, artistic and political texts. Remaining conscious throughout the surgical procedures, Orlan continues to read for as long as she is able to during the operation, 'even when they are working on my face, which gives my latest operations the image of a corpse being subjected to an autopsy but which continues to speak, as if detached from the body' (Miglietti 2003: 173).

CASE STUDY 1.15: ORLAN

Orlan (1947–) is one of the most extreme and challenging performers of her time. French-born, Orlan's career in art started when, at the age of 17 she staged photographs of her own body. This has subsequently become the leitmotif for all of her work. The drive behind Orlan's programme of performance is a form of total self-transformation, one that is at once revolting and revolutionary and which tackles taboos about the body through a series of major surgical operations. In these subversions of standardised cosmetic surgery Orlan re-shapes her features to fit computer representations of mythic icons, based at times on Renaissance paintings such as the *Mona Lisa* and Botticelli's *Venus*. During these surgical procedures/performances Orlan remains awake and lucid, reading text to camera whilst surgeons, costumed theatrically, peel back portions of her face.

$\rightarrow$

→

A performer who has been described as a 'beauty morph' and the 'doyenne of cyberspace', Orlan combines new technologies, cosmetic surgery and virtual reality to question the illusion of beauty and notions of identity construction. In defiance of conventions of medical surgery and art practice her work asks controversial questions about the status of the body, alongside conceptual ideas of body image in an age of genetic manipulation.

Orlan's surgical performances began in 1979 when she was diagnosed as having an ectopic pregnancy, which necessitated an emergency procedure. By the time Orlan went into the operating theatre she had commissioned a video camera operator to record the event, which was subsequently presented at an arts centre in Lyon. The links with Frida Khalo's paintings is apparent, as is the current penchant for photographic and filmic 'evidence' rather than painterly representations.

Chronology (Selected):
One-Off Striptease with Trousseau Sheets (1975)
Mise-en-scene for a saint (1980)
Histoires Saintes de l'Art (1985)
The Reincarnation of Saint Orlan (1990)
Operation Reussie (1991)
Sacrifice (1993)
This is My Body ... This is My Software (1996)
Le sang, le Coeur et le nid de l'aigle (1999)

Recommended Reading:
Butler, Judith. 1990. *Gender Trouble: Feminism and the Subversion of Identity*. London & New York: Routledge.
Brentano, Robyn and Olivia Georgia. 1994. *Outside the Frame: Performance and the Object*. Cleveland: Cleveland Center for Contemporary Art.
Ince, Kate. 2000. *Orlan: Millennial Female*. Oxford. Berg.
Pitts, Victoria. 2003. *In the Flesh: The Cultural Politics of Body Modification*. New York: Palgrave Macmillan.
Durand, Regis and Eleanor Heartney. 2004. *Orlan: Carnal Art*. Paris: Flammarion.

Luce Irigaray's argument that female performers need to find ways of representing themselves through forms that expose the materiality of their bodies reads like a programme note to Orlan and also to Marina Abramović (Irigaray 1985: 14). Irigaray's comments are given added weight through Rebecca Schneider's argument that 'Any body bearing female markings is automatically shadowed by the history of that body's signification, its delimitation as a signifier of sexuality either explicitly (literally) in porn, or implicitly (symbolically) in art' (Schneider 1997: 17). Postmodern, auto-biographical and feminist performance is marked as political not primarily because of what words are spoken so much as by who speaks them. This is so because the work forms an implicit critique to the idea that women in performance are essentially man-made constructs, bodies turned into 'objects of male desire ... for men to gaze upon' (Case 1988: 66) or, as John Berger describes it, the one-sided situation whereby 'Men look at women. Women watch themselves being looked at' (Berger 1985: 47). The contemporary female body-in-performance is used increasingly as a form through which to challenge the norms of a culture (and not least a culture of art and performance) which is dominated by men. As Giovanna Nicoletti puts it, the female performer's 'body is no longer interpreted and represented through artistic material, but is itself used as a material, as protagonist and linguistic instrument' (Nicoletti 1972: 135).

In art and theatre history, the voices of women have been virtually disregarded. As we saw at the start of this chapter, things began to change at the point when female artists such as Yoko Ono started to utilise live art as a medium through which culturally accepted roles could be examined and changed. Live art provided a platform for the deconstruction of systematically phallocentric representational modes, which had up until that time insidiously governed the ways in which women in performance were seen, indeed, the ways in which they were *allowed to be seen*. Feminist practitioners challenged the imposition of masculinist readings on their work and the ways in which these readings attached pre-determined and centuries-old ways of seeing and hearing. According to Judy Chicago, prior to this there had been 'no acknowledgement within the art community that a woman might have a different point of view from a man, or if a difference was acknowledged, that difference meant inferiority' (Sayre 1992: 98).

Feminist performers attempted to free their work from the patriarchal vocabulary provided in the vast majority of plays. Rejecting the limitations of those male-drawn characterisations which saw them as evil, vengeful, or wanton, practitioners began addressing their spectators directly, articulating their own experiences and by assuming control of the ways in which they were seen and heard. This signalled a shift away from the objectification of the to-be-seen towards the subjectification of the to-be-heard. Lizbeth Goodman – writing from experience as both performer and scholar – sees feminist performance as a form 'through which she [the artist] invents and interprets her own sense of self' (Goodman 1993: 182). This 'self' is a body reclaimed from the male gaze. This is significant, as many female performers present those same naked images of women's bodies that might in other contexts be regarded as existing for precisely that same objectification by men. Lucy Hughes-Hallett is aware of this when she points to a feminist sensitivity towards the 'potentially exploitative nature' of the naked female body, arguing that 'it makes sense to use your own image if you are expressing your own emotions' (Hughes-Hallett 1992: 24). The context in which the body is seen changes its own image and changes the ways in which it is read, or at least changes the ways in which it seeks to be read. The fact that two images or events might look the same can be used as a means of exposing the massive differences between them, or of questioning our spectatorial assumptions. In the Duchampian sense, the image is recontextualised and given new thoughts. In asking us to address the question of how an image can mean *this* and also *this* content is always renegotiable, always made subject to the postmodern icons of concept and context. In this way, a live artist such as Helen Paris is able to 'fully inhabit the "erotic" stereotyped female body on stage, only to subvert those images once they were in place, opening up the flesh to expose what is abject' (Hughes 2000: 21).

For the past 40 years, women have been creating performance work that confronts and overturns male-generated scopophilia, making work that has been at the forefront of major developments in performance and politics. Approaches to performance by practitioners such as Paris, Abramović and Orlan function as a means of confronting a series of prejudicial takes on the female body, and this 'notion of performance as directly accessing an artist's real self continues the project to bring the everyday directly into art – which has been part of the agenda of avant-garde art in the twentieth century' (MacDonald 1997: 188).

Marina Abramović began making relational performance work with her partner Ulay (Uwe Laysiepen) in 1975, creating a single unit 'androgyne' within which their sexual opposites were contained, alongside a doubling of personas that cut across life and work. Citing Freud's idea of the double as insurance against the destruction of the ego and a denial of the power of death, Chrissie Iles suggests that 'if death can be said to be the outer limits of one's body, the self-lesionism inflicted by artists working with the body in the early seventies, including Marina Abramović and Ulay, could be argued to be a physical expression of this desire for transcendence. … The double reverses its aspect and becomes a tool for observing and criticizing the self'

(Abramović and Ulay 1997: 9). Abramović found with Ulay a means of developing further those issues of gender, identity and the body she had previously explored through role-reversal with an Amsterdam prostitute in *Role Exchange* (1975), passive manipulation at the hands of spectators in *Rhythm O* (1974) and violent assaults on her own body in *Art Must be Beautiful, Artist Must be Beautiful* (1975).

Unlike Orlan, for whom – and despite appearances to the contrary – pain and discomfort need to be kept to an absolute minimum, Abramović has always felt that the subject of her work needs to be the limits of her body's capacity to endure, that she would use performance to push her mental and physical limits beyond consciousness (Abramović 1998: 15). Accepting of the possibility of dying during her work, Abramović consistently pushes herself to her durational, psychological and physical limits: 'She cuts herself, she combs her hair ... remains motionless for hours, she marks herself, slips and falls, she allows herself to be crawled upon by snakes ... she carves her skin' (Miglietti 2003: 95); 'Art should be done,' Abramović feels, 'from that extraordinary state of mind one could only get to physically, through exhaustion or pain or repetition' (Carr 1994: 45).

CASE STUDY 1.16: MARINA ABRAMOVIĆ

Born in Belgrade in 1946, Abramović's early performances were a form of rebellion against her strict upbringing as well as against the repressive culture she encountered in post-war Yugoslavia. This initial work set the pattern for a series of performances which were, above all, ritualistic and durational purifications designed in part to free Abramović from the constraints of her past.

In 1975 Abramović met Ulay, an artist who shared her date of birth as well as her artistic interests and passions. Over the next two decades they lived and collaborated together, performing and travelling throughout the world, until they marked the ending of their relationship by walking the Wall of China from separate ends. Throughout their time together their performances sought to expose and explore the parameters of power and dependency between artists and audience, as well as between the artists themselves. A consequence of this was

→

→

that Abramović became known for works which took her to physical and emotional limits, many of which involved the artist exposing herself to genuine risk and pain. Abramović regards performance as something occurring as a type of energy dialogue in which works are not rehearsed or even repeated but done once (despite the fact that many of her own works have been repeated over periods of years). The performer has a concept to follow, but at the same time the outcome of the performance is never fully known. It is in this way that, for Abramović at least, performance differs from theatre.

Abramović describes herself as the 'Grandmother of Performance Art', and she remains probably the most active and influential of those practitioners who came to public attention in the early 1970s. In 1997 Abramović presented the video installation and performance *Balkan Baroque* at the Venice Biennale, where she received the Golden Lion Award for Best Artist.

Chronology (Selected):
Come to Wash with Me (1969)
Rhythm 10 (1973)
Rhythm 0 (1974)
Art Must be Beautiful, Artist Must be Beautiful (1975)
Role Exchange (1975)
Thomas' Lips (1975)
Breathing in/Breathing out (1977)
Incision (1978)
Rest Energy (1980)
Nightsea Crossing (1981)
The Lovers: The Great Wall of China (1988)
Cleaning the Mirror I (1995)
Insomnia (1997)

Recommended Reading:
Schneider, Rebecca. 1997. *The Explicit Body in Performance*. London & New York: Routledge.

→

→

Abramović, Marina, and Ulay. 1997. *Ulay/Abramovic: Performances 1976–1988*. Eindhoven: Stedelijk Van Abbemuseum.

Abramović, Marina. 1998. *Performing Body: Marina Abramovic*. Milan: Charta Edizioni.

Schimmel, Paul. 1998. *Out of Actions: Between Performance and the Object*, 1949–79, Los Angeles: The Museum of Contemporary Art (MOCA).

The naked body reveals itself, just as the wounded body bleeds. For Kira O'Reilly, Franko B, Ron Athey and Orlan, the blood, whilst real, is controlled. But such is not always the case. Rabih Mroué tells of a performer whose wounded eye began to bleed profusely mid-performance, to the extent that his fellow actors and spectators alike asked that he leave the stage and seek immediate medical attention. Despite his suffering, the performer refused and the performance continued until the 'bloody eye became a spectacle in itself, reality and fiction mingling in an exceptional way to offer the public's voyeurism a rare and curious object' (Mroué 2003: 13). At the conclusion of the performance the audience applauded, 'expressing their admiration for his abnegation, their gratitude for his sacrifice, and saluting the risks he had deliberately run. ... Nobody noticed his eye lying on the stage, staring fixedly at the audience' (Ibid.). According to Mroué this amounts to a crime in which all present have been willing participants, and there is a clear sense where his judgment is correct. It is through events such as these that the act of spectatorship assumes the status of witness: we see something only once, something that does not end safely with the bringing down of the curtain and the bowing to applause.

The shift from spectating to witnessing turns the act of watching into an act of complicity. Tim Etchells talks about 'the distinction between being an audience member, a spectator and a witness' (de Wend Fenton and Neal 2005: 157). For Etchells, 'To witness an event ... is to be present at it in some fundamentally ethical way, as an onlooker. The art-work that turns us into witnesses leaves us, above all, unable to stop thinking, talking, reporting what we've seen ... borne on by our responsibility to events' (Ibid.: 157–8). There is, as Etchells acknowledges, more to the distinction than post-performance resonance. Audience members and spectators are, after all, as likely to feel compelled to re-live the events taking place in a play as a 'witness' might be to Ron Athey's acts of ritualistic self-harm or Forced Entertainment's own theatricalised and knowingly difficult endurance pieces. The distinction that

Etchells points us to lies in the area of ethical responsibility. Not only might we be able to stop the things we have paid to see from taking place (or taking place in the particular ways that they do), but it may well be that it is only our continued attendance that brings them about at all. With work where the theatre's 'as if' is transformed into the more performance-driven 'is', we are compelled to attend with a different type of focus. Seeing the character of Othello stage-strangling the character named Desdemona is something to be watched, seeing and smelling Franko B's blood is something to be witnessed.

For Artaud, the image of a violent act portrayed in the theatre was infinitely more powerful than the real act of violence carried out elsewhere. The 'real' act carried out in the theatre has a different power still, not emphatically more or less, but markedly different.

As the real has entered the spaces of theatre and art, so the artistic and the theatrical have infiltrated mainstream life. We see this to the extent where 'to pierce oneself is no longer a bold statement: fashion models, sugary pop singers, and sportsmen now wear their piercings ostentatiously, and so do weekend-Bohemian yuppies and upper-class students from Yale or Harvard ... America's afternoon talk shows have become more outrageous than any performance art piece I ever saw' (Gómez-Peña 2000: 272–3). It may well be the case that we blink once, if at all, when we witness body modification and adornment in 'life', whereas we blink hard and look away when the same act or image is presented to us within the frame of art. It is precisely this framing aspect of art that makes the things we see so often difficult to bear. The frame both provides and demands a focus, creating a contract which we are not always willing or capable of honouring. It is for this reason that an image in a gallery can be both difficult and shocking in ways that are absent when we encounter the same image in a newspaper. The image is, of course, in no way the same, just as an event in the theatre is in no way the same as that event taking place elsewhere. Content means nothing to us without context.

Placing the body in harm's way as an intention rather than a possible consequence of performance – in the line of fire as Chris Burden once had it –emerged as something akin to a movement in the post-Artaudian 1960s. Gina Pane began working with her body in performance in 1968, subjecting it to wounds most famously with *Escalade Sanglante* in 1971. Pane's performances 'were based on a certain kind of danger', within which Pane recalls testing 'some pretty extreme limits ... I was exhibiting the danger, my limits, but I never offered answers. The result was not genuine danger, but only a structure that I had created. And this structure gave the viewer a certain type of shock. The viewer no longer felt safe. He or she would be caught off balance, and this would give them a certain internal emptiness. And they were obliged to remain in that void. I would give them nothing' (Donald 1990: 62). Pane's assumptions about spectators notwithstanding, her comments about danger being carefully controlled within performance structures are important. The blood and gore of body art has assumed its own mythology, and it is one that often disguises the fact that most art of this kind is made up of confessional performances in situations where any kind of danger to the artist is minimal and where danger to spectators is no more likely than at any theatre event.

Chris Burden's 1989 work *Samson* is a case in point. In this piece each spectator enters the space through a turnstile, hooked up to a 100-ton jack, which forces two large timbers out against the gallery walls. The idea is that any one spectator might be one spectator too many, an unknowing Samson bringing the building down on the heads of all present. The reality was different. The jack was geared down and the number of spectators needed to place any strain on the wall was so far in excess of all expectations as to make the projected outcome impossible. Danger was no more than a concept, as illusionistic in its own way as the live rounds fired in Siegfried and Roy's Las Vegas act, and maybe more so. Abramović stopped doing performances that involved cutting when she became so skilled in the act that the work lost its painful charge, even though spectators were unaware of the distinction. The sight of blood within the performance space disguises its own occasional ordinariness, suggesting pain and discomfort even when none exists. Orlan is clear about this, telling spectators that the only pain she experiences is the pain of watching, with us, her own operations on film: 'I am sorry to make you suffer,' she explains, 'but remember, I am not suffering, except like you, when I look at the images' (Ince 2000: 63).

The most fabled of all Burden's performances and possibly the most fabled act of all contemporary performance, was his *Shoot* of 1971. For many people Burden's bullet in the arm stands as a metaphor for the excesses of performance art. Where the notion of suffering for one's art is regarded as a laudable trait – and where Robert de Niro's 60lb weight gain for the Schrader/Scorsese movie *Raging Bull* contributed in no small part to the actor's Oscar win – this type of suffering, it seems, is only acceptable when the aim is one we approve. Throwing oneself headlong into method absorption, like launching into a tackle on the sports field, skiing down a mountain, or driving a Formula One Ferrari at 200 miles per hour is thus regarded by the public as praiseworthy and even heroic, whereas taking far fewer risks in non-mainstream performance is tantamount to insanity. Burden's scar has assumed iconic status, with spectators queuing for hours to gape at the entry and exit holes in his 1981 work *Show the Hole*. Burden has acknowledged that his intentions for the work were somewhat different: 'The way it was supposed to happen was that the bullet would go by and scratch my arm, and one drop of blood would come out so there would be this grey zone like – was I shot? Or was I not? I'd convinced all the people around me so much that no one even brought a first-aid kit. I practised with the man who shot me for a couple of weeks, to shoot near me, close to me, so he got used to doing that. My fear was that he'd miss. He'd pick up the rifle and actually be so nervous that he'd miss. So the bullet went in and out, it didn't hurt, but to look at your arm and see a smoking hole in it is kind of horrific' (Burden 1993: 19). Picking up on the work some months later from *Esquire* magazine, *Newsweek* ran a feature carrying a claim, with no evidence in support, that Burden's future work would involve acts of violence against the audience. And so, in no small part as a consequence of a nervous marksman, a trembling target and journalistic hype the micro of Burden and the macro of performance art went from strength to strength.

Performance has the capacity to transcend its own safety net, regardless of the care with which that net has been assembled, and consequence will often find a way of getting in on the act. One of Burden's early orchestrations was his *220*, performed in the F Space, Santa Ana, California in October 1971. The title of the piece referred to the 220 Volt electric cable that ran live into a deeply flooded studio floor as Burden and his co-performers spent the night atop a number of wooden stepladders. The structured risk element, that if a performer fell to the floor in the night electrocution would occur, was minimal as long as the performers remained awake, which they did. The unstructured risk occurred when the bone-dry ladders began to absorb water, which crept upwards through the night.

Another unexpected consequence took place in a 1994 performance of *The Cruci-Fiction Project* at San Francisco's Rodeo Beach. For this work Guillermo Gómez-Peña and Roberto Sifuentes were placed on wooden crosses in front of an audience of some 300. Programmes were handed out among the crowd, inviting spectators to free the performers from their martyrdom and to expedite their release as a political gesture. The performers had expected to be freed within an hour. It was not until some three hours later, by which time Gómez-Peña's right shoulder had become dislocated, and both he and Sifuentes had lost consciousness, that a group of Japanese drummers took sympathetic action, climbing on each other's shoulders to release them. As Gómez-Peña recovered consciousness he heard a number of spectators in the crowd shouting 'Let them die' (Gómez-Peña 2000: 64).

In many ways body art is still regarded as a phenomenon that belongs in the 1960s and 1970s. The 1960s were radical years, and the 1968 student uprising in Paris serves as a useful historical catalyst for the excesses in art that took place around that time. Of at least equal significance is the fact that artists such as Pane, Burden, Schneemann and Acconci were people who felt their Post-War status acutely. At a time when the world had suffered as much as it had, when images of mass-graves were being assimilated with painful slowness into the cultural psyche, performers responded to this through the methods they deemed most appropriate. The barked instruction 'Don't tell me, show me' remains the staple of actor-training in the West, despite Heiner Müller's protestations that description is always more honest than representation. Yves Klein's early 1960s *Anthropometries* can read as male fantasy fulfillment in their use of naked female bodies daubed in his patented blue and pressed against canvas, until they are regarded in the light of his visit to Japan, where the traces of nuclear-blasted bodies remained etched into walls. Once seen this way Klein's limbless torsos assume a terrible significance that does much to aid our understanding of the work.

Derrida felt that words were to be drawn from the body like blood from a syringe; Harold Pinter says that words are the things we deploy to cover our nakedness. Words and the body, words and the body that bleeds. Unlike the camera on which *Shoot* was recorded and unlike the words we use to describe it, the bullet hole in Burden's arm provides its own testament, and the text that abides is not written in ink. As a form that deals with the flesh of the seen, performance knows that the bodies it displays function as the limits of possibility. The body as marked, the body as 'other', the body as our most familiar and most strange. The obscene body placed centre-stage subverts the very form that frames it, forcing us into a relationship with the forbidden and the unspoken, with the ordinariness of everyday behaviour and the extraordinary focus that comes with performance.

4
Writing the Written, Writing the Group

Critical terms change the ways that we think, talk and write. Interdisciplinarity, for example, largely replaced the term experimental, just as postmodernism and performance displaced interdisciplinarity and theatre. In Britain the term 'Live Art' describes that which elsewhere is identified as Performance Art. The study of contemporary performance seems at times like a job-creation scheme for linguists and lexicologists, an endless re-theorisation. As it is with terminology, so is it with practice. Collaborative group work and devising, which until relatively recently were looked upon as something exotic, as practices that deviated from the norm of playwriting, have become relatively commonplace activities.

Not every writer is suited to this sharing of the authorial voice: Arnold Wesker argues that this 'is not a method of working to which [he] could adapt' (Wesker 1985: 69). In Wesker's opinion, 'to create by committee is a procedure few artists can tolerate ... art is the last and only human activity where the individual's spirit and imagination must not be called upon to compromise its vision of the human condition. Group theatre, needing to accommodate the perceptions and sensibilities of many, inevitably results in such compromise' (Ibid.: 70). Wesker makes a valid point, one that conforms to his belief that 'the miracle [of theatre] takes place when all energies are directed towards realizing the writer's intentions' (Ibid.). Nevertheless, the phenomenon of the writer-in-residence, where theatre texts are created in response to and/or with target communities is no longer regarded as a gimmick dressed up as initiative, and the case for writing-in-action and in-situ has been well made. Tim Etchells and the members of Forced Entertainment, for instance, have an 'unspoken agreement that no one would bring anything too completed to the [devising] process – a few scraps or fragments of text, an idea or two for action, a costume, an idea about space, a sketched out piece of music – everything unfinished, distinctly incomplete – so there'd be more spaces for other things to fill in … more dots to join' (Etchells 1999: 51). Key here is that the period of making shifts from a concentration on creative interpretation to one where the task is to interpret what is being created. Allan Owens regards as most vital those processes where participants in drama forms work in collectives that are not necessarily consensual (Owens 2005: 9), arguing that what is required is not the imposition of an individual worldview so much as a pretext to engage all involved 'in a dramatic situation where they [can] actively consider issues, problems, concepts and ideas from a wide range of perspectives in order to (re)consider their own' (Ibid.: 12).

Owens' work is primarily in the areas of intercultural applied drama, in a variety of global educational and community settings. It reminds us that the tradition of performers collaborating through devising and improvisation in the writing process is not limited to the narrow range of contemporary practice focussed on in this book. Many film writers and directors, for example, encourage actors to work around scripts, rather than following lines to the letter, and some are happy to let the entire script emerge through the type of organic group work that Wesker sees as compromise.

The British writer/director Mike Leigh has achieved considerable success through approaches that draw on and from the group, rather than arriving at rehearsal with a script full of intentions to be realised.

CASE STUDY 1.17:   MIKE LEIGH

Mike Leigh was born in Salford in 1943 and was educated at Salford Grammar School, before gaining a scholarship to the Royal Academy of Dramatic Art in 1960. Leigh went from here to Camberwell School of Arts and Crafts, the Central School of Art and Design, and the London Film School. In 1965 he began devising and directing his own plays, completing nine before the production of *Bleak Moments* at the Open Space Theatre in 1970. Directing nothing other than his own material, Leigh is perhaps the closest that contemporary British film, theatre and television has to an auteur. His closest domestic rival in this area (though clearly not in style of work) is Steven Berkoff.

→

→

In the years between *Bleak Moments* (1970) and *High Hopes* (1988), his next film for cinema, Leigh made nine feature-length television plays, as well as shorts and theatrical productions. Leigh encouraged actors to go beyond the conventionally naturalistic in their characterisations, depicting through this process a series of desperate situations, tempered by humour, which are captured by dramatic lighting and an often static but precisely positioned camera.

Leigh has often been accused of patronising his characters and encouraging the audience to look down at their responses to the situations they find themselves in. A counter-argument is that most of Leigh's characters, despite their eccentricities, are ordinary people struggling with courage, resolve and limited resources to confront particular problems. The character quirks of speech, gesture, and appearance encouraged in his actors (something Leigh describes as a 'running condition') has at times inspired acting that plays close to a type of neo-realism. This is facilitated by lengthy periods of improvised rehearsal, honed by Leigh into dramatic scripts that capture the idiosyncratic nature of his performers' speech patterns and rhythms.

Leigh received an OBE in 1993 for his dedication and services to British filmmaking and, in 2005, the Joseph Plateau Award for Outstanding Achievement in Filmmaking at the Flanders International Film Festival.

To date, Mike Leigh has written 25 plays.

Chronology (plays):
The Box Play (1965)
The Last Crusade of the Five Little Nuns (1966)
My Parents Have Gone to Carlisle (1966)
Waste Paper Guards (1966)
NENAA (1967)
Down Here and Up There (1968)
Individual Fruit Pies (1968)
Epilogue (1969)
Big Basil (1969)
Bleak Moments (1970)

→

→
A Rancid Pong (1971)
Dick Whittington and his Cat (1973)
The Jaws of Death (1973)
Wholesome Glory (1973)
Babies Grow Old (1974)
The Silent Majority (1974)
Abigail's Party (1977)
Ecstasy (1979)
Goose Pimples (1981)
Smelling a Rat (1988)
Greek Tragedy (1989)
It's a Great Big Shame (1993)
Naked (1995)
Career Girls (1997)
Two Thousand Years (2005)

Recommended Reading:
Clements, Paul. 1983. *The Improvised Play*. London: Methuen.
Coveney, Michael. 1996. *The World According to Mike Leigh*.
   London: HarperCollins.
Carney, Ray and Leonard Quart. 2000. *The Films of Mike
   Leigh – Embracing the World*. Cambridge: Cambridge
   University Press.
Movshovitz, Howie (ed.) 2000. *Mike Leigh Interviews*. Missis-
   sippi: University Press of Mississippi.

Steve Dixon has emphasised the extent to which 'Devising a performance is a difficult, often painful process: a creative and emotional pendulum of ups and downs; a battle to distil essences and to articulate the intangible; a birth with invariable complications. Certain approaches and agreed philosophies help anchor the process, unifying the ensemble through shared ideology, methodology, or aesthetic. Starting points – themes, stories, characters – provide foundations from which to build, and protect from the discomforting fear of the 'blank page' or empty space' (Dixon 1998: 61). Whilst remaining cognisant of the freedoms afforded to actors in the devising process, Dixon makes the telling point that certain key moments and ideas will almost always be pre-determined and worked towards.

For Alison Oddey, 'Devising theatre … can cause heartache, joy, frustration, and satisfaction. It can make an individual wonder why she or he ever had this notion of wanting to create work that is unique to a particular group and interests. What is this constant appeal of wanting to begin from the germ of an idea, and develop it into a full-scale piece of theatre? It is the need to say something, to express oneself, to give a voice to ideas, thoughts and feelings about the world; to capture the essence of a particular group of people making and creating theatre' (Oddey 1994: 200). Oddey's words convey a little more than they intend. Capturing the essence of a particular group of people may well be an aim, but it falls some way short of being the universal given that Oddey's text implies. That there is often a feel good factor to the devising process is undoubtedly true, but it is useful to step back from this and focus on the rigorous processes that devising demands.

Devising has become something of the lingua franca of university theatre because of its natural accommodation to any size of group and any gender breakdown. Anthony Frost uses the terms *aleatoric* and *ungendered* to refer to the casting of plays in a way that is randomised and in which 'any performer, male or female [is] prepared to play any role at any time' (Frost 1998: 151). Most of us will have seen and be familiar with examples of this in student productions, where versions of *Hamlet* contain half a dozen Danish princes, alongside at least as many Ophelias. If situations such as these are problematic, then no such problems exist with devising, and if they do, they are deliberately and knowingly inscribed, so that 'performers are *merely* persons of masculine or feminine gender whose personal features are deliberately effaced. They may be said to represent certain states of mind or currents of thought circulating through consciousness; in other words, they are internalized representations of a consciousness engaged in an objective clarification of the self' (Rabkin 1999: 41).

This is an approach often utilised in devising and group writing, where material is composed in order to fit the size, capabilities and interests of the group members, but, process aside, it is the finished product that matters most (if not exclusively) to the majority of spectators. This is as demanding of performance skills as one would expect to see in the realisation of a conventionally scripted play. Sarah-Jane Dickenson voices the concerns of many, when she writes that 'Student numbers and gender breakdown have made the use of many texts in the received canon distant from the needs of students in a practical context' (Dickenson 1995: 38). Study of the text through practice is often sacrificed to the cut and paste of student bodies, whilst performative efficacy plays a poor second fiddle to the requirement that everyone is afforded equal opportunities to take part, with all of the attendant issues of assessment that this implies. What is more, 'The distortion, manipulation and interpretation of many recognised texts to fit the large group tends to further underline an uneven gender bias, particularly in focus and content' (Ibid.). Dickenson is correct to highlight the gender bias in scripted plays. As we well know, the history of playwriting is also the his-story of plays. Despite the acceleration of plays by women, and those which can accommodate female performers, the shelves of university libraries, certainly in Britain and the U.S., continue to buckle under the sheer bulk of plays by white, male writers. The temptation to stage 'male' plays is as strong as it is because the pool is so wide: quality is always an issue when it comes to selecting a play for a group to perform, but quantity also counts, and often counts more.

Despite the considerable majority of undergraduates in Theatre, Drama and Performance programmes in Britain and the U.S. being female, most tutors are male. This male bias extends beyond tutors: there are relatively few female heads of department, heads of school, deans and pro-vice chancellors. The sensibilities and power bases in most of our universities, faculties and departments, like the plays on the shelves, remain resolutely male, white and middle-class. Under circumstances such as these, the possibilities for empowering the individuals involved that come with choosing group devising and *group scripting* become even more persuasive.

Companies have such diverse methods of devising performance material that generalisations, as ever, are problematic. The two companies whose work forms the spine of this chapter are Forced Entertainment and the Wooster Group. Certain similarities between the companies and their approaches exist, whilst others are often massaged to fit. Each company works, usually, with a long-term director whose fingerprints are eminently visible. For Forced Entertainment this is Tim Etchells; for the Wooster Group, Elizabeth LeCompte. Each company has a core membership that has worked together for many years. Each has a unique, immediately recognisable and endlessly imitated house-style. Each has come to represent, in their respective countries, and depending upon which critics we read, the best of experimentation and the worst of excess.

There is a sense whereby the constant focus on these companies blinds us to work taking place elsewhere and with different agendas, as though the present and immediate future of Western performance lay in the hands of two companies working out of Sheffield and New York City. Knowing that this is not true, like knowing that John Osborne's *Look Back in Anger* was just one thin slice of British theatre in 1956, provides us with some safeguard. The reality is that the critical focus these companies receive does as much to make their work important as the theatre work they produce.

Since its emergence out of the process-orientated and Grotowski-inspired interests of Richard Schechner's Performance Group, 'The Wooster Group have been deconstructing – and disrupting – the dramatic classics that animate theatre history, filtering them through a late-twentieth-century sensibility' (de Wend Fenton and Neal 2005: 167).

CASE STUDY 1.18:   THE WOOSTER GROUP

Elizabeth LeCompte first directed Schechner's Performance Group in 1974. In 1980 the decision was made to rename group after the address of their Wooster Street studio in Manhattan's Soho district. LeCompte's interest in creating a visual language that was not reliant upon psychological realism was echoed by her performers, and the company began to make work which, to paraphrase Savran, broke all the rules of theatre. The group's use of 'bad taste' material, not least their utilisation of blackface routines in *Route 1 & 9* has offended and polarised their audiences. The group's early work resulted in huge controversy, with their funding being cut by 40 per cent for allegedly presenting (in *Route 1 & 9*) 'harsh and caricatured portrayals of a racial minority'.

The group's working process includes – even centres around – the deconstructing of classic and established texts and the exploration of the points at which mimesis and reality meet. Because the group's original members were not Stanislavski-trained performers, there was no prior assimilation of naturalistic techniques to work against. This freed the work from a number of restraints, as did LeCompte's insistence that the *mise en scene* did not need to be subordinate to any previously written script. The Wooster Group's performances have always stemmed from a variety of sources, including autobiography and the personalities and preoccupations of core members. The work is collaborative in the extreme.

The Wooster Group's approach to written text is no different to the approach taken to space, lighting and personnel: everything is up for grabs, and nothing is regarded as sacred. The adoption of this stance landed the group in trouble with Arthur Miller's legal team, when the writer took exception to the radically deconstructionist approach taken to *The Crucible*. The Wooster Group's response to this resulted in *LSD*

→

→

(*...Just the High Points...*) a production regarded by many as their seminal work.

Chronology (Selected):
Sakonnet Point (1975)
Rumstick Road (1977)
Nayatt School (1978)
Point Judith (an epilog) (1979)
Route 1 & 9 (The Last Act) (1981)
Hula (1981)
For the Good Times (1982)
L.S.D. (...Just the High Points...) (1984)
North Atlantic (1984)
Frank Dell's The Temptation of St. Antony (1987)
Brace Up! (1991)
The Emperor Jones (1993)
Fish Story (1994)
The Hairy Ape (1995)
Hose/Lights (1998)
North Atlantic (1999)
To You, The Birdie! (Phedre)(2001)
Poor Theater (2003)
Hamlet (2007)
La Didone (2007)

Recommended Reading:
Savran, David. 1988. *Breaking the Rules: The Wooster Group*. New York: Theatre Communications Group.
Auslander, Philip. 1994. *Presence and Resistance, Postmodernism and Cultural Politics in Contemporary American Performance*. Michigan: Michigan University Press.
Cole, Susan Letzler. 1992. *Directors in Rehearsal*. London & New York: Routledge.
Zarrilli, Phillip (ed.) 1995. *Acting (Re)Considered*. London & New York: Routledge.
Campbell, Patrick (ed.) 1996. *Analysing Performance: a Critical Reader*. Manchester: Manchester University Press.

→

→
Aronson, Arnold. 2000. *American Avant-Garde Theatre: a History*. London & New York: Routledge.
Callens, Johan (ed.) 2004. *The Wooster Group and its Traditions*. Brussels: Peter Lang.

However much we might like to state the opposite, the theatre world for most of us and for most of the time is a fundamentally conservative place. Consequently, the Wooster Group's upsetting of certain spectators is in some ways the thing that most pleases the rest. Richard Eyre, who was at that time Director of the National Theatre, thought the group's performance of a multimedia-heavy deconstruction of Chekhov's *Three Sisters*, which they re-imagined into *Brace Up!* was a pointless exercise and a facile postmodern conceit; Nicholas de Jongh took a similarly unimpressed view of the work, regarding it as a sub-Brechtian and intrinsically incoherent mess of meaningless technology. Dominic Cavendish, writing in The *Telegraph*, complains that the manner in which the company presents the texts they use 'would give purists a collective seizure' (Cavendish 2002: 22), not least through their transformation of classic dramatic material into 'flip, colloquial turns of phrase, muttered nonchalantly into microphones' (Ibid.). This British criticism echoed the responses of earlier U.S. critics. 'The two lead theatre critics for the (New York) *Times* in the eighties, Frank Rich and Mel Gussow, loathed and ridiculed the group for their "vapid" and "stale" "assaults on classics"' (Callens 2004: 66). By the late 1980s, however, 'Stephen Holden took over the avant-garde beat and penned somewhat more thoughtful critiques of the work directed by the now – "intrepid Elizabeth LeCompte"' (Ibid.). Even more latterly, reviews of the Wooster Group in the *New York Times* read more like sanctification than criticism. Yesterday's pariahs become today's champions. And so it goes.

It is in the nature of innovative and progressive performance to be a step or two ahead of the critics who read it. The famous critical response to the first London performance of Beckett's two-act *Waiting for Godot* was after all that nothing happens twice, and few forward-thinking practitioners find early support in either the popular or heavyweight press. In responding to work, we can do no more than draw upon what we know, making sense of the new through our understanding of the old. It takes time for cultural shifts to become recognisable enough to describe and longer still for a critical vocabulary to emerge that allows the description to adopt as comfortable a place in the columns of our newspapers as it does in specialist journals. All theatrical performance is a conventionalised activity, and yet the relationship between the postmodern practice exemplified by the Wooster Group and its modernist past demonstrated a significant enough distinction to unfix the expectations of all but the most radical of viewers.

The Wooster Group was different enough from the norm to alienate their share of theatre critics, but not so different as to make that alienation permanent. For Derrida a performance would be unlikely to work if it did not 'repeat a "coded" or iterable utterance' (Derrida 1988: 18), making the work identifiable in some way as a "citation" (Ibid.). In this way a company such as the Wooster Group subvert the conventional expectations of theatre, but do so in the service of recognisable principles. We can see through this that it is the Wooster Group's 'reliance on the avant-garde's aesthetic strategies, which tend to preserve the very structures and principles they subvert' (Callens 2004: 47). A consequence of this is that 'LeCompte's early radical deconstructions and later reframings of canonical texts very much confirm their cultural capital' (Ibid.). Shocking as a piece such as the 1981 project *Route 1 & 9* was, with its immediately infamous and subsidy-halting re-presentation (complete with blackface) of a Pigmeat Markham minstrel routine, it did not take long for this event to assume respectability and even cult status. This has certainly been the case amongst British academics. The company rapidly became the most identifiable peg on which to hang a series of conference papers and articles on postmodern performance. Glasgow's Tramway and London's Riverside Studios played host to performances such as *L.S.D (...Just the High Points...)*, *House/Lights* and *To You, The Birdie! (Phedre)*, and the undergraduate essays on deconstruction rolled in.

Change is the lifeblood of theatre. It is at once its most troubling and most essential element. Inasmuch as it is possible to speak of a break in tradition, we do so in the context of a loss of faith in historically transmitted authority. Chekhov had famously called for new forms of theatre or no theatre at all, arguing that a theatre that rested on its laurels was not a theatre worth having. Chekhov's call for realism was subversive in its way and at its time, although our current feelings may be that its subversion was ultimately invidious. In making things seem 'like life' and therefore objective, realism actually disguised its own subjectivity, to the extent that its subversion was one of inversion, with the form offering one type of illusion as an all-seeing truth. Brecht recognised this when in 1938 he offered the following still timely warnings that the new is never new for long:

> The concept of realism ... is an old concept which has been much used by many men and for many purposes, and before it can be applied we must spring-clean it too ... For time flows on ... methods wear out, stimuli fail. New problems loom

up and demand new techniques. Reality alters; to represent it the means of representation must alter too ... What was popular yesterday is no longer so today. Anybody who is not bound by formal prejudices knows that there are many ways of suppressing truth and many ways of stating it ... great experiments in the theatre ... involved the exploding of conventional forms and the intelligibility of a work is not ensured exclusively by its being written in exactly the same way as other works which people have understood. These other works were not invariably written just like the works before them.

(Brecht 1964: 108–9)

Adrian Heathfield's analysis of the Chicago-based performance collective Goat Island, in his essay *Coming Undone* could be equally applied to the Wooster Group, and it goes some way towards identifying the ubiquity of recent innovations in performance, alongside performance critique. Heathfield suggests that 'The approach to making a performance work is one which does not set out with identified objectives of meaning, but involves instead a negotiation of intentions and knowledges through collaborative practice. ... Sources enter the evolving aesthetic and are then interrogated within it, until their place and relation is solidified' (Goat Island 2001: 17). Heathfield develops his argument by saying that Goat Island 'do not set out to deliver the meaning of their work, but rather they undertake a process of the discovery of meaning *in* their work, and implicate their spectators within this process' (Ibid.: 17–18). In a similar vein, descriptions of Richard Foreman's *Evidence* read for all the world as an early Wooster Group or Forced Entertainment design: 'The theater set-up looks grim, what with bare walls, bare light bulbs, found furniture in a spare rigid arrangement ... a blackboard on the upstage wall ... the whole effect anti-decorative, leading one to expect maybe an abstract court martial' (Rabkin 1983: 69).

It is at this point that those distinctions between the Wooster Group, Goat Island and Foreman's Ontological-Hysteric Theater, which are so apparent when the work is seen, appear to collapse inside a critical mass. This is not about derivation, anymore than one naturalistic play is derived from another. Instead, it evidences the fact that we are struggling, each of us, with an analytical vocabulary that, try as it might for precision, renders the complexities and subtle nuance of performance with broad linguistic strokes.

The Wooster Group spent three years devising *To You, The Birdie!*, which amounts to a fairly typical rehearsal period for the company. For all this careful and considered endeavour, the group members are relatively circumspect when it comes to describing the developmental processes. This is not about the secrecy of rehearsal or keeping the complexities of process hidden from the outside world. It has much more to do with those differences between the vocabularies of making and description, which Melrose and Jackson have gone to some lengths to expose and explore. For Melrose critical thinking about performance needs to 'move on from the notion that the "theoretical" is necessarily commensurable with the writing which has tended to serve it as vehicle' (Melrose 2005). Arguing that expert practitioners such as LeCompte theorise in and through their work, in practice, rather than after the event, in writing, Melrose is vehement in her belief that 'the writerly habitus of many of us in the university, a complex mind-set enabling and applauding certain sorts of actions, and not others, actually prevents many of us ... from contemplating the possibility that the expert-arts-practitioner-*other* might *theorise* in modes and registers of complex practice which operate wholly or in significant part outside of writing' (Ibid.). Annie-B Parson succinctly says that 'certain artists formalize their work on paper and there are other artists like ... Liz LeCompte, who couldn't be less interested in writing it down and creating a pedagogical format' (Liska, Parson et al. 2006: 51).

In articulating his own negotiation of the relationship between professional directing practice with the performance company Optik and the perceived demands of academic theory, Barry Edwards suggests that in performance work 'the need to make contact is at the heart of the enterprise' (Edwards 1999). Developing this theme, Edwards asks, 'Is contact possible via writing? *I am writing this in order to make contact*, not to theorise my own work. I develop my practical work in the absence of theory *as separate*. Though I am well aware that theorists would have a field day objecting to that statement. No doubt a theoretical position underpins what I am writing at this very moment, but *I am not aware of it*, or *I choose to ignore it*. So there is no theoretical starting point, no hypothesis which can be used as a reference point for the writing. But there is a starting point, there is always a starting point' (Ibid.).

The Wooster Group's lengthy periods of rehearsal are exceptional. Finances always play their part and the Wooster Group, as well as receiving funding and owning their own performance and rehearsal space outright, happily acknowledge the financial cushion provided by Willem Dafoe's earnings from his Hollywood film career. The rehearsal process for someone like Gómez-Peña is a very different matter. Defining his work as first and foremost being concerned with the conceptual, Gómez-Peña claims that he always departs 'from a theoretical proposal, an idea which first becomes a blueprint for action, and eventually becomes a performance piece; I don't spend that much time in the rehearsal room. What we do instead is write, brainstorm, debate with other artists and activists, and every now and then we rehearse. We usually only rehearse physically the month before launching a new project' (Gómez-Peña 2000: 171). 'Our discussions during the creative process are not just about the work itself. We talk about what we saw on TV the night before, about a new book we are reading, about cinema, computers, sex, anthropology … And then, out of these eclectic discussions, where language and ideas are like personas in a conceptual mini-proscenium, the stage of the dinner table or the bar table, a new image or a new text begins to emerge' (Ibid.: 173). When asked by Nick Kaye to discuss her rehearsal process, Joan Jonas explains, 'The difference between my rehearsals and, say, theatre rehearsals, is that my rehearsals are just about working the piece out. I don't really rehearse' (Kaye 1992: 59).

The Wooster Group has become famous for their radical treatment of a number of texts, not least those classics of American theatre, Thornton Wilder's *Our Town* and Arthur Miller's *The Crucible*. Lyn Gardner gives a sense of Miller's response to LeCompte's deconstructionist treatment of his work: 'Miller decided it was a deconstruction too far and got an injunction preventing use of the text. Saucily, the Woosters responded by using a timer to mark each of the one-minute segments of copyrighted text that they were allowed by law to use. The Wooster Group's approach to classic texts is an attempt to rescue them from the museum, and even Miller eventually came to see the importance of this. "They were swinging on swings and speaking at a rate of speed that I could not follow. It just seemed to me to be kidding around with an important theme, and negating it. But I have to confess that I ran into young people who had seen it and were tremendously moved by it. I just had to think: my sensibility must be totally at variance to this"' (Gardner 2003: 19). Miller's sensibilities, conditioned as they inevitably were to relatively straightforward directorial interpretations of his work were unprepared for that which Susan Broadhurst recognises as an 'appropriation' that was 'not easily incorporated into traditional understandings of the text–production relationship of the theatre' (Broadhurst 1999: 146).

As befitting their status as the darlings of postmodern performance, the Wooster Group's working practice continues to place together fragments of their previous product in order to relocate the characters, situations and themes developed within them. This allows for the possibility of questioning and challenging not only the fabrication of the work, but also the spectators' reading of it. It also creates a climate of such endless self-reflexivity that the company effectively engages in its own deconstruction, as narrative emerges as a continuum over many pieces of work. The company exposes the rehearsal process in the act of performance, merging past and present realities through connections between the text in performance and the various materials they have constructed it from. Susan Letzler Cole gives as an example of this as the 'reading aloud of text on text-making in the process of creating scripts that allude to other scripts, subtexts that allude to other subtexts' (Cole 1992: 92). The 'script' that the Wooster Group arrives at is fluid and unfixed, open to potentially radical modification throughout rehearsal and performance. Sense is sacrificed for resonance in text and delivery, with LeCompte undercutting the work whenever the material begins to feel like a play, whenever the work appears in danger of furnishing spectators with too many straightforward directorial clues. For LeCompte this is about the provision of a 'safety valve', a means of interrupting and disrupting the flow of the text, allowing a shifting between acting (in the moment) and quoting (in the past).

In productions such as *Rumstick Road*, LeCompte's directorial and compositional approach clearly revels in the unexpected and disjunctive, seeing both rehearsal and performance as opportunities to 'do the wrong thing' (LeCompte 1992: 130). The back-stage paraphernalia and technical devices used during performance remain visible to the spectators; the performers make no attempt to conceal them and often operate technical equipment themselves. Consequently, the performance offers a rehearsal quality, despite the assiduously rehearsed nature of the work. The company's work reflects the possibility for development and change, not least the shifting 'real life' circumstances of the performers. Crohn Schmitt sees the group's work as 'an illusion of reality (where) any reality breaks the spell of illusion' (Crohn Schmitt 1990: 46). The Wooster Group does not try to hide its status as illusionistic stagers of the performed and it rarely, if ever, invites its audience to suspend an individual or collective disbelief. Rather, it makes the statement: 'look this is not real, so you make up your mind' (Ibid.), drawing attention to itself and subverting the very reality that theatre generally purports to represent.

The Wooster Group's visit to Britain with *L.S.D. (...Just the High Points...)* was marked by a London Weekend Television South Bank Show documentary on the work, and this hour-long programme became at least as influential on a generation of British practitioners as did the live work. Scratchy, desperately copied cassettes were passed to and fro between performers whose own work quickly began to echo the edginess of LeCompte's anarchic approach to mise en scène. That the new never stays new for long is art's blessing and curse, and as with all other practitioners of note, the Wooster Group's aesthetic was rapidly codified to the point where we recognise the following description as a type of postmodern performance paradigm. 'The exposed rows of harsh fluorescent lighting; the metal, skeletal grid ... dance as an interruption device; the use of audio samples. ... actors, either sitting at tables or standing, speaking into microphones, while facing out towards the audience; an ironic mode of acting. ... And of course the use of video and sound technology to alter the visual and auditory landscapes of performance' (Callens 2004: 265).

Tim Etchells, director of The British group, Forced Entertainment (the group began as a 'co-operative', dropping the word along the way) describes the impact of seeing the Wooster Group for the first time in 1987. 'We were excited by the work because it came from such a different aesthetic and formal place compared to so much of the work from Europe and UK that we'd been influenced by directly or from a distance' (Helmer and Malzacher 2004: 38).

Forced Entertainment was formed in 1984, when seven graduates of Drama at Exeter University moved from the South West of England to the post-industrial 'Steel City' of Sheffield. Writer, director (and sometime performer) Tim Etchells cites Claire MacDonald's 1986 description of the company as developing a 'new visual grammar' in order to 'prise open ... the media-glutted consumer culture of the city' as clarification of their intent (Etchells 1999: 19). Like a collection of flaneurs, the company members were part of their new community, as well as being observers of the world they had opted to inhabit. Seen in this light, MacDonald's reading of their work was also confirmation and vindication of the reasons behind their decision to relocate. The city, in all its manifestations, became the subject of much of the company's work, as well as furnishing them with content. Fragments of texts found in bus shelters, a reassembled letter sent from a prisoner, pencil-drawn routes to the motorway, the gaudy, the grim and the derelict – all of these and more were integrated into the making process, to the extent where the poeticisation of banality, often given a Buster Keatonesque deadpan delivery, became *the* voice of Forced Entertainment. A voice as recognisably their own as the video monitors that flanked the playing space of their early productions.

CASE STUDY 1.19:   FORCED ENTERTAINMENT

The chronology that follows makes no distinction between durational projects, digital media and the company's more conventional   theatre-based work. Forced Entertainment's video and film projects are highlighted in bold.

Chronology:
Jessica in the Room of Lights (1984)
The Set-Up (1985)
Nighthawks (1985)

→

$\rightarrow$

The Day that Serenity Returned to the Ground (1986)
*(Let the Water Run its Course) to the Sea that Made the
Promise* (1986)
200% and Bloody Thirsty (1988)
Some Confusions in the Law about Love (1989)
Marina and Lee (1991)
Welcome to Dreamland (1991)
*Emanuelle Enchanted (or a Description of this World as if it
Were a Beautiful Place)* (1992)
Club of No Regrets (1993)
Red Room (1993)
12 am: Awake and Looking Down (1993)
Dreams' Winter (1994)
Hidden J (1994)
Ground Plans for Paradise (1994)
Speak Bitterness (1994)
A Decade of Forced Entertainment (1994)
Nights in this City (1995)
Break In! (1996)
Showtime (1996)
Quizoola (1996)
DIY (1997)
Pleasure (1997)
Filthy Words and Phrases (1998)
Paradise (1998)
Dirty Work (1998)
Nightwalks (1998)
Who Can Sing a Song to Unfrighten Me? (1999)
Disco Relax (1999)
Spin (1999)
Frozen Palaces (1999)
Scar Stories (2000)
Hotel Binary (2000)
And on the Thousandth Night ... (2000)
Kent Beeson is a Classic & an Absolutely New Thing (2001)
My Eyes Were Like the Stars (2001)
Starfucker (2001)
The Last Mile Home (2001)

$\rightarrow$

→

Instructions for Forgetting (2001)
Down Time (2001)
Starfucker (2001)
First Night (2001)
The Travels (2002)
Everything (2003)
Mark Does Lear (2003)
Miles Magic (2003)
Miles Titanic (2003)
So Small (2003)
Erasure (2003)
The Voices (2003)
Bloody Mess (2003)
Imaginary Evidence (2003)
Marathon Lexicon (2003)
Exquisite Pain (2005)
The World in Pictures (2006)

Recommended Reading:

Etchells, Tim. 1999. *Certain Fragments: Contemporary Performance and Forced Entertainment*. London & New York: Routledge.

Heathfield, Adrian. 2000. *Small Acts: Performance, the Millennium, and the Marking of Time*. London: Black Dog Publishing.

Kaye, Nick. 2000. *Site Specific Art: Performance, Place and Documentation*. London & New York: Routledge.

Helmer, Judith and Florian Malzacher (eds) 2004. *Not Even a game Anymore: The Theatre of Forced Entertainment*. Berlin: Alexander Verlag.

A sub-heading of Etchell's *Certain Fragments* is 'You Play with what Scares You' (1999: 66). The term refers to specific incidents in the group's history and yet the feeling remains that the idea of playing with what they fear has a wider implication for the work than is suggested by the brief one-page examples offered on this subject by Etchells. The act of relocation, of being cast adrift, carries its own inevitable sense of trepidation, albeit one tempered by the chance to re-invent one's self with relative impunity. Any of this book's readers who have travelled to Exeter and Sheffield will be aware of how different these locations are, and it is difficult to imagine the post-holocaustic anxieties that make up the 1992 project *Emanuelle Enchanted*, emerging from the leafy environs of Exeter. Working without the safety net of text is in and of itself an act of faith in the face of fear.

Plato believed that the Muses inspired artists; Freud believed that the same type of unconsciousness that inspired artists could be found in the defence mechanisms of his neurotic patients. These overly romanticised ideas of the artist's otherness, of art arising out of inspirational leaps taken by the innately creative, appear to make some sense of Forced Entertainment's working approach. And yet these same ideas fuel the belief that creativity is intrinsically beyond analysis, that the ways of making performance are instinctive rather than reflective. We can recognise for ourselves and from our own experiences the way that creative insights can occur 'unexpectedly without effort, like an inspiration' (Wallas 1926: 84). That these occasions are commonly regarded and referred to as inspirational is not in doubt. However, inspiration does not always arrive with this immediacy, and it may be the case that what passes for inspiration is in many instances no more than a dawning realisation of concepts that have been germinating silently in the subconscious for some time. Viewed in this way, the creative activity entered into by Forced Entertainment is not quite the leap in the dark that it might at first appear. As with the Wooster Group, work builds on previous work, and the larger the back catalogue, the more unused ideas exist to fuel new work. And this is logical enough. Italian art critics have adopted the term *pentimento* to describe the phenomenon, whereby an earlier pencilled sketch can show through the surface of subsequent paintings, so that lines of text can bleed through the painted faces of saints, and this is what we see with the work of Forced Entertainment. The traces we see in the work are the traces of process and Etchells' written texts, misleadingly disingenuous as they are, expose constructedness and provisionality in every line. As tinned spaghetti stands in for blood, cardboard signs denote characters and talcum powder is offered up as gunsmoke, so spoken text is neither representational nor precious. Performance texts as Etchells sees them 'are ghosts ... made in the midst of clumsy and long performance-making processes – in the midst of group rehearsal and improvisation, soundtrack-making, "choreography", argument and set-building. They were not made for other people to "do" them, and they were never really made to stand alone' (Etchells 1999: 133).

As the company grew, they 'became less interested in the idea of writing as a separate function – more interested in the kind of "writing" that one does either improvising or in condensing or ripping off stuff that's already written ... Reading them in different sequences ... or cutting backwards and forwards between texts' (Helmer and Malzachar 2004: 46). Text becomes a set of rules: words to be spoken. Delivered in differing ways, these can invite spectators in or repel. In *First Night* (2001), spectators are addressed individually, pointed at and subjected to predictions as to the inevitable manner of their deaths: cancer, car crash, suicide. That we know we are in a theatre watching professional actors act does little to dilute the impact of the words and the mode of address. Unbridled artifice is everywhere in the work, from fixed and painted smiles and pantomime trees to lurid costumes straight out of a cable television nightmare, but the shock of Etchells' words cut through all of this. Like Brecht for the 21st century, Forced Entertainment exploits empathy, distance and the ethics of performance with humour, attitude and conviction. As spectators, we are left with no real option but to buy in or walk out.

With no consistent characterisations to conceal or subdue the performers, it is easy to believe that what we are given through the work is an insight into the cast members' lives. The accessibility of the group and the easy familiarity they have with spectators adds to this feeling. As with Jeanette Winterson's claim that *Oranges Are Not the Only Fruit* is autobiographical and non-autobiographical throughout, personas are revealed and concealed through Forced Entertainment's work in equal measures. As Laura Marcus states, 'The self does not pre-exist the text but is constructed by it ... the self 'finds' itself in its acts of self-expression' (Marcus 1994: 180). The role of performing artist is one which allows for the assuming of a series of transitory identities at the same time as the performer's own live presence is being signalled. According to Kwame Anthony Appiah, 'Every human identity is constructed, historical; invented biologies, invented cultural affinities, come with every identity; each is a kind of role that has to be scripted, structured by conventions of narrative to which the world never quite conforms' (Appiah 1992: 96).

For experienced and innovative practitioners the uncertainty of rehearsal is always a given and space for imaginative deviation will always exist. As Peter Brook notes, 'The rehearsal work should create a climate in which the actors feel free to produce everything they can bring to the play. That's why in the early stages of rehearsal everything is open and I impose nothing at all. In a sense this is diametrically opposed to the technique in which, the first day, the director gives a speech on what the play's about and the ways he's going to approach it' (Brook 1988: 3). The situation Brook describes and which Forced Entertainment use is relatively uncommon. It requires a climate of structured and supportive independence, in which a variety of elements and concepts can be successfully explored in order that performers, directors, designers and writers are afforded the opportunities and space to pursue the types of lateral and divergent creative thinking championed by those such as Edward de Bono (1995).

Postmodernism notwithstanding, creativity stands for more than regurgitation and recycling. When Etchells and the performers begin their process of making work with nothing more than what is at hand – the space, the personnel and a given time scale – they create for themselves an invitation, almost an *imperative*, to explore and challenge the very models and modes of address that the group clings to. They attempt to revisit their past endeavours without repeating them. The potential for frustration at not being provided with the type of direct route towards successful completion that Wesker feels is provided by a play is an integral part of Forced Entertainment's process, for it is at the point of creative frustration that 'crucial decisions are made ... which directly affect the outcome of the creative product or concept' (Kneller 1965: 105).

The educational philosophers Torrance and Ball (1984) have identified five 'creativity skills': originality, fluency, abstracting, elaboration and openness. And we are able to use these to understand some of the reasons why even their fiercest detractors will often hail the work of Forced Entertainment and the Wooster Group as original. Originality is a loaded word, and never more so than when it is applied to performance. Yet we can identify originality in performance work as a departing from the obvious and the conventional. Originality is located in the area of the psychologically rather than the historically creative (Boden 1996: 17), where, in order for creativity to flourish, the people involved need to be open to multiple possibilities, to display a lack of rigidity, and a permeability of boundaries in concepts, beliefs, perceptions and hypotheses, alongside a highly developed tolerance for ambiguity. This leads practitioners away from (simply) building on what they know. In instances such as these – and Forced Entertainment's devising process is a prime example – performers ask questions of what it is that they know and why this knowledge is valued in the ways that it is.

I am aware that I am engaging here in the type of critic-speak that Shannon Jackson exposes to such scathing rebuke in her reading of Nick Kaye's interview with Elizabeth LeCompte. Jackson refers to Kaye's repeated 'effort to make an artist's process available for reflection' (Jackson 2004: 111) as a conversational misfire, 'where the ever-sought hope for artist-scholar exchange is ever-deferred'(Ibid.). Such may be so, and I, like Kaye (and a great many others) may be falling into the trap of adscitition described at the start of Chapter 2. Gómez-Peña refers to 'the bittersweet relationship between artists and academicians' (Gómez-Peña 2000: 264), arguing that academics and theorists 'secretly resent the fact that we (artists) can theorize about our own work rather than waiting for them to explain it for us' (Ibid.). If this is so, so be it. The vocabularies of critique inevitably differ from the vocabularies of practice, in the same ways that the rhythms of writing alone are distinct from the rhythms of making with others. Differences in terminology, therefore, have more to do with the demands imposed by different modes of address than with contradictory views on the ways that work gets made.

The five 'creativity skills' suggested by Torrance and Ball are indicative of Forced Entertainment's making process. *Originality* takes place when practitioners make the types of imaginative leaps that deny any significant reliance on the conventional and the everyday, when performance problems are considered in unusual and surprising ways. *Fluency* can be regarded as the ability the company has repeatedly demonstrated of arriving at a number of ways of addressing the problems as and when they are encountered, of consideration without prior judgement. *Abstracting* takes place when the writer/director and performers identify the most effective and appropriate solution to the problem, of distilling a wide array of possibilities into a plan of creative attack. *Elaboration* occurs when the ideas for performance are made viable through a series of increasingly detailed approaches to rehearsal. *Openness* is evidenced in the company's resistance to the idea of premature closure, to a reluctance to regard production work as 'finished'.

The fact that Forced Entertainment's work proceeds without a clear plan or end point is no handicap: the company has been consistently and increasingly prolific, making work across a range of media, including theatre, installation, interactive performance, durational work, critical writing and film. The absence of rigidity provides space for progression, which is always impossible to predict. This is paradigmatic of divergent thinking, with its characteristic freedoms. For Forced Entertainment this leads to 'an irregular process where we do the same thing for three days and then the fourth day we change it radically, the fifth day it stays the same, the sixth day we change it again. ... nothing in the rehearsal room is safe' (Etchells 2006: 5).

As a self-styled and self-confessed outsider, it is appropriate that Steven Berkoff features at the very edge of this book, as a practitioner who is half-in, half-out of innovation and always three-quarters out of favour. Berkoff's contribution to the areas of text and performance are virtually without parallel in contemporary theatre, and yet his work is critically ignored, certainly in most British universities, academic papers and articles. Naseem Khan's contribution to the 2005 book *The Turning World* encapsulates the grudging regard – so grudging as to be at times nakedly dismissive – in which Steven Berkoff is held in Britain. Paying tribute to the London International Festival of Theatre (LIFT) specifically and to domestic theatrical experimentation at large, Khan informs us that 'The avant-garde movement that burst over London from the later 1960s on, breaking free of text-based constraints, had spawned a wealth of physical-based and radical theatre – Lumiere and Son, Pip Simmons, Natalie Yavin's The Other Theatre, even Steven Berkoff's own experiments with his London Theatre Company (de Wend Fenton and Neal 2005: 61). In any company, Khan's 'even' writes Berkoff out of the frame at the same time as she purports to write him in. It is hard to see a logical reason for this. Berkoff has, after all, carved for himself a unique position in the British, European and North American theatre landscape. His own claims notwithstanding, as writer, director, actor and production journalist, there is, domestically at least, no one out there to touch him. What he does best, he does better than anybody else.

Berkoff's alienated position owes more than a little to his own pugnacious and bombastic manner. His concern has always been about making performance rather than friends. This spills over into every aspect of his life, to the extent that he continuously makes enemies of his peers, the public and of the press. In 1979 Berkoff threatened to kill the journalist Nicholas de Jongh for being critical of his production of *Hamlet* (De Jongh 1989: 21). Berkoff's opinion of playwrights is that their work is 'all about spew' (Freeman 2004b: 16). Warming to his own theme he goes on to say that 'British theatre churns out work that's a form of torture. We feel theatre is a kind of medicine that will assuage our cultural guilt. It's the theatre of medicine' (Ibid.). Critics are people who speak from positions of privilege and safety, aligned to ignorance and the British public, he feels sure, are filled with loathing and envy.

Berkoff's is a defence mechanism born of isolation and of loneliness, and it is as permanent and visible as skin. He feels that all actors and writers are lonely, given shape and defined by spectators, only fully complete in the act of performance. His written texts exemplify this, with their larger than life characters speaking a blend of Shakespearean pentameter and working class London argot with lyrical brutality and imagistic profanity. Berkoff's respect for the traditions of physical theatre taught by the likes of Jacques Lecoq is every bit as strong as his disregard for what he regards as the insipid irresponsibility of faux naturalistic text, a theatre form he believes to be as dangerous to our spectatorial health as smoking.

Berkoff's approach to group work reads, from the outside at least, less like ensemble practice and more like an extended act of guru-driven self-homage. And there is nothing wrong with this: group dynamics are arrived at and defined in differing ways, and since when was an overbearing ego out of place in the theatre? Precious few writers in theatre are identified on the page as immediately as Berkoff and fewer still – if any at all – have created their own equally identifiable performance styles. The term 'Pinteresque' makes a writerly sense, as does 'Beckettian': Mamet's style, and Shepard's, are no less linked to the rhythms and cadence of their words without an attendant physical vocabulary that would reveal its origins to us through a performer's delivery. Under these circumstances, in light of Berkoff's creation of a major theatrical voice, one that is as physical and performative as it is writerly and textual, it is right and proper that mention of his work draws the body of this book to a near-close.

When the organisers of LIFT 2004 asked their visitors what meaning theatre had to them and, crucially, what, if theatre was no longer available, would be missing from their lives, the responses were somewhat predictable. Predictable inasmuch at least as the people asked had already expressed commitment to attending a festival of challenging and progressive theatre work. The respondents said that for them theatre was 'a place of survival, an intimate space of exchange across cultural barriers, of renewal, of play, of resistance, reconciliation, joy, and confrontation with painful pasts' (de Wend Fenton and Neal 2005: 202). For Eric Bogosian the value of theatre lies in its unique qualities of shared experience: a ritual and sacred form, 'something we make together every time it happens. Theater is holy. Instead of being bombarded by a cathode ray tube we are speaking to ourselves. Human language, not electronic noise' (Bogosian 1994: xii). Bogosian is stressing theatre's once-only nature, where text is what happens in the here and now, in the absence of geographical, technical or ideological barriers between the s/he who sees and the s/he who is there to be seen, between words spoken and words heard. Acknowledging the particular vitality of small-scale and one-off performance, Patrice Pavis goes as far as suggesting that a theatre work is reduced in direct relation to the number of times it is repeated (Pavis 1992: 100–1). Reading the runes of body art and autobiographical performance, Jean Baudrillard warns us that in our age of simulacra, where everything is forever already a copy of the done-to-death, we are searching for the real and the true more than ever before (Baudrillard 1983). Richard Foreman makes distinctions between the reliance on immediacy and entertainment found in mainstream theatre work and the attempts made by progressive performance to aspire to something that spectators have not yet become (Rabkin 1983: 136).

In this sense, performance is always ahead of the game, always just beyond the horizons of its spectators. Howard Barker recognises the fact that playwrights have to create work, which can accommodate the 'habits of perception, reflexes [and] expectations' of an audience (Barker 1989: 151). Accordingly, he feels it is unlikely that the writing of plays will be the 'instrument by which theatre undergoes profound changes of function'

(Ibid.). The more abstract, fluid and poetic qualities of text for performance, on the other hand, possess the potential to 'lead the audience ... into new relations with the stage ... [for] only by infringing the rules of playwrighting was the theatre able to shed its utilitarian functions' (Ibid.: 152). In 2000, Gerry Robinson, Chairman of the Arts Council of England, served warning that 'theatres doing average performances ... doing unadventurous shows may struggle to survive' (Robinson 2000: 4). Robinson is emphatic in his belief that whilst we are right to glory in theatre's success stories, these 'occasional stabs of thrilling theatre' blind us to the reality that theatre is in crisis (Ibid.: 13). For Robinson, 'Too much [theatre] still relies on the recollection of a postwar golden era, which claims a status that has long since been lost' (Ibid.). And this is a useful reminder of how pedestrian, not to say moribund the bulk of Western theatre remains. In any given year of the 21st century, new product has accounted for no more than 15 per cent of all theatre produced. Beyond the tourist bubbles of the West End and Broadway, audiences continue to fall, and touring work in Britain is at its lowest ebb in 30 years.

This makes for bleak reading, but hope always remains. Gurpreet Kaur Bhatti, whose 2004 play *Behzti* was withdrawn from the Birmingham Repertory Theatre, following a series of heated demonstrations, threats and violent attacks, claimed that 'Theatre is not necessarily a cosy space, designed to make us feel good about ourselves. It is a place where the most basic human expression – that of the imagination – must be allowed to flourish' (Kaur Bhatti 2005: 17). An activity through which our imaginations are provided with space to flourish. Perhaps this is enough for us to know. Performance has no notable value in terms of survival, and yet it seems to have been around as long as people have. We can either accept this as a given, as evidence of the essentiality of performance to life or we can question why it is that humankind has always demonstrated the urge to engage in something so seemingly unimportant. And maybe the nourishment of our individual and collective powers of imagination is the uncomplicated answer we all seek.

That we know that theatre *can* matter to us is not the same thing as believing that it automatically *does*. One of the intentions of this book (spreading, it seems, like a Rorschach inkblot) has been to suggest that the continuance of theatre is linked inextricably to an embracing of the *now* of lived experience, rather than the *then* of dubious historicity. That an imaginative concentration on the present should be evidenced in performance writing is not an add-on to this belief, but it is central to it. Beyond the certainty that performance will always continue to exceed our expectations, no certainties exist. The cautious approach to history undertaken in this book might seem to provide us with some ground rules, even if these have shown themselves as rules to be broken. Historical contextualisation, as we have seen in Chapter 1, might aid an understanding of what it is that performance *does*, and that in turn might assist our consideration of what performance *is*. And yet what it is that constitutes performance has been structured by a series of beliefs, and these have shifted through time, so that our reading of the past is always informed and corrupted by the lens of the present.

The present belongs to those who live in it, and this is our only reality. At the stubbed out cigarette end of postmodernism's multi-channel, multi-plex filled world, the last thing we need is another dose of artifice. The fact that interplay between a performer's presentation of her or his performative self (the self-portrait) and the presentation of ordinariness (the human readymade) is not 'new' does not render it redundant. As this book has attempted to show, performance writing has given the relationship of self to art a renewed potency through its relocating of artists from the realms of their customary practice to one where they are brought into direct contact with spectators. In this way tensions are created between '*being oneself and acting a role*, between material reality and symbol or metaphor. This change signalled two great desires: the artist's desire to rescue the vitality of communication from an art system increasingly besotted with the commodity, and the *ordinary person's* to come to know himself or herself through their lived experience, particular history, identity and subjectivity' (Schimmel 1998: 221). Allan Kaprow suggested that 'As art becomes less art, it takes on philosophy's role as a critique of life. ... Precisely because art can be confused with life, it forces attention upon the aim of its ambi-guities, to *reveal* experience' (Kaprow 1966: 13). And the 40-something years that have gone by have done little to reduce the insightfulness of his words. John Deeney cuts to the heart of the matter when he asks 'How can mere representations of reality be trusted anymore?' (Deeney 1998: 19) The same point is taken further by Auslander in his recognition that the space between simply *being* and *representing* the performative self is crucial to an understanding of contemporary performance culture (Auslander 1994: 81).

The postmodern performance we are currently making, watching and writing about is nothing if it is not the conflation of old and new modes, where realism as a style brushes up against the new real of autobiographical delivery, where the physical and the verbal, the spatial and the temporal are (con)fused into work that functions as a subversive interstice, critiquing the very representational modes it creates. Performance remains as interrogative as it ever was, but the subject of interrogation has, for many, moved away from wider social and political concerns, towards a focus on the role of performance and the re-presentational concerns of performers. The relationship between 'text' as something written/spoken and 'performance text' as the entire event becomes a type of textual playground, where nothing is sacrosanct and everything is up for grabs. Performance of our time has become a network of increasingly polysemic possibilities, forever nudging at the conceptual frames that define it, to the extent that on occasions it is so removed from conventional notions of theatre that we cannot recognise the work as performance at all. For some this will always be a case of The Emperor's New Clothes, and for the rest of us there are times when suspicion gnaws away, when it is hard, too hard even, to believe in the worth of the work that we see.

The bottom line is that it is all about faith. To say that our faith is a faith in doubt invites misreading. What is meant is that doubt is our central condition and occasional bouts of disbelief are as necessary as breath. Performance is an act of faith and faith in an act. In a world where the probable plays second fiddle to the possible, there is little to be gained by playing safe. Performance that concerns itself with newness and renewal does not distance itself from popular taste and popular culture; on the contrary, our collective willingness to embrace the new in other forms is a wake-up call to the type of critical spectatorship theatre demands. Performance makers and writers, as ever, heard the call a long time ago.

5
Writing Exercises

The following exercises relate broadly to chapter-content, in that they draw on elements of space, self, group-work and automatism. Some are relatively detailed, with the type of contextualisation that might be provided in educational contexts; others give suggestions with less rationale, and some have none at all. In these instances the ideas are left to speak for themselves.

Taken overall, the sessions, tested in rehearsal studios, workshops and classes, can be used to make up the practical elements of a course in performance writing. Nevertheless, they are offered here as prompts for practice, not prescription. Readers are recommended to take what is useful, and modify, merge, adapt and develop to suit particular needs.

1. Naming

We are on dangerous ground when we assume that performance texts, no matter how personal they may seem, offer a reliable image of writers' lives. A performance text is always in some ways 'invented', a construction. With this in mind, write a list of all of the names you are known by. How did you come by your names? How do your different names make you feel and how do they make you behave? Which names best describe or define you?

2. Automating

When writing text for performance, there is awareness that what one is doing is on one level controlled and on another surprising, almost accidental. Writing therefore involves sensitivity to correspondences and resonance, even when words have been arrived at without conscious thought. As we have seen, this is not quite the same thing as automatic writing. Whereas automatic writing denies the possibility of editorial interference, performance writing involves recognition that the act of writing is itself in part a process of discovery and that new ideas may stem from writing, as much as it functions as the articulation of ideas. There is no fixed sequence in the process of writing and all that is written is not pre-planned; indeed, one can write in order to discover what it is that one thinks.

SECRETS OF THE MAGICAL SURREALIST ART

Written Surrealist composition
Or
First and Last Draft

After you have settled yourself in a place as favourable as possible to the mind's concentration upon itself, order writing material to be brought to you. Let your state of mind be as passive and receptive as possible. Forget your genius, your talents, as well as the genius and talents of others. Repeat to yourself that literature is pretty well the sorriest road that leads to everywhere. Write quickly without any previously chosen subject, quickly enough not to dwell on, and not to be tempted to read over, what you have written. The first sentence will come of itself; and this is self-evidently true, because there is never a moment but some sentence alien to our conscious thought clamours for outward expression. It is rather difficult to speak of the sentence to follow, since it doubtless comes in for a share of our conscious activity and so the other sentences, if it is conceded that the writing of the first sentence must have involved even a minimum of consciousness. But that should in the long run matter little, because therein precisely lies the greatest interest in the surrealist exercise. Punctuation of course necessarily hinders the stream of absolute continuity which preoccupies us. But you should particularly distrust the prompting whisper. If through a fault ever so trifling there is a forewarning of silence to come, a fault let us say, of inattention, break off unhesitatingly the line that has become too lucid. After the word whose origin seems suspect you should place a letter, any letter, 'L' for example, always the letter 'L', and restore the arbitrary flux by making that letter the initial of the word to follow.

(Breton 1972: 29–30)

3. Finding

Work with found text, words lifted from the world around you. Let the craft here be in the areas of selection and editing. Make notes of spoken dialogue you overhear in the street; compose a text from the words found on pages of a magazine or as you channel-hop, with a notebook and pen in hand: write down what you hear and remember, not worrying, in the first instance, about any gaps.

You can add formality and rules as you go. Regard these as liberating, rather than limiting devices, inasmuch as they remove the possibility of writer's block – a term used most often as a means of disguising a lack of confidence in ideas. Select numbers, from your date of birth, telephone number, bank account, passport, library card etc, and use these to choose library books by reference numbers. Use more of these numbers to choose certain pages and translate the words you find into actions and speech.

4. Behaving

Write a series of six actions that are suggestive of character. Create these without adding any spoken words. Think in terms of behaviour, and think directorially.

5. Omitting

In your own time and space, compose a narrative based on a significant aspect of your life. Loss and conflict are useful keynotes here, because conflict between intention and obstacle forms the core of drama. Aim to write on at least half a side of an A4 paper. The only stipulations are that you do not use the letter 'e' and that you are prepared to share the results. There are no other rules. Truth, or what counts for truth in autobiographical writing, is not what is sought here. What you are being asked to do here is to create lipograms, techniques of writing with a letter missing. There are literary precedents for this exercise: Ernest Vincent Wright's *Gadsby* and G. Perec's *A Void* are two noted examples.

As with any exercise, this one can be developed in a variety of ways. Instead of eliminating a vowel, try creating text that denies something else. No downstage movements, for example, or, if you are working as part of a group, no gender division of lines, no conversational language or words that describe anything a performer could reasonably show, no reference to life outside the performance space or no repeated words.

Reducing one's options is often a useful way of moving work forwards.

6. Documenting

Work in a verbatim fashion, creating text based exclusively on material gleaned through interview. Be aware of the ethical responsibilities bound up in this. Be aware also that there are no hard and fast rules here. What is unethical in one set of circumstances is, perhaps, right and proper in another. This is about taking responsibility for your actions and considering the impact these have on people around you. As a general rule it's safest to let your subjects know your intentions before you start.

Regardless of the authenticity of the words you use, the relocation of material into performance renders its own peculiar falsity, substituting ideas of form and content into form and context. What happens when the words stay the same but everything else changes?

7. Reassembling

Borrow from the Dadaists by treating text as collage. Charles Marowitz did this when he shattered *Hamlet* like a vase, reassembling the material in a seemingly random way. Marowitz was questioning the extent to which a play might retain its essential elements regardless of the way it was cut up and reconfigured. Try this with an example of a text you have written previously. Print it out, cut it up and piece it back together randomly. Consider the ways in which this new content suggests new forms and explore these practically.

8. Physicalising

The exercise is about encouraging writing that is visual, spatial and active in its approach.

Choose a scene from a previously published dramatic text. Re-write it, omitting as many lines as you can without altering the essential sense of this or subsequent scenes. Consider the ways in which actions might be used as replacement for words, turning dialogue-driven information into something more physical. This is an exercise, remember: a means towards an end rather than an end in itself and, so long as the material is used in workshops and not public performance, plagiarism and copyright are not issues here.

9. Locating

Write a monologue in the present tense and first person that runs in real time and which refers directly to the space in which it plays, where the playing space – be it studio theatre, corridor or kitchen – is employed for its own intrinsic qualities, rather than functioning as a surrogate for another place. This is about site-specificity (or site-sympathy), about drawing on and exploiting the tangible fabric of the space.

Develop the piece now by including sections that play with the notion of time so that your words and/or actions relate to events in the past as well as the present. Make things hard for yourself by linking the past with another space and making your performance accommodate that difference. Resist the temptation to start from scratch with your writing as this is about developing rather than re-inventing material.

10. Timing

Write a sequence that plays for eight minutes exactly and which includes the following elements: a revelation, a risk, a question, repetition, development and restricted movement. Keep to these rules whether you are writing for one performer or several. Add any other elements that you choose, as long as these six are in place.

Bibliography

Abramović, Marina. 1998. *Artist Body*. Milan: Leva spa.
——. 1998. *Performing Body: Marina Abramović*. Milan: Charta Edizioni.
Abramović, Marina, and Ulay. 1997. *Ulay/Abramovic: Performances 1976–1988*. Eindhoven: Stedelijk Van Abbemuseum.
Acconci, Vito. 1993. 'Performing after the Fact'. *New Observations*. 95: 20–30.
Adorno, Theodor. 1984. *8*. C. Lenhardt (trans.) New York: Routledge & Kegan Paul.
Allain, Paul and Jen Harvie. 2006. *The Routledge Companion to Theatre and Performance*. London & New York: Routledge.
Allen, Graham. 2003. *Roland Barthes*. London & New York: Routledge.
Anderson, H. H. (ed.) 1959. *Creativity and Its Cultivation*. New York: Harper.
Anderson, Laurie and Germano Celant. 1998. *Laurie Anderson: Dal Vivo*. Milan: Fondazione Prada.
Anderson, Linda. 2001. *Autobiography*. London & New York: Routledge.
Apollonio, Umbro. 1973. *Futurist Manifestoes*. New York: Viking Press.
Appiah, Kwame Anthony. 1992. *In My Father's House: Africa in the Philosophy of Culture*. Oxford: Oxford University Press.
Aronson, Arnold. 2000. *American Avant-Garde Theatre: A History*. London: Routledge.
Artaud, Antonin. 1958. *The Theatre and Its Double*. M. C. Richards (trans.) New York: Grove Press.
Aston, Elaine and George Savona. 1991. *Theatre as Sign-System*. London & New York: Routledge.
Auslander, Philip. 1994. *Presence and Resistance: Postmodernism and Cultural Politics in Contemporary American Performance*. Ann Arbor: University of Michigan Press.
——. 1997. *From Acting to Performance: Essays in Modernism and Postmodernism*. London & New York: Routledge.
——. 1999. *Liveness: Performance in a Mediatized Culture*. London & New York: Routledge.
Austin, John L. 1975. *How to Do Things with Words*. 2nd Edn. Cambridge, MA.: Harvard University Press.
Baggini, Julian and Peter S. Fosl. 2002. *The Philosopher's Toolkit: A Compendium of Philosophical Concepts and Methods*. Oxford: Blackwell Publishing.
Barba, Eugenio and Nicola Savarese. 1991. *The Secret Art of the Performer: A Dictionary of Theatre Anthropology*. London & New York: Routledge.
Barker, Howard. 1989. *Arguments for a Theatre*. Manchester: Manchester University Press.

Barranger, Milly. 1995. *Theatre: A Way of Seeing*. Belmont, CA: Wadsworth.

Barry, Peter. 1995. *Beginning Theory*. Manchester: Manchester University Press.

Barthes, Roland. 1973. *Mythologies*. London: Granada.

———. 1974. *S/Z*. Oxford: Blackwell.

———. 1975. 'An Introduction to the Structural Analysis of Narrative'. *New Literary History*. 6: 237–72.

———. 1977a. *Image, Music, Text*. Stephen Heath (ed.) London: Fontana Press.

———. 1977b. *Roland Barthes by Roland Barthes*. London: Macmillan.

Battcock, Gregory and Robert Nickas (eds).1998. *The Art of Performance*. New York: Dutton.

Baudrillard, Jean. 1983. *Simulations*. Paul Foss, Paul Patton and Philip Beitchman (trans.) New York: Semiotext(e).

———. 1994. *Simulacra and Simulation*. Shiela Faria (trans.) Ann Arbor: University of Michigan Press.

Bauman, Zygmunt. 1978. *Hermeneutics and Social Science: Approaches to Understanding*. London: Hutchinson.

———. 1988. 'Is There a Postmodern Sociology?'. *Theory, Culture & Society*. 5: 217–37.

———. 1990. *Thinking Sociologically*. Oxford: Blackwell.

BBC News Archive. 14 February 1998. 02:43 GMT. *Death Threat Author Says 'Life Goes On'*. http://news.bbc.co.uk

Beckerman, Bernard. 1970. *Dynamics of Drama: Theory and Methods of Analysis*. New York: Alfred A. Knopf.

Beckett, Samuel. 2006. *The Complete Dramatic Works of Samuel Beckett*. London: Faber & Faber.

Bell, David and Barbara M. Kennedy (eds) 2000. *The Cybercultures Reader*. London: Routledge.

Benedetti, Jean. 1982. *Stanislavski: An Introduction*. London: Methuen.

Benjamin, Walter. 1969. *Illuminations*. Hannah Arendt (ed.) New York: Shocken Books.

Bennett, Susan. 1990. *Theatre Audiences: A Theory of Production and Reception*. London & New York: Routledge.

Bentley, Eric. 1965. *The Life of the Drama*. London: Methuen.

Berger, John. 1972. *Ways of Seeing*. New York: Penguin Books.

———. 1985. *The Sense of Sight: Writings by John Berger*. New York: Pantheon Books.

Betterton, Rosemary. 1996. *Intimate Distance: Women, Artists and the Body*. London & New York: Routledge.

Bial, Henry (ed.) 2004. *The Performance Studies Reader*. London & New York: Routledge.

Birringer, Johannes. 1993. *Theatre, Theory, Postmodernism*. Bloomington: Indiana University Press.

———. 1998. *Media and Performance*. Baltimore: Johns Hopkins University Press.

Blau, Herbert. 1982. *Blooded Thought: Occasions of Theatre*. New York: PAJ Publications.

———. 1990. *The Audience*. Baltimore: Johns Hopkins University Press.

——. 1992. *To All Appearances: Ideology and Performance*. London & New York: Routledge.

——. 1996. 'Who's There? – Community of the Question'. *Performing Arts Journal* 83. Vol. 28, No. 2: 1–12.

——. 2002. *The Dubious Spectacle: Extremities of Theatre, 1976–2000*. Minneapolis: University of Minnesota Press.

Boal, Augusto. 1992. *Games for Actors and Non-Actors*. London: Routledge.

——. 1994. *The Rainbow of Desire*. London: Routledge.

——. 1998. *Legislative Theatre*. London & New York: Routledge.

——. 2000. *Theatre of the Oppressed*. London: Pluto Press.

Boden, Margaret. 1996. *Dimensions of Creativity*. Cambridge, MA: MIT Press.

Bogosian, Eric. 1994. *Pounding Nails in the Floor with My Forehead*. New York: Theatre Communications Group.

Bonney, Jo (ed.) 2000. *Extreme Exposures: An Anthology of Solo Performance Texts from the Twentieth Century*. New York: Theater Communications Group.

Bourdieu, Pierre. 1977. *Outline of a Theory of Practice*. R. Nice (trans.) Cambridge: Cambridge University Press.

Bradby, David and David Williams. 1988. *Directors' Theatre*. London: Macmillan.

Bragg, Melvyn. 1987. 'The Wooster Group'. *The South Bank Show*. ITV. 22 February 1987.

Brater, Enoch and Ruby Cohn (eds) 1992. *Around the Absurd: Essays on Modern and Postmodern Drama*. Ann Arbor: University of Michigan Press.

Brecht, Bertolt. 1964. *Brecht on Theatre*. John Willett (ed. & trans.) London: Eyre Methuen.

Brecht, Stefan. 1978. *The Theatre of Visions: Robert Wilson*. Frankfurt: Suhrkamp Verlag.

Brentano, Robyn and Olivia Georgia. 1994. *Outside the Frame: Performance and the Object*. Cleveland: Cleveland Center for Contemporary Art.

Breton, André. 1965. 'The Artistic Genesis and Perspective of Surrealism'. Richard Hurley (trans.) in *Surrealism and Painting*. No. 3: 26–36.

——. 1972. *Manifestoes of Surrealism*. Richard Seaver and Helen R. Lane (trans.) Ann Arbor: University of Michigan Press.

Brewer, Mary. 2005. *Staging Whiteness*. Middletown, Connecticut: Wesleyan University Press.

Broadhurst, Susan. 1999. *Liminal Acts: A Critical Overview of Contemporary Performance and Theory*. London & New York: Cassell.

Brockett, Oscar G. 1995. *History of Theatre*. Boston: Allyn and Bacon.

Brook, Peter. 1968. *The Empty Space*. London: Macgibbon & Kee.

——. 1988. *The Shifting Point: Forty Years of Theatrical Exploration 1946–1987*. London: Methuen.

Bruno, Giulianna. 2002. *Atlas of Emotion: Journeys in Art, Architecture, and Film*. London & New York: Verso.

Buchloh, Benjamin H. D., Judith F. Rodenbeck & Robert Haywood. 2000. *Experiments in the Everyday: Allan Kaprow & Robert Watts*. California: Miriam & IRA D. Wallach Art Gallery.

Bullough, Edward. 1912. 'Psychical Distance as a Factor in Art and as an Aesthetic Principle'. *British Journal of Psychology*. Vol. 5: 87–117.

Bunuel, Luis. 1984. *My Last Breath*. Abigail Israel (trans.) London: Vintage.

Burden, Chris. 1993. 'Chris Burden'. *Talking Art 1*. Adrian Searle (ed.) London: ICA: 15–27.

Burden, Chris, Fred Hoffman and Paul Schimmel. 2000. *Chris Burden*. New York: Distributed Art Publishers Inc.

Burger, Peter. 1984. *Theory of the Avant-Garde*. Michael Shaw (trans.) Minneapolis: University of Minnesota Press.

Burns, Tom. 1992. *Erving Goffman*. London & New York: Routledge.

Buse, Peter. 2001. *Drama + Theory: Critical Approaches to Modern British Drama*. Manchester: Manchester University Press.

Butler, Judith. 1990. *Gender Trouble: Feminism and the Subversion of Identity*. London & New York: Routledge.

——. 1993. *Bodies that Matter: On the Discursive Limits of 'Sex'*. London & New York: Routledge.

——. 1997. *Excitable Speech*. New York: Routledge.

Cabanne, Pierre. 1997. *Duchamp & Co*. Paris: Editions Terrail SA.

Cage, John. 1995. *Silence*. London: Marion Boyars.

Calle, Sophie. 2004. *Exquisite Pain*. London: Thames & Hudson.

Callens, Johan (ed.) 2004. *The Wooster Group and Its Traditions*. Brussels: Peter Lang.

Cameron, Kenneth and Theodore J. C. Hoffmann. 1974. *The Theatrical Response*. London: Macmillan.

Campbell, Sue. 2003. *Relational Remembering: Rethinking the Memory Wars*. Maryland: Rowman & Littlefield.

Carney, Ray and Leonard Quart. 2000. *The Films of Mike Leigh – Embracing the World*. Cambridge: Cambridge University Press.

Carlson, Marvin. 1984. *Theories of the Theatre: A Historical and Critical Survey from the Greeks to the Present*. Ithaca & London: Cornell University Press.

——. 1996. *Performance: A Critical Introduction*. London & New York: Routledge.

——. 2001. *The Haunted Stage: The Theatre as Memory Machine*. Ann Arbor: Michigan University Press.

Carr, Cindy. 1994. *On Edge: Performance at the End of the Twentieth Century*. Hanover: University Press of New England.

Case, Sue Ellen. 1988. *Feminism and Theatre*. London: Macmillan.

Castells, Manuel. 2004. *The Power of Identity*. Oxford: Blackwell.

Cavendish, Dominic. 2002. 'The Avant-Garde is Alive and Well – If a Little Grumpy'. *The Telegraph*. 16 March 2002: 22.

Chambers, Colin (ed.) 2002. *The Continuum Companion to Twentieth Century Theatre*. London & New York: Continuum.

Cixous, Hélène. 2005. *Stigmata: Escaping Texts*. London & New York: Routledge.

Clark, Romy and Roz Ivanic. 1997. *The Politics of Writing*. London & New York: Routledge.

Clements, Paul. 1983. *The Improvised Play*. London: Methuen.

Coe, Richard. 1985. *When the Grass was Taller: Autobiography and the Experience of Childhood*. London: Yale University Press.

Cohn, Ruby. 1969. *Currents in Contemporary Drama*. Bloomington: Indiana University Press.

Cole, Susan Letzler. 1992. *Directors in Rehearsal*. London & New York: Routledge.

Constantinidis, Stratos. 1993. *Theatre Under Deconstruction: A Question of Approach*. New York: Garland.

Conquergood, Dwight. 1989. 'Poetics, Play, Process and Power: The Performative Turn in Anthropology'. *Text and Performance Quarterly* 1: 82–95.

Counsell, Colin. 1996. *Signs of Performance: An Introduction to Twentieth-Century Theatre*. London & New York: Routledge.

Coveney, Michael. 1996. *The World According to Mike Leigh*. London: Harper Collins.

Crimp, Donald. 1993. *On the Museum's Ruins*. Cambridge: MIT Press.

Crohn Schmitt, Natalie. 1990. *Actors and Onlookers: Theater and Twentieth Century Scientific Views of Nature*. Evanston, Ill.: Northwestern University Press.

Cronin, Anthony. 1997. *Samuel Beckett: The Last Modernist*. London: Harper Collins.

Crow, Thomas. 1996. *Rise of the Sixties*. New York: Harry N. Abrams Inc.

Davis, Tracy C. and Thomas Postlewait (eds) 2003. *Theatricality*. Cambridge: Cambridge University Press.

Darwin, Charles. 1979. *The Origin of Species*. New York: Gramercy Books.

De Bono, Edward. 1995. *Serious Creativity*. London: Harper Collins.

Deeney, John. 1998. *Writing Live*. London: London Arts Board.

De Marinis, Marco. 2004. 'The Performance Text'. *The Performance Studies Reader*. Bial, H (ed.) London: Routledge.

De Oliveira, Nicolas, Nicola Oxley and Michael Petry. *Installation Art in the New Millennium*. London: Thames & Hudson.

De Wend Fenton, Rose and Lucy Neal. 2005. *The Turning World: Stories From the London International Festival of Theatre*. London: Calouste Gulbenkian Foundation.

Delgado, Maria M. and Caridad Svich. 2002. *Theatre in Crisis?* Manchester: Manchester University Press.

Derrida, Jacques. 1978. *Writing and Difference*. Alan Bass (trans.) Chicago: University of Chicago Press.

——. 1988. *Limited Inc*. Samuel Weber and Jeffrey Mehiman (trans.) Evanston: Northwestern University Press.

Dery, Mark. 1996. *Escape Velocity: Cyberculture at the End of the Century*. New York: Grove Press.

Dickenson, Sarah-Jane. 1995. 'Writing for the Large Group Production'. *Studies in Theatre Production*. No. 12: 33–46.

Ditton, Jason (ed.) 1980. *The View from Goffman*. New York: St. Martin's Press.

Dixon, Steve. 1995. 'The Actor as Chameleon: experiments in style, genre and multi-media'. *Studies in Theatre Production*. No. 12: 54–64.

——. 1998. 'Autonomy and Automatism: Devising Multi-Media Theatre with Multiple Protagonists'. *Studies in Theatre Production*. No. 18: 60–80.

——. 2007. *Digital Performance: A History of New Media in Theatre, Dance, Performance Art and Installation.* Cambridge, Massachusetts: MIT Press.

Donald, James (ed.) 1990. *Psychoanalysis and Cultural Theory: Thresholds.* Macmillan: London.

Dromgoole, Dominic. 2002. *The Full Room: An A–Z of Contemporary Playwriting.* London: Methuen.

Durand, Regis and Eleanor Heartney. 2004. *Orlan: Carnal Art.* Paris: Flammarion.

Durgnat, Raymond. 1988. 'Defetishizing Buñuel'. *Cineaste.* Vol. XXIII, No. 4: 2–18.

Eagleton, Terry. 1991. *Ideology: An Introduction.* London: Verso.

——. 1996. *Literary Theory: An Introduction.* Minneapolis: University of Minnesota Press.

Eco, Umberto. 1977. 115 'Semiotics of Theatrical Performance'. *The Drama Review.* Vol. 21, No. 1: 112–22.

——. 1986. *Semiotics and the Philosophy of Language.* London: Palgrave Macmillan.

Edwards, Barry. 1999. *Embodied Performer Practice.* PSI Workshop, Aberystwyth. http://www.optik.tv

Egan, Susanna. 1984. *Patterns of Experience in Autobiography.* Chapel Hill. University of North Carolina Press.

Eiger, Dietmar. 2004. *Dadaism.* Koln: Taschen.

Emin, Tracey. 2005. *Strangeland.* London: Hodder & Stoughton.

Esslin, Martin. 1973. *The Theatre of the Absurd.* New York: Overlook Press.

——. 1987. *The Field of Drama: How the Signs of Drama Create Meaning on Stage and Screen.* London: Methuen.

Etchells, Tim. 1999. *Certain Fragments: Contemporary Performance and Forced Entertainment.* London & New York: Routledge.

——. 2006. *The World in Pictures: Contextualising Pack.* www.forcedentertainment.com

Eyre, Richard. 2001. *Changing Stages: A View of British Theatre in the Twentieth Century.* London: Bloomsbury.

Feral, Josette. 1992. 'What is Left of Performance Art? Autopsy of a Function, Birth of a Genre'. *Discourse.* Vol. 14: 148–60.

Finley, Karen. 1988. 'The Constant State of Desire'. *The Drama Review.* Vol. 32, No. 1: 139–51.

——. 2000. *A Different Kind of Intimacy: The Collected Writings of Karen Finley.* New York: Thunder's Mouth Press.

Fischer-Lichte, Erika. 1996. 'From Theatre to Theatricality – How to Construct Reality'. *Theatre Research International.* Vol. 20, No. 2: 97–105.

Fitzpatrick, Tim. 1989. 'The Dialectics of Space-Time: Dramaturgical and Directorial Strategies for Performance and Fictional World'. *Performance from Product to Process.* Tim Fitzpatrick (ed.) Sydney: Frederick May Foundation: 49–112.

Fletcher and Spurling. 1972. *Beckett: A Study of His Plays.* New York: Hill & Wang.

Forced Entertainment. 1996. 'A Decade of Forced Entertainment'. *Performance Research.* Vol. 1, No. 1: 73–88.

Foreman, Richard. 1992. *Unbalancing Acts: Foundations for a Theatre*. New York: Pantheon Books.

Fortier, Mark. 1997. *Theory/Theatre: An Introduction*. London & New York: Routledge.

Foster, Hal. (ed.) 1983. *Postmodern Culture*. London: Pluto Press.

—— (ed.) 1988. *Vision and Visuality*. Seattle: Bay Press.

——. 1993. *Compulsive Beauty*. Cambridge: MIT Press.

——. 1996. *The Return of the Real: Avant-Garde at the End of the Century*. Cambridge, Massachusetts: MIT Press.

Foucault, Michel. 1972. *The Archaeology of Knowledge and the Discourse on Language*. A. M. Sheridan Smith (trans.) London: Tavistock Press.

Fraser, Mariam and Monica Greco (eds) 2004. *The Body: A Reader*. London & New York: Routledge.

Freeman, John. 1998. 'The Location and Theory of Looking'. *Journal of Dramatic Theory and Criticism*. Vol. XII, No. 2: 129–41.

——. 2003a. *Tracing the Footprints: Documenting the Process of Performance*. Maryland: University Press of America.

——. 2003b. 'Suffering from Certainty'. *Research in Post-Compulsory Education*. Vol. 8, No. 1: 39–52.

——. 2004a. 'Performatised Secrets, Performatised Selves'. *Contemporary Theatre Review*. Vol. 14, No. 4: 64–77.

——. 2004b. 'Battling with Berkoff'. *Total Theatre*. Vol. 15, No. 4: 16–17.

——. 2005. 'Fading Away: Remembering to Forget What Theatre Was'. *Journal of Dramatic Theory and Criticism*. Spring 2005: 31–42.

——. 2006. 'First Insights: Fostering Creativity in University Performance'. *Arts & Humanities in Higher Education*. Spring 2006: 91–103.

Fried, Michael. 1998. *Art and Objecthood: Essays and Reviews*. Chicago: University of Chicago Press.

Frost, Anthony. 1998. 'Timor Mortis Conturbuit Nos: Improvising Tragedy and Epic'. *Theatre Praxis*. Christopher McCullough (ed.) Basingstoke: Macmillan, 151–73.

Frost, Anthony and Ralph Yarrow. 1990. *Improvisation in Drama*. London: Macmillan.

Fuchs, Elinor. 1989. 'Staging the Obscene Body'. *The Drama Review*. Vol. 33, No. 1: 33–58.

Gale, Maggie B. and Viv Gardner. 2005. *Auto/Biography and Identity*. Manchester: Manchester University Press.

Gardner, Lyn. 2003. 'Do Not Disturb'. The *Guardian*. 13 December 2003: 19.

Garrard, Rose (ed.) 1980. *About Time*. London: Institute of Contemporary Arts.

Geertz, Clifford. 2000. *Local Knowledge*. New York: Basic Books.

Gilmore, Leigh. 2001. *The Limits of Autobiography, Trauma and Testimony*. Ithaca: Cornell University Press.

Gladwell, Malcolm. 2005. *Blink*. New York & London: Penguin.

Goffman, Erving. 1959. *The Presentation of Self in Everyday Life*. New York: Doubleday.

Goat Island. 2001. *It's an Earthquake in My Heart: A Reading Companion*. Chicago: Illinois Arts Council.

Goldberg, RoseLee. 1988. *Performance Art: From Futurism to the Present*. New York: Harry N. Abrams Inc.

Goldberg, RoseLee and Laurie Anderson. 2000. *Laurie Anderson*. New York: Harry N. Abrams Inc.

Gómez-Peña, Guillermo. 1997. *New World Border*. California: City Lights.

——. 2000. *Dangerous Border Crossers: The Artist Talks Back*. London & New York: Routledge.

——. 2005. *Ethno-Techno: Writings on Performance, Activism and Pedagogy*. London & New York: Routledge.

Goodman, Lizbeth. 1993. *Contemporary Feminist Theatre: To Each Her Own*. London: Routledge.

——. 1998. *The Routledge Reader in Gender and Performance*. London & New York: Routledge.

Gorchakov, Nikolai M. 1954. *Stanislavski Directs*. New York: Minerva Press.

Grace, Sherrill and Jerry Wasserman. 2006. *Theatre and Autobiography*. Vancouver: Talon Books.

Gray, John. 1993. *Action Art: A Bibliography of Artist's Performance from Futurism to Fluxux and Beyond*. Connecticut: Greenwood Press.

Gray, Katherine M. 1995. 'Troubling the Body: Towards a Theory of Beckett's Use of the Human Body Onstage'. *Journal of Beckett Studies*. Vol. 5, No. 1: 1–17.

Gray, Spalding. 1979. 'About *Three Places in Rhode Island*'. *The Drama Review*. Vol. 23, No. 1: 31–42.

——. 1994. *Gray's Anatomy*. New York: Picador.

——. 2005. *Swimming to Cambodia*. New York: Theatre Communications Group.

——. 2006. *Life Interrupted*. New York: Crown.

Grosenick, Uta (ed.) 2005. *Women Artists in the 20th and 21st Century*. Koln: Taschen.

Grotowski, Jerzy. 1969. *Towards a Poor Theatre*. London: Macmillan.

Hall, Stuart. 1993. 'Communities, Nation and Culture'. *Cultural Studies*. 7.3: 349–63.

Hare, David. 1991. *Writing Left-Handed*. London & Boston: Faber & Faber.

Harrop, Peter. 1996. 'Notes for a Topography of Theatre'. *Occasional Papers in the Arts and Education*. Vol. 6: 125–7.

Harvie, Jen. 2005. *Staging the UK*. Manchester: Manchester University Press.

Hassan, I and S. Hassan (eds) 1983. *Innovation/Renovation*. Madison: University of Wisconsin Press.

Heathfield, Adrian (ed.) 2004. *Live: Art and Performance*. London: Tate Publishing.

Heddon, Deirdre. 1998. 'What's in a Name?…' *Studies in Theatre Production*. No. 18: 49–58.

Helmer, Judith, and Floorian Malzacher (eds) 2004. *Not Even a Game Anymore: The Theatre of Forced Entertainment*. Berlin: Alexander Verlag.

Henri, Adrian. 1974. *Total Art: Environments, Happenings and Performance*. New York: Praeger.

Hoffmann, Jens and Joan Jonas. 2005. *Perform*. London: Thames & Hudson.

Hopkins, Jerry. 1986. *Yoko Ono*. New York: Macmillan.

Hough, Michael. 1990. *Out of Place: Restoring Identity to the Regional Landscape.* New Haven: Yale University Press.

Hughes, David (ed.) 2000. 'Research in Process'. *Live Art Magazine.* London: Arts Council of England.

———. 2002. 'Editorial'. *Live Art Magazine.* No. 41: 2.

Hughes, Robert. 1980. *The Shock of the New: Art and the Century of Change.* London: British Broadcasting Corporation.

Hughes-Hallett, Lucy. 1992. 'The Battlefields of Love: Insights in the Work of Roberta Graham'. *Performance.* No. 65/66, Spring 1992.

Ince, Kate. 2000. *Orlan: Millennial Female.* Oxford: Berg.

Invirne, James. 1997. *Jack Tinker: A Life in Review.* Ottowa: Oberon.

Irigaray, Luce. 1985. *This Sex Which is Not One.* C. Porter (trans.) New York: Cornell University Press.

Issacharoff, Michael. 1989. *Discourse as Performance.* Stanford: Stanford University Press.

Jackson, Shannon. 2004. *Professing Performance: Theatre in the Academy from Philology to Performativity.* Cambridge: Cambridge University Press.

Jahn, Wolf. *The Art of Gilbert & George or an Aesthetic of Existence.* London: Thames & Hudson.

Jameson, Frederic (ed.) 1977. *Aesthetics and Politics: Ernst Bloch, Georg Lukacs, Bertolt Brecht, Walter Benjamin, Theodor Adorno.* R. Taylor (trans.) London & New York: Verso.

———. 1991. *Postmodernism, or, the Cultural Logic of Late Capitalism.* Durham: Duke University Press.

———. 2000. *A Jameson Reader.* Oxford: Blackwell.

Jeffries, Stuart. 2005. 'Imagined Sensibilities'. *Guardian.* 26 September 2005: 7.

Jencks, Charles. 1987. *Modern Movements in Architecture.* London: Penguin.

Johnson, Randall (ed.) 1993. *The Field of Cultural Production: Essays on Art and Literature.* New York: Columbia University Press.

Jones, Amelia. 1995. *Postmodernism and the En Gendering of Marcel Duchamp.* Cambridge: Cambridge University Press.

———. 1998. *Body Art/Performing the Subject.* Minneapolis: The University of Michigan Press.

Jones, Amelia, and Andrew Stephenson (eds) 1999. *Performing the Body/Performing the Text.* London & New York: Routledge.

Judd, Donald. 1975. *Complete Writings: 1955–1975.* New York: New York University Press.

Kane, Sarah. 2001. *Sarah Kane: Complete Plays.* London: London: Methuen.

Kaprow, Allan. 1966a. *Manifestoes.* New York: Something Else Press.

———. 1966b. *Assemblage, Environments and Happenings.* New York: Harry. N. Abrams.

———. 1993. *Essays on the Blurring of Art and Life.* Berkeley: University of California Press.

Kaur Bhatti, Gurpreet. 2005. 'This Warrior is Fighting On'. *Guardian.* 13 January 2005: 17.

Kaye, Nick. 1992. 'Mask, Role and Narrative: An Interview with Joan Jonas'. *Performance*. No. 65/66, Spring 1992: 49–59.

———. 1994. *Postmodernism and Performance*. London: Macmillan.

———. 2000. *Site-specific Art: Performance, Place and Documentation*. London & New York: Routledge.

Kellein, Thomas. 1995. *Fluxus*. New York: Thames & Hudson.

Kelley, Jeff. 2004. *Childsplay: The Art of Allan Kaprow*. California: University of California Press.

Kelly, Alex. 2000. 'Third Angel: Class of '76'. *Small Acts: Performance, the Millennium and the Marking of Time*. Heathfield, A. (ed.) London: Black Dog Publishing.

Kieran, Matthew. 2004. *Revealing Art*. London & New York: Routledge.

King, Nicola. 2000. *Memory, Narrative, Identity: Remembering the Self*. Edinburgh: Edinburgh University Press.

Kirby, Michael. 1965a. *Happenings: An Illustrated Anthology*. London: Sidgwick and Jackson.

———. 1965b. 'The New Theatre'. *The Drama Review*. Vol. 10, No. 2: 32–43.

———. 1987. *A Formalist Theatre*. Pennsylvania University Press: Pennsylvania.

Kneller, G. F. 1965. *The Art of Science and Creativity*. New York: Holt, Reinhart & Winston.

Knowles, Ric. 1999. *The Theatre of Form and the Production of Meaning: Contemporary Canadian Dramaturgies*. Toronto: ECW Press.

———. 2004. *Reading the Material Theatre*. Cambridge: Cambridge University Press.

Knowlson, James. 1996. *Damned to Fame: The Life of Samuel Beckett*. London: Bloomsbury.

Kwon, Miwon. 2004. *One Place after Another: Site-Specific Art and Locational Identity*. Cambridge, Massachusetts: MIT Press.

Lacan, Jacques. 1977. *The Four Fundamental Concepts of Psychoanalysis*. Alan Sheridan (trans.) London: Hogarth Press.

Langellier, Kristen. 1999. 'Personal Narratives: Perspectives on Theory and Research'. *Text and Performance Quarterly* 19: 125–44.

Layzell, Richard. 1998. *Enhanced Performance*. London: Black Dog Publishing.

LeCompte, Elizabeth. 1992. 'Island Hopping: Rehearsing the Wooster Group's *Brace Up!*'. *The Drama Review*. Vol. 36, No. 4: 128–37.

Lefebvre, Henri. 1991. *The Production of Space*. Donald Nicholson-Smith (trans.) Oxford: Blackwell.

Lennard, John and Mary Luckhurst. 2002. *The Drama Handbook*. Oxford: Oxford University Press.

Levy, Deborah (ed.) 1992. *Walks on Water*. London: Methuen.

Linker, Kate. 1994. *Vito Acconci*. New York: Rizzoli International Publications, Inc.

Lippard, Lucy. 1997. *The Lure of the Local: The Sense of Place in a Multicultural Society*. New York: New Press.

———. 1984. *Overlay: Contemporary Art & the Art of Prehistory*. New York: Pantheon Books.

Liska, Pavol, Ruth Margraff, Annie-B Parson, Tory Vasquez and Sarah Benson. 2006. 'Working Downtown'. *Performing Arts Journal* 83. Vol. 28, No. 2: 42–60.

Lyotard, Jean-François. 1979. 'That Part of Cinema Called Television: An Assessment of Television'. *Framework*. 11, Autumn 1979: 7–19.

——. 1984. *The Postmodern Condition: A Report on Knowledge*. Geoff Bennington and Brian Massumi (trans.) Manchester: Manchester University Press.

——. 1989. *The Lyotard Reader*. Oxford: Blackwell Publishing.

MacDonald, Claire. 1997. *Women and Performance*. London & New York: Routledge.

MacDonald, Erik. 1993. *Theatre at the Margins*. Ann Arbor: University of Michigan Press.

Malkin, Jeanette R. 1999. *Memory-Theatre and Postmodern Drama*. Ann Arbor: University of Michigan Press.

Manning, Philip. 1992. *Erving Goffman and Modern Sociology*. Cambridge: Polity Press.

Marcus, Laura.1994. *Autobiographical Discourses: Theory, Criticism and Practice*. Manchester: Manchester University Press.

Margolis, Joseph (ed.) 1978. *Philosophy Looks at the Arts: Contemporary Readings in Aesthetics*. Philadelphia: Temple University Press.

Marowitz, Charles. 1991. *Recycling Shakespeare*. London: Macmillan Education Ltd.

Marranca, Bonnie. 1979. 'The Self as Text: Uses of Autobiography in the Theatre'. *Performing Arts Journal* 10/11: 9–22.

——. 1984. *Theatrewritings*. New York: PAJ Publications.

Martin, Jacqueline. 1991.*Voice in Modern Drama*. London & New York: Routledge.

——. 1994. *Towards a Multidisciplinary Approach to Acting*. Amsterdam: Uitgeverij International Theatre & Film Books.

——. 2005. Performance Anaysis: A Strategy for Understanding Traditional and Contemprary Forms of Performance'. *The IDEA Papers*. Research Monograph Series, 3. Brisbane: IDEA Publications.

Marx, Karl. 1995. *Selected Writings*. Indianapolis: Hackett.

McAuley, Gay. 1999. *Space in Performance: Making Meaning in the Theatre*. Ann Arbor: University of Michigan Press.

McCullough, Christopher (ed.) 1998. *Theatre Praxis: Teaching Drama Through Practice*. London: Macmillan.

McKenzie, Jon. 2001. *Perform or Else: From Discipline to Performance*. New York: Routledge.

Melrose, Susan. 1999. 'Restaging "Theory" in the Postgraduate Performance Studies Workshop'. *New Theatre Quarterly*. Vol. 15, No. 57: 39–56.

——. 2005. 'Words Fail Me: Dancing with the Other's Familiar'. Keynote Address: Centre for Performance Research Symposium, Aberystwyth. 6–10 April 2005. http://www.sfmelrose.u-net.com/wordsfailme

Miglietti, Francesca Alfano. 2003. *Extreme Bodies: The Use and Abuse of the Body in Art*. Milan: Skira Editore S.p.A.

Mink, Janis.1995. *Duchamp*. Koln: Taschen.

Montano, Linda. 2000. *Performance Artists Talking in the Eighties*. Los Angeles: University of California Press.

Monteith, Moira. 1986. *Women's Writing: A Challenge to Theory*. Brighton: Harvester Press.

Morris, Frances, Chris Burden, Nicholas Serota and Tom Horton. 1999. *Chris Burden: When Robots Rule – The Two Minute Airplane Factory*. London: Tate Gallery Publishing.

Morse, Margaret. 1998. *Virtualities: Television, Media Art, and Cyberculture*. Bloomingdale: Indiana University Press.

Movshovitz, Howie (ed.) 2000. *Mike Leigh Interviews*. Mississippi: University Press of Mississippi.

Mroué, Rabih. 2003. 'The Fabrication of "Truth"'. *Beyond Borders: European Cultural Foundation* No 5: 7–12.

Müller, Heiner. 1984. *Hamlet-Machine and Other Texts for the Stage*. New York: PAJ Publications.

——. 1994. 'Contexts and History'. *German Studies Review*, Vol. 22, No. 1: 181–2.

Mulvey, Laura. 1989. *Visual and Other Pleasures*. Basingstoke: Macmillan.

Munroe, Alexandra and Joe Hendricks. 2000.*Yes: Yoko Ono*. New York: Harry N. Abrams, Inc.

Naumann, Francis. 1999. *Marcel Duchamp*. New York: Harry N. Abrams Inc.

Nicoletti, Giovanna. 1972. *Skin Deep*. Milan: Skira Editore S.p.A.

Nochlin, Linda. 1971. *Realism*. New York: Penguin.

Noever, Peter (ed.) 1996. *Chris Burden: Beyond the Limits*. New York: Distributed Art Publishers.

Oddey, Alison. 1994. *Devising Theatre: A Practical and Theoretical Handbook*. London: Routledge.

Olney, James. 1972. *Metaphors of Self: The Meaning of Autobiography*. Princeton: Princeton University Press.

Ono, Yoko. 1970. *Grapefruit*. 2nd edn. New York: Simon & Schuster.

Owens, Allan. 2005. 'Planning for the Possibilities of Dissensus in Process Drama'. *Hyva hankaus – teatterilahtoiset meneelmat oppimisen ja osallisuuden mahdollisuuksina*. Helsinki: Draamatyo: 9–14.

Owens, Allan and Clive Holtham. 2006. *Enhancing Management Knowledge through Extra-Rational Theatrical Tools: Beyond Consensus of Theatrics to Dissensus of Dialogue*. International Organisation, Knowledge and Learning Conference. University of Warwick.

Page, Edwin. 2006. *Quintessential Tarantino*. London: Marion Boyars.

Pavis, Patrice. 1992. *Theatre at the Crossroads of Culture*. Leon Kruger (trans.) London & New York: Routledge.

——. 1998. *Dictionary of the Theatre: Terms, Concepts and Analysis*. Toronto & Buffalo: University of Toronto Press.

——. 2003. *Analyzing Performance: Theater, Dance and Film*. David Williamson (trans.) Ann Arbor: Michigan University Press.

Pearson, Mike, and Michael Shanks. 2001. *Theatre/Archaeology*. London & New York: Routledge.

Pepper, Arthur. 1949. *Drama*. New York: Harcourt Brace.

Peters, John. 1988. *Vladimir's Carrot*. London: Methuen.

Phelan, Peggy. 1993. *Unmarked: The Politics of Performance*. London & New York: Routledge.

——. 2004. 'On seeing the Invisible: Marina Abramović's *The House with the Ocean View*'. *Live: Art and Performance*. Heathfield, A (ed.) London: Tate Publishing.

Phelan, Peggy and Jill Lane (eds) 1998. *The Ends of Performance*. New York: New York University Press.

Pitts, Victoria. 2003. *In the Flesh: The Cultural Politics of Body Modification*. New York: Palgrave Macmillan.

Postlewait, Thomas and Bruce A. McConachie (eds) 1989. *Interpreting the Theatrical Past: Essays in the Historiography of Performance*. Iowa: University of Iowa Press.

Pronko, Leonard. 1967. *Theater East and West: Perspectives toward a Total Theater*. California: University of California Press.

Quadri, Franco, Franco Bertoni and Robert Stearns. 1997. *Robert Wilson*. New York: Rizzoli International Publications, Inc.

Rae, Paul. 1997. *'Presencing' in Presence*. University of Middlesex. www/epai/presencesite/html/rae01.html

Rabkin, Gerald. 1983. 'The Play of Misreading: Text/Theater/Deconstruction'. *Performing Arts Journal* 19. Vol. 7, No. 2: 42–7.

Rabey, David Ian. 2003. *English Drama Since 1940*. Harlow: Pearson.

Reinelt, Janelle G. and Joseph R. Roach (eds) 1992. *Critical Theory and Performance*. Michigan: University of Michigan Press.

Reiss, Julie. H. 1999. *From Margin to Center: The Spaces of Installation Art, 1969–1996*. Cambridge, Massachusets: MIT Press.

Riggins, Stephen Harold. 1990. *Beyond Goffman: Studies on Communication, Institution, and Social Interaction*. New York: Mouton de Gruyter.

Roach, Joseph. 1996. *Cities of the Dead*. New York: Columbia University Press.

——. 1999. 'Reconstructing Theatre/History'. *Theatre Topics*. 9.1: 3–10.

Robinson, Gerry. 2000. *The Creativity Imperative: Investing in the Arts in the 21st Century*. London: Arts Council of England.

Rose, Barbara. 1979. 'Hans Namuth's Photograph and the Jackson Pollock Myth: Part One: Media Impact and the Failure of Criticism'. *Arts Magazine*. Vol. 53, No. 7: 23–32.

Rosemont, Penelope. 1998. *Surrealist Women*. Texas: University of Texas Press.

Ross, Sheldon. 1988. *A First Course in Probability*. 4th edn. New York: Macmillan.

Russell Brown, John (ed.) 1997. *The Oxford Illustrated History of Theatre*. Oxford & New York: Oxford University Press.

Rylance, Rick. 1994. *Roland Barthes*. Hemel Hempstead: Harvester Wheatsheaf.

Sachs, Hans. 1942. *The Creative Unconsciousness*. Chicago: Crown.

Sandford, Mariellen. R. 1995. *Happenings and Other Acts*. London & New York: Routledge.

Sartre, Jean Paul. 1990. *Being and Nothingness*. Hazel Barnes (trans.) London: Routledge.

Saunders, Graham. 2002. *Love Me or Kill Me: Sarah Kane and the Theatre of Extremes*. Manchester: Manchester University Press.

Savran, David. 1985. *Breaking the Rules: The Wooster Group 1975–1985*. Ann Arbor: UMI Research Press.

Sayre, Henry M. 1992. *The Object of Performance*. Chicago: University of Chicago Press.

Scarry, Elaine. 1985. *The Body in Pain: The Making and Unmaking of the World*. New York: Oxford University Press.

Schechner, Richard. 1973. *Environmental Theater*. New York: Hawthorn Books.

——. 1977. *Essays on Performance Theory, 1970–1976*. New York: Drama Book Specialists.

——. 1982. *The End of Humanism*. New York: PAJ Publications.

——. 1985. *Between Theatre and Anthropology*. Philadelphia: University of Pennsylvania Press.

——. 2002. 'My Art in Life: Interviewing Spalding Gray'. *The Drama Review*. Vol. 46, No. 4: 161–76.

Schechner, Richard, and Willa Appel (eds) 1990. *By Means of Performance: Intercultural Studies of Theatre and Ritual*. Cambridge: Cambridge University Press.

Schimmel, Paul. 1998. *Out of Actions: Between Performance and the Object: 1949–1979*. Los Angeles: the Museum of Contemporary Art.

Schneemann, Carolee. 2002. *Carolee Schneemann: Imaging Her Erotics: Interviews, Projects*. Cambridge, Massachusets: MIT Press.

——. 1979. *More than Meat Joy: Complete Performance Works and Selected Writings*. New York: McPherson & Company.

Schneider, Rebecca. 1997. *The Explicit Body in Performance*. London & New York: Routledge.

Schumacher, C. 1989. *Artaud on Theatre*. London: Methuen.

Schutzman, Mady and Jan Cohen-Cruz. 1993. *Playing Boal: Theatre, Therapy, Activism*. London: Taylor & Francis.

Scruton, Roger. 1986. *Sexual Desire*. London: Weidenfield & Nicolson.

Searle, Adrian. (ed.) 1993. *Talking Art 1*. London: Institute of Contemporary Arts.

Shank, Theodore. 2002. *Beyond the Boundaries: American Alternative Theatre*. Ann Arbor: The University of Michigan Press.

Shapiro, Gary (ed.) 1990. *After the Future: Postmodern Times and Places*. Albany: SUNY Press.

Sheppard, Anne. 1987. *Aesthetics*. Oxford: Oxford University Press.

Sierz, Alex. 2001. *In-Yer-Face Theatre: British Drama Today*. London: Faber & Faber.

Singleton, John and Mary Luckhurst. 2000. *The Creative Writing Handbook*. London: Palgrave Macmillan.

Smith, David. 1999. *Zygmunt Bauman, Prophet of Postmodernity*. Cambridge: Polity Press.

Smith, Hazel and Roger Dean. 1997. *Improvisation, Hypermedia and the Arts since 1945*. Amsterdam: Harwood Academic Press.

Smith, Marquard (ed.) 2005. *Stelarc: The Monograph*. Cambridge, Massachusetts: MIT Press.

Smith, Sidonie and Julia Watson. 2002. *Interfaces – Women/Autobiography/Image/ Performance*. Ann Arbor: University of Michigan Press.

—— (eds) 1998. *Women, Autobiography, Theory: A Reader*. Madison: University of Wisconsin Press.

Sokel, Walter. 1963. *An Anthology of German Expressionist Drama: A Prelude to the Absurd*. Joseph M. Bernstein (trans.) New York: Garden City.

Sprinkle, Annie. 1991. *Annie Sprinkle: Post Porn Modernist*. Amsterdam: Torch Books.

——. 2001. *Hardcore from the Heart: The Pleasures, Profits and Politics of Sex in Performance*. Gabrielle Cody (ed.) London & New York: Continuum.

Spurling, John and John Fletcher. 1972. *Forces in Modern French Drama*. London: University Press.

Stanley, Liz. 1992. *The Auto/Biographical I*. Manchester: Manchester University Press.

Stanton, William and Christopher McCullough. 1998. 'Theology of Authorship?' *Studies in Theatre Production*. No. 17: 21–9.

States, Bert O. 1985. *Great Reckonings in Little Rooms: On the Phenomenology of Theater*. Berkeley: University of California Press.

Stathos, John. 1999. *Tate*. London: Tate Publishing.

Steiner, Barbara and Jun Wang. 2004. *Autobiography*. London: Thames & Hudson.

Stelarc and James D. Paffrath (eds) 1984. *Obsolete Body/Suspensions/Stelarc*. Davis, CA.: JP Publications.

Stephenson, Heidi and Natasha Langridge. 1997. *Rage and Reason: Women Play- wrights on Playwiting*. London: Methuen.

Steyn, Julian (ed.) 1997. *Other than Identity: The Subject, Politics and Art*. Manchester: Manchester University Press.

Styan, J. L. 1981. *Modern Drama in Theory and Practice*. Vols. 1, 2 & 3. Cambridge: Cambridge University Press.

Swindells, Julia (ed.) 1995. *The Uses of Autobiography*. London: Taylor & Francis.

Taylor, Charles. 1985. *Human Agency and Language*. Cambridge: Cambridge University Press.

ten Cate, Ritsaert. 1996. *Man Looking for Words*. Amsterdam: Theater Instituut Nederland.

Thomas, Helen. 2005. *The Body and Everyday Life*. London & New York: Routledge.

Tillman, Frank and S. Cahn. 1969. *Philosophy of Art and Aesthetics, from Plato to Wittgenstein*. New York: Harpers & Row.

Tomkins, Calvin. 1997. *Duchamp*. London: Chatto & Windus.

Torrance, E. P. and O. Ball. 1984. *Torrance Tests of Creative Thinking, Streamlined Manual Including Norms and Directions for Administering and Scoring Figural A and B*. Bensenville, Illinois: Scholastic Testing Service.

Tzara, Tristran. 1981. *Seven Dada Manifestos*. London: Calder.

Unwin, Stephen and Carole Woddis. 2001. *A Pocket Guide to 20th Century Drama*. London: Faber & Faber.

Vergine, Lea. 1974. 'Bodylanguage'. *Art and Artists*. September 1974: 22–100.

Wallas, George. 1926. *The Art of Thought*. New York: Harcourt Brace.

Warnock, Mary. 1987. *Memory*. London: Faber & Faber.

Wasserman, George. W. 1989. *The Ecstasies of Roland Barthes*. London: Routledge.

Wesker, Arnold. 1985. *Distinctions*. London: Jonathan Cape.

Whitmore, Jon. 1994. *Directing Postmodern Theatre: Shaping Signification in Performance*. Ann Arbor: University of Michigan Press.

Wilshire, Bruce. 1982. *Role Playing and Identity*. Bloomington: Indiana University Press.

——. 1990. 'The Concept of the Paratheatrical'. *The Drama Review*. Vol. 34, No. 4: 160–9.

Wilson, Robert. 1970. *Deafman Glance: Programme Notes*. New York. Brooklyn Academy of Music Opera House.

Wilson, Timothy and Jonathan Schooler. 1991. 'Thinking Too Much: Introspection Can Reduce the Quality of Preferences and Decisions'. *Journal of Personality and Social Psychology*. Vol. 60, No. 2: 181–92.

Worthen, W. B. 1998. 'Drama, Performativity, and Performance'. *PMLA*. Vol. 113, No. 5: 1093–107.

Worthen, W.B. and Peter Holland. 2004. *Theorizing Practice: Redefining Theatre History*. London: Palgrave Macmillan.

Wrights and Sites. 2000. *The Quay Thing Documented: Studies in Theatre and Performance*. Supplement 5. Wiltshire: Antony Rowe Limited.

Yates, Francis. 1966. *The Art of Memory*. London: Routledge & Kegan Paul.

Zarrilli, Phillip B. (ed.) 1995. *Acting (Re)Considered: Theories and Practices*. London & New York: Routledge.

Zinder, David. 1980. *The Surrealist Connection: An Approach to a Surrealist Aesthetic of Theater*. Michigan: UMI Research Press.

Zurbrugg, Nicholas. 2000. *Critical Vices: The Myths of Postmodern Theory*. London & New York: Routledge.

Index